The Song of

Annie Moses

A Musical Quest
A Mother's Gift

Robin Donica Wolaver

Guideposts

New York

The Song of Annie Moses

ISBN-10: 0-8249-3483-0
ISBN-13: 978-0-8249-3483-5

Published by Guideposts
16 East 34th Street
New York, New York 10016
Guideposts.org

Distributed by Ideals Publications, a Guideposts company
2630 Elm Hill Pike, Suite 100
Nashville, Tennessee 37214

Guideposts and *Ideals* are registered trademarks of Guideposts.

Acknowledgments

Every attempt has been made to credit the sources of copyrighted material used in this book. If any such acknowledgment has been inadvertently omitted or miscredited, receipt of such information would be appreciated.

Scripture quotations marked (ESV) are taken from the *Holy Bible, English Standard Version*, copyright © 2001 by Crossway Bibles, a division of Good News Publishers. Used by permission. All rights reserved.

Scripture quotations marked (KJV) are taken from *The King James Version of the Bible*.

Scripture quotations marked (NIV) are taken from *The Holy Bible, New International Version*. Copyright © 1973, 1978, 1984, 2011 by Biblica, Inc. Used by permission of Zondervan. All rights reserved worldwide. www.zondervan.com

Lyrics on page 17 are from "A Little on the Lonely Side," words and music by Frank Weldon/Dick Robertson/James Cavanaugh and "I Can't Begin to Tell You," words and music by James V. Monaco and Mack Gordon.

Library of Congress Cataloging-in-Publication Data

Wolaver, Robin.
  The song of Annie Moses : a musical quest, a mother's gift / Robin Donica Wolaver.
    pages cm
  ISBN 978-0-8249-3483-5
  1. Wolaver, Robin. 2. Contemporary Christian musicians–United States–Biography. I. Title.
  ML420.W646A3 2013
  780.92–dc23
  [B]
                                                      2013018255

Cover and interior design by Müllerhaus
Cover photograph by Shutterstock Images
Typeset by Aptara, Inc.

Printed and bound in the United States of America
10 9 8 7 6 5 4 3 2 1

To my beautiful mother,
Ethel Jane Moses Donica,
who didn't pick cotton for nothin'.

Contents

Colossus and Cow Pies

With conquering limbs astride from land to land
EMMA LAZARUS IN *THE NEW COLOSSUS*

Every Saturday morning, after I escort my children to their classes, I linger in the wide, fluorescent-lit corridor simply to enjoy the magic. On either side of me stretches a row of doors with small windows, many of which have been covered with a sheet of music or a piece of paper.

It is the occupant's way of saying, "Please do not stare at me."

But I want to stare, to scour the edges of the glass for a peek, a tiny glimpse of the musical marvel that hides inside the room behind the door. A photo-ID card with bright young eyes shining out at me rests in the lower left-hand corner of each covered window. Across the top of a card, I read: "The Juilliard School, Precollege Student."

There are few places like this on earth.

As I stroll the hall, music fades from the doors behind me and swells from the doors in front of me—a cacophony of mingled virtuosity: scales and arpeggios; fiery melodies; the bittersweet beauty of Mendelssohn's Violin Concerto; the harmonic genius of Bach's keyboard calculus. My lungs expand with energy; the practice rooms exude life.

Every year, thousands of students from across the globe audition to become a part of the musical circle within this world-renowned conservatory. Only a handful are accepted, many from foreign countries. Some are children of the poor who are willing to sacrifice everything for the golden door of opportunity. Others are children of the wealthy: architects, engineers, physicians, and financiers.

I peek inside an uncovered window to my left. A little Asian girl, so tiny she cannot effectively reach the pedals of the baby grand, practices with fierce concentration. Her fingers scurry sideways over the ivories with stunning speed. Her glossy black hair radiates health, and her eyes sear the keys. On the floor beside her lies a backpack covered with brightly colored stickers, the only evidence of childhood.

Behind her, in the shadows, sits her mother, eyes closed, head sagging, shoulders slumped loosely with fatigue. She is the hub of her daughter's world, the substance of her success.

A young man approaches up the hall, and I recognize him as a newcomer, a profoundly talented pianist from Russia who plays in a chamber-music group with my son, Alex, a violist, and my daughter, Annie, a violinist. Their group will be performing a Brahms piano quintet in the Juilliard Theatre tonight.

The young Russian smiles at me, nodding hello. He is sixteen years old, speaks little English, and sleeps at the YMCA. His family gave him the few rubles they had, and in a jumble of joy and sadness, sent him alone across the ocean to study music.

Several times a week, he hauls a tin cup and a cheap, battery-powered keyboard onto the platforms of the New York City subway and plays for strangers who have loose change to spare. He is a serious, quiet boy, never late for rehearsal. In performance, he wears a frayed, oversize tuxedo that transforms, somewhere in the sweep of sound, into Prince Charming attire, offering an arm to escort you to a musical epiphany.

I arrive at the theater early for the quintet, hoping for a good seat. The theater fills, and the quintet takes the stage. My daughter plays first violin, and she is a poised and confident leader: Her face animated, her eyes wide, she communicates without words, leading the group in the musical phrasing and nuance that creates a unified performance. My son plays viola. He is two years younger than Annie, and his music rises and falls in concert with her leadership. The unity is powerful.

When the last passionate note of Brahms has died away, I find myself in tears and blow my nose. Where I grew up, in the Kiamichi Mountains of southeastern Oklahoma, a high-caliber performance was a local yokel winning a turkey shoot with a big gun. My family's daily musical feasts from our high-fidelity home stereo were country fried: Johnny Cash's *Ride This Train,* Marty Robbins' *Gunfighter Ballads* and *More Gunfighter Ballads,* Tex Ritter's "Blood on the Saddle," and Roger Miller's southern twang chanting:

> *Chug-a-Lug, Chug-a-Lug*
> *Makes ya wanna holler hi-dee-ho*
> *Burns yer tummy, don't ya know*
> *Chug-a-Lug, Chug-a-Lug.*

My mother frowned at this song. She disapproved of Mr. Miller's humor and insisted that lyrics extolling moonshine whiskey were entirely inappropriate for the children of the preacher of our little mountain church.

Daddy hadn't thought of that. Although he did not "Chug-a-Lug," he was a native son, and moonshine whiskey was as commonplace as spittoons, copperheads, and outhouses.

Mama's point exactly.

So Daddy retired Mr. Miller and augmented our record collection with a Jimmy Durante rendition of "Jingle Bells." I, along with my two older sisters, Cindy and Sherry, loved to hear Jimmy's gravelly voice rasping the beloved lyrics as we decorated the Christmas tree. But our toddler brother, David, stood at the hi-fi, frightened and crying, the way young children sometimes get frightened at strange, scary sounds, like Jimmy's rough tones griping, *"Jingle bells. Jingle bells. Jingle all the way."*

So Mama retired even Jimmy and played instead her own selection of cultured vinyl, a recording called *Jane Morgan Time.* Jane's powerful, ewe-like vibrato bleated of love, in English, French, and Spanish. Her ability to sing in multiple languages qualified her, in Mama's mind, as an educated musician.

To me, Jane Morgan was a platinum-blonde siren; I loved to sit and stare at her on the album cover. If my childhood had a soundtrack, it would be her gutsy alto, commanding from the deep grooves of a crackling LP, *"Kiss me once and kiss me twice and kiss me once again; it's been a long, long time."* I could imagine her perfectly drawn red lips puckering up to smooch out the words. Her lips were like the fat, red wax lips Mama would occasionally buy for me at the grocery. I loved to grip those lips between my teeth and run wild, trying to kiss someone. When Mama put an end to my antics, I'd pop the lips into my mouth and chew the cherry-flavored wax until *rigor mortis* threatened my jaws.

Holding second place in Mama's library of cultured music was the voluminous tenor voice of Mario Lanza. Mario wailed from the bottom of his diaphragm, as if he were about to swallow his tonsils. *"Drink, drink, drink, to lips that are red and sweet as the fruit on the tree."* Did Mario know about Jane Morgan's red lips?

Daddy cleaned his guns and listened. His first date with Mama, when they were living in Dallas, had included tickets to a Mario movie. But "Drink, Drink, Drink" was not his favorite tune.

He'd pull Mama into his lap. "For a hypocrite, you sure are good-looking! So tell me, what's the difference between Roger Miller's 'Chug-a-Lug' and Mario Lanza's rum-mug salute?"

Mama would not be deterred. Her children would be exposed to the most excellent music she could find. For us, Mario was grand opera, his songs on a par with "Love Is a Many Splendored Thing" and "Born Free."

As we grew, Mama began to probe the meager depths of Christian recording artists and discovered Word, Inc. Now a staple in the industry, Word was a toddling record company then, struggling to build the foundations of contemporary Christian music. Their artists influenced our lives greatly: Ethel Waters, The White Sisters, The Good Twins, Polly Johnson, and comedian Don Loney. My sisters and I memorized *Don Loney Talks* and *Don Loney Talks Again,* practicing stand-up comedy as we quoted his lines:

> *I pressed a kiss to her lips*
> *What could I do but linger?*
> *And as I ran my hand through her hair*
> *A cootie bit my finger.*

Our family held another ritual that shaped my musical tastes more deeply than the collection of phonograph records. Every Sunday, we marched down a mountain trail to the little rock church house where my father ministered as a missionary. He led the singing, while Mama played an old black upright piano. We sang four-part harmony from the shaped notes of the Stamps-Baxter hymnal, an opus ubiquitous in country churches in those days, holding old-fashioned favorites like "I'll Fly Away" and "Will the Circle Be Unbroken?"

Many of the church members were Native American, Choctaw to be exact, one of what the European settlers labeled the "five civilized tribes" because of their friendly ways and openness to adopting new customs. In the event of death, they would bring their Choctaw hymnals and croon the most melancholy rendition of "Amazing Grace" I've ever heard. Their voices would find the melody by sliding from note to note with a soft wail. The whole thing sounded so sad to me that I would cry even if I didn't know the poor person lying in the box.

The mountain people I grew up with had their own music, and most of us didn't know or care that there was such a thing as the Juilliard School. Even if we'd known it, there was no map to take us there.

And yet, here we are. I sit back in my seat in the theater and hum a line from "Blood on the Saddle," while the kids stash their instruments.

Only minutes away, Lady Liberty stretches her lantern to the sky, her base engraved with the poetry of Emma Lazarus:

Not like the brazen giant of Greek fame,
With conquering limbs astride from land to land.

The lines refer to one of the seven wonders of the ancient world, the Colossus of Apollo, a giant statue that stood with one foot planted on either side of the harbor in the Grecian city of Rhodes.

In a strange sort of way, I can relate to Colossus doing the splits. Facing south, my left foot is firmly planted at Lincoln Center in New York City—the high-roller, high-stakes, high-falutin', highbrow, capital of the music world—while my right foot is stuck in a cow pie on a muddy mountain road in my hometown of Zafra, Oklahoma. Yes, I am an incognito cowgirl, a lover of country music, hillbilly gospel, and Choctaw hymns. Yet on this evening in New York, I have three children studying stringed instruments with world-famous teachers at a world-famous conservatory, two younger children studying violin and piano down the street at the Manhattan School for Strings, and a baby boy listening from my lap, clapping his hands, insisting we hurry up and let him have his turn. As an education-minded mom, music schools are valuable to me. The learning offered within their walls enjoys an iconic reputation, the hauteur of hype.

But I am not cowed by that fact. That cow pie underneath my right foot has acted as a strong fertilizer, growing authentic musical roots.

No highbrows for me: The songs of home are the most beautiful songs in the world.

On the other hand, I cannot stomach the ornery redneck who spits artistic ignorance like tobacco juice. The study of classical repertoire offers students an opportunity to reach for the pinnacle of skill and advanced technique. Classical scores contain a multitextured depth of form and exposition that challenges the brain, enhancing its potential, building a sort of internal, "broad-brain" connection. Simply put, to listen to and learn classical music is to grow smarter, grow faster, and grow more talented than one would ordinarily grow.

So there is stability and balance in my Colossus stance. From this posture I can serve God most effectively. I earnestly hold on to the common touch that is so important to the ministry of Jesus, and I have not shirked the scriptural mandate to "play skillfully" (Psalm 33:3, NIV) and to "make his praise glorious" (Psalm 66:2, NIV). God is not only the Creator of all kinds of music; He is a demanding patron of the arts who has been doing some serious upgrading of my family's musical offerings for more than a century.

A miraculous musical journey spanning four generations has brought my children and me to Juilliard and on to world stages as diverse as Carnegie Hall and the Grand Ole Opry. When I look back over my life and the lives of family members who preceded us, I can clearly see the finger of God, stuck in the dirt, plowing a path before us, shaping our music and our message for His purposes. It is a path of switchbacks and surprises, of talent lost then found, of hopeless poverty kicked aside by grim determination, of musical opportunities withheld by God's left hand only to be purified and reissued with His right.

The music in my life began with a soft hum in the black dirt of a Texas cotton field. It crescendoed under the influence of the gentle, mournful songs of the Choctaw Indians and the happy gospel hymns of a small church in the Oklahoma hills. Then it was tailored by a university's erudite guidance, tested by Nashville, Tennessee's music elite, joined by my own brood of children, and carried halfway across a continent to this place.

I have learned more than I ever thought possible.

Many parents witness the fruit of God's work in the music of our family and approach me with questions about how to achieve greater success with their children. I hear questions like, "My son loved playing the piano until he went to high school. Now he wants to quit. Should I let him?" "How did you choose instruments for your children? Did you choose for them?" "Did you force your children to study music?" Or, "How did you find a good teacher?"

Some parents or grandparents make grievous and misguided remarks such as, "Your family is so talented. Our family has no talent. We can't carry a tune in a bucket." Or, "My kid is only nine years old. She's got plenty of time." "My children are all just going to take piano lessons. I figure it's the most basic musical instrument."

I do my best to answer, but as I look at God's work through the generations of our family, I realize that there's much more to our success than a single-minded interest in music. It starts with something far richer and much deeper: the grace of God gradually unfolding His wisdom and His love. His guidance has equipped our family to take our passion for music and grow it in ways we never could have imagined. It can do the same for your family.

The Song of Annie Moses is my story of being a wife, a mother, and, most of all, a woman who was given a gift by her own mother, and her mother's mother. It is the story of how I was led by God to honor that gift by passing it on to others through the testimony of our family's story and the life-changing power of music.

Love's Legacy

But the effect of her being on those around her was incalculably diffusive:
for the growing good of the world is partly dependent on unhistoric acts;
and that things are not so ill with you and me as they might have been,
is half owing to the number who lived faithfully a hidden life,
and rest in unvisited tombs.

MIDDLEMARCH BY GEORGE ELIOT

Annie Moses. Prettiest baby.

Our family's love of music can be traced in many directions, but one of the richest legacies comes from my maternal grandmother, Annie Moses. Born in Melissa, a cotton town in north Texas, Annie exhibited exceptional beauty, winning first place in the prettiest baby contest at the county fair. God had used His most rare palette of colors when He wove her together in the secret place. Fiery red hair framed her face with soft, spongy curls. Her eyes, soft green and brushed with bits of topaz, grabbed you by the heart, compelling you to look.

Yet Annie's delicate beauty did not mean she would lead a delicate life. The eldest of eleven children, she humbly took her place as a slave of necessity and became the lead worker in her family's sparse field of dreams. She hoed corn, picked cotton, and bucked hay with the muscle of a man.

Cruel poverty staked a claim early, driving its flag into Annie's heart, signing its name across her winsome face. The simple folk music that reached her was meager amid the black and white of Texas dirt and cotton bales. The callous cuff of hard manual labor and the yellow teeth of the southern sun bit into her fair skin.

The fields set a brutal backdrop for Annie's life, but they were not the only challenge she faced. Her mother, Mary Fortner, wore a tight bun and a tighter heart, and her father, William, could be quick-tempered and demanding. When Annie was twenty, they frowned on her attachment to her beau, Buddy Moses. But Annie loved the jolly, lumbering man, and her hard life spurred her to escape. She was conscientious. He was carefree. She was hard-working. He was happy-go-lucky. She was poor. He was poorer.

Annie left the field early one day to attend a small-town carnival. Buddy walked her home. She would pay for that.

"You can't whip her!" Annie's mother cried, gripping her father's arm. "She's twenty years old."

But he did. He whipped her for walking home with Buddy, for holding hands with someone no-good for her, for choosing a feller on her own and defying his will. He whipped her for the family who needed her strong back, for her selfishness, and for himself.

It was over in a minute, and as Annie Fortner climbed into bed, the welts on her back swelled her resolve to marry Buddy Moses—as soon as possible.

It was a hard start. Marriage didn't free Buddy and Annie from field labor; other types of work were not readily available. Around the time the first baby came, a boy she named George William, Othar Harris hired the couple to work on his estate. Othar and his wife, Leona, lived just a few miles away from Melissa, in Chambersville, Texas, and were some of the largest landholders in the area. Five houses lined their property—four of them nothing more than laborers' shacks. Working for the Harrises was a move that would prove to be a strategic one on God's part.

On a hot August evening, in a tiny bedroom of one of those shacks, my mother was born. Annie Moses gave birth to her second child, a beautiful baby girl whom she named Ethel Jane, after her mother and grandmother. God is always constructing a new beginning.

He filled Jane's eyes with the same beautiful topaz he had sprinkled throughout Annie's, covered her finely shaped head with glossy chestnut hair, and brushed the alabaster skin with an apricot blush. Then, in His lavish, wonderful way, God piled on the talent. He strung Jane's voice with finely spun silver, a high, light soprano—reminiscent of Shirley Jones or Julie Andrews—and wrote on her heart a passion for music.

Hope is born with a child, and, despite her poverty, Annie dreamed of providing the education and opportunity necessary to develop her daughter's potential. It would take two more generations of God's guidance for the sound to build, but with my mother's birth, the song of Annie Moses had begun.

The year was 1933. The Great Depression that had devoured the American economy hardly affected the Moses family; they simply carried on. The cotton fields, like God, were no respecter of persons. Not even a pretty little girl who could sing like a lark escaped them. Like the slaves of the Deep South a century before, Jane began her musical education by singing in a cotton patch.

> *Oh, I don' pick the cotton*
> *Ol' cotton, he pick me*
> *Ain't it a cotton-pickin' shame*
> *That devil cotton know my name.*
> *Oh, I don' pick the cotton*
> *Ol' cotton, he pick me.*

The fields had their own music when the heat fairly whistled and the steam rose, clammy and sour, from underneath Jane's hair. The ground, wet and cold before dawn, was by noon so burning hot on her little bare feet that she stepped from milkweed to milkweed to avoid blisters. The flies and crickets buzzed, gossiping along with friendly pickers who chatted, hats bobbing, laughter floating from afar—boss watching.

And God, too big to be seen, stood right there in the middle, cultivating the heart of this little girl whom He had lavished with talent. The casual observer might have said that the odds were against Jane, that her talents would come to nothing. But her life would testify that the odds are trumped when God steps in. It would take time—generations—but He was slowly and lovingly changing the landscape, activating the most simple and unlikely people to implement His plan.

For landowner Leona Harris, the Great Depression was nothing more than a pothole slowing the brand-new Cadillac she graciously received every year from her doting husband. Educated and refined, Leona wore white lace gloves, cashmere sweaters in soft April colors, and big hats nestled elegantly into her dark, upswept coiffure.

Othar Harris was brilliant, a quiet and fair man who invented such sophisticated machinery as a conveyer belt made from a straight-eight Packard engine off one of his own discarded luxury automobiles, and a hay truck carved out of last-year's cut-in-half Cadillac. Othar's tractor bragged dual wheels before dual wheels were invented—and a purring Oldsmobile engine he installed himself. He never sold his or his wife's used automobiles.

Throughout the Great Depression, when jobs and cash were scarce, Othar employed the full-time services of four men who housed their families in the clapboard dwellings on his property. They were grateful, in such hard times, to work the vast fields, planting in the spring and harvesting in the summer. They enjoyed Othar's leadership and innovation, as well as his accommodations. The house occupied by the family of Buddy and Annie Moses sat close to the Harris' beautiful white Victorian.

The Harris home murmured of wealth. A great clock ticked steadily in the entry hall, and fragile glass vases held fresh-cut flowers. No toys littered the manicured lawn, no cradle creaked beside the velvet sofas: No children occupied the bedrooms. There had been a baby, once, growing inside Leona, with all the promise of blessings that a child bestows on a couple. But the day of the birth brought no first gulp of breath, no first cry of surprise, no happy exclamations from Othar—only silence. The doctor came gravely to Leona's bedside, leaned over, and told her that the baby had died.

For some reason known only to God, there were no more babies after that.

So Leona's heart yearned, until one hot August afternoon, the cries she longed to hear came streaming from the bedroom window of the humble dwelling down the path. Leona quickly ascertained Jane's talents and reached out to her with the wealth of love she had stored up for her own lost child.

Thus began afternoons of high culture for a little girl who had seemed destined only for the cotton patch. While her daddy painted the Harris' wraparound porch, Leona painted Jane's mind with Monet images of another world. While Annie planted the Harris' fields, Leona planted dreams in Jane's heart. Annie relished the arrangement and worked harder than ever, knowing her little girl would benefit from the unveiling of new horizons. Leona took Jane in unconditionally, as though it was the most natural thing in the world for a boss's wife to nanny a laborer's daughter.

The French doors of Leona's boudoir opened to the fragrance of her beloved rose garden, and she took Jane for walks there, holding her hand, teaching her the intricacies of each bloom. In the hall, Leona's rare vase collection blinked between the beveled glass and mirrors of a cherrywood china cabinet, and each piece provided an opportunity for show and tell. Leona sat beside Jane, pointing out the artistry, the colors, the unique history. Her contralto voice was melodious, her silver bridgework flashed, and her eyes spoke to Jane as if she were the only other person alive. Jane's heart swelled with love.

One Christmas, Leona took Jane by the hand and led her into the dining room, where a cherrywood table stretched like a limousine under a shimmering chandelier. Beside the table, beautifully arranged on the matching buffet, sat dolls of every sort: baby dolls, big-girl dolls, country dolls, and rich city dolls. But the most beautiful doll of all stood straight, with big brown eyes and sun-blushed cheeks. Her thick chestnut braids were tied with blue grosgrain ribbon, and the blue-and-white floral fabric on the band of her yellow straw hat matched that of her dress. She wore brown leather shoes and a blue apron edged with ruffles. She was a portrait of her new owner.

For a poor girl in the gray days of the Great Depression, one might think a new china doll would hold the key to heaven on earth. But though Jane loved the doll, something else came to eclipse her. Jane's brightest moments, the times she loved most, were when Leona pulled a small, ladder-backed chair close beside the keyboard of her ebony baby grand and seated Jane there on a soft pillow. Then Leona would play.

Thus was the light lit.

Much later, I came to see that Leona was my mother's patron—her Medici or Archduke Rudolf—a woman of means who moved in not to fund a professional but to demonstrate the miracle of art and music to the soul of a child. Through her love, she illuminated the destinies of generations.

Following the death of her husband many years later, Leona became terminally ill with Alzheimer's disease. My mother is still moved to tears when she recalls the elegant lady, her gray eyes empty and fearful, standing at the second-story window of a nursing home in Texas, waving a tissue, imploring in pale, pitiful tones to passersby, "Oh, help me. Someone, please help me."

Leona's body would fail and her mind would let go of its purpose, but the love she gave was food in the hands of God, nourishing a legacy. How much she would have enjoyed sitting by my side in the performance halls of the Juilliard School, seeing the small light of hope she lit, more than a half-century earlier, gather brightness as the torch passed to a new generation.

The comforts of Leona's world provided Jane with a reprieve from the frustrating cycles of her extended family's harshness. Buddy and Annie's strained start, their union disfavored by Annie's parents, had cast a pall over their children—George, Jane, and Othar, the baby, named after Mr. Harris. Distrust between Annie's parents and her husband rankled. Often, Annie had to overlook her parents' slights, to forgive and forget, but still, they found fault not only with her husband but with her children.

One warm, sunny Easter, however, all hearts were softened and all slights set aside as the Fortner family gathered, including aunts and uncles and cousins. The house was aired and the table spread, a farmhouse feast as only a farm family can prepare. The Moses family arrived along with the others, set on having a good time.

In the front of the house sat Grandmother Fortner's special *Room*, a hallowed sanctuary whose walls protruded gracefully from the rest of the house, a wraparound porch curving to cradle and shade it. The door to the *Room* remained locked at all times, the curtains closed on its mysteries. No children ever so much as jiggled the handle for fear of Grandmother Fortner. So everyone was astonished when, in a rare quirk of conviviality, the stiff-backed old woman coughed up the key, unlocked the door, and invited her guests inside. Porcelain figurines and etched glass gleamed from the top of every dresser, lined every table, and hung from the walls. Beckoning and forbidding, they tempted Jane to touch them, but she wouldn't risk Grandmother's wrath, and besides, something else interested her more. Her eyes slid past the adornments to the carved mahogany cabinet of an upright piano at the far side of the room. A piano! A piano? Grandmother Fortner owned a piano?

Annie Moses made her way through the crowd, patting her daughter's head as she passed. She sat down at the instrument and opened a hymnal.

"I'll try, sisters," she said, "but you have to remember, I've only had eight lessons." Eight lessons? Jane couldn't believe it. Her mother had studied piano!

Her head bobbed as her eyes moved from the notes on the page to the notes on the keyboard, searching for the right chords. Halting at first, then with more confidence, she played. Annie began to sing. "Christ the Lord is Risen today. Ahh-le-lu-ia!"

Jane stood transfixed. Her mother's voice sounded throaty and natural, as though it had grown out of the rich earth she worked with her hands.

"Sons of men and angels say: Ahh-le-lu-ia!" Annie's voice soared, and one by one, the aunts joined her.

"Raise your joys and triumphs high. Ahh-le-lu-ia!" They sounded, to Jane, like angels, the deep strong chords of the piano reaching up to support them.

"Sing ye heavens and earth reply. Ahh-le-lu-ia!" Mother could play the piano like Leona Harris? Mother could sing? The blended voices pulled Jane forward to her mother's knees, and she stared up in rapt attention. It was the sweetest song she had ever heard.

When the room had cleared, Jane stood quietly. The minutes ticked by. Silence. Nobody came to shoo her away. All alone and enveloped in grace, she gingerly touched the piano. With two fingers of each hand, she pressed the keys. It sounded beautiful—her music. Love welled up. She had watched Leona play, but Leona had never invited her to play. When had her mother learned to play—to sing? One day, Jane vowed, she might play and sing too, like her mother.

It was a day of miracles, in which Grandmother Fortner, for all her gruffness, played no small part. Grandmother Fortner was off her game! She'd neglected to clear the room, after the singing, and lock the door. She'd left a child untended in a domestic sanctuary. She'd left Jane to absorb the full effect of her mother's debut, and to touch the keys herself.

Somewhere in the course of her life, the Fortner family's earnings had afforded Annie Moses those eight beautiful lessons. But her parents had never really believed in her music and when harvest time hit, the fields reigned supreme. She rarely got to touch a piano after that, but she harbored no grief for her own overlooked talent. Instead she watched the natural unfolding of her daughter's: the lilting voice, the white smile, the graceful bearing. Jane loved to climb on the woodpile and perform for the chickens: "Oh, look at the moon, it's shining up there; Oh, Mama, it looks like a lamp in the air. Last week it was small and shaped like a bow; but now it's grown bigger and round like an OOOOOO!" Jane rounded her lips and flung her arms wide in a Broadway-style finale.

Annie, watching from the window, would tuck her head and smile. She had learned to keep special moments hidden, lest the world snatch them away.

Jane dreamed of singing on a real stage. Her woodpile stage lacked prestige, and the chickens didn't seem to notice the new white satin blouse, and the red velvet skirt and bolero vest her mother had sewn for her. She lifted her chin and sang with all her might, "Some-wheeeeeere over the rainbow…bluebirds fly; Birds fly over the rainbow, why then oh why can't I?"

The question pounded in her heart. What good is a look, if no one is looking? What good is a song, if no one is listening? Did anybody care about her music? Was there anybody out there who wanted to teach her to play and to sing?

When Jane was in the seventh grade at the Chambersville school, God answered her cry by sending a second angel, one as sweet and unlikely as Leona. Petite and frail, Miss Madie Francis looked light enough to fly without wings.

She had never married and lived with her mother. Ill health had made her hair thin and dingy, and her eyelids fluttered uncontrollably.

But Miss Francis' musical intuition and artistic sensitivity overcame her physical challenges. She quickly assessed Jane's gifts, rolled up her sleeves, and pulled out the music. Within a month, Jane was on the school's piano, hammering the notes of the Hanon études and running slow, steady scales up and down the keyboard.

Then came another gift. One bright afternoon, Jane skipped home from school to find a mahogany miracle sitting in the front room of the house. How could it be? Grandmother Fortner, with the tight bun and the tighter heart, had given Jane's mother the piano. The lonely old upright, decorative and beautiful, had been locked away for decades, begging to be played. Now Jane would have an instrument at the ready on which to practice, to prepare, and to play.

The piano, however, established another dilemma. The house was small, and the front room doubled as a bedroom. Worn out from long hours on Mr. Harris' rough, noisy tractor, Buddy wanted peace and quiet at home. When Jane began to play, he would gripe, "Get off that noisy thing."

So Jane practiced immediately after school, before her daddy came home, and on Monday nights when he would suit up the boys, George and Othar, and hustle them off to Boy Scout meetings, leaving Jane alone with her mother. Annie would sit in her rocker and sew quietly while Jane played. Occasionally, Jane would turn to her mother and ask, "Does that sound right?" A woman of few words, Annie would smile, nod, and return to her stitching, delighted. Monday nights were precious.

During lessons at school, Miss Francis insisted that Jane count out loud as she played, accenting the proper notes. "One-and-two-AND-three-and-four-AND...." Instead of mere counting, Jane *sang* the numbers with natural ease, revealing a new layer of talent.

"Why, Jane! You sing beautifully." Miss Francis' face showed happy surprise. "Would you like to sing at the recital? Let's see." She began to thumb through a stack of sheet music. "Your voice sounds light and agile." Her eyelids fluttered wildly. "Very, very pretty! And I hear vibrato...unusual for a girl your age. A sign of prodigy—Here!" She pulled a piece of music from the stack. "Here's a sweet song that I love. The lyrics are for someone a bit older. But...well, take a listen."

Miss Francis began to play and sing, a lilting tempo. "How do you like this?

> *I'm a little on the lonely, a little on the lonely side*
> *I keep thinking of you only and wishing you were by my side*
> *You know my dear when you're not here there's no one to romance with*
> *So if I'm seen with someone else, it's just someone to dance with....*

"Sing with me, Jane.

> *. . . Every letter that you send me I read a dozen times or more*
> *Any wonder that I love you more and more*
> *Oh, how I miss your tender kiss and long to hold you tight*
> *I'm a little on the lonely side tonight...."*

The words might have been written for Miss Francis; for a moment, her face was wistful. Then the mood evaporated, and she applauded, "Lovely! Just lovely! That one's a for-sure!"

She searched the stack again. "There aren't that many numbers in the recital, so I believe you'll have time to sing two." She pulled out a piece. "This one is slower, and very popular, 'I Can't Begin to Tell You.'" Her eyelids fluttered with excitement. "Actually," she whispered, leaning close, "I can begin to tell you… the audience will probably wish the whole recital belonged to you!" She ran a scale up the keyboard and began the song:

> *I can't begin to tell you how much you mean to me*
> *My world would end if ever we were through*
> *I can't begin to tell you how happy I would be*
> *If I could speak my mind like others do*

She paused, "Take it away, Jane!"
Jane's lyric soprano took up the lines.

So take the sweetest phrases the world has ever known
And make believe I've said 'em all to you.

Re-ci-tal. Re-ci-tal. Re-ci-tal. Every heartbeat drummed the word. Jane learned her songs, returning to her woodpile stage to practice on the chickens. In addition to the two vocal numbers, she prepared a piano piece, "Woodland Echoes," performing it for her mother during their Monday nights together. She still plays the song today, and I marvel that she played it then, with only one year of lessons. The piece is in 3/4 meter and contains what I call a "grab-and-go" left hand, the type made famous in pieces like Scott Joplin's "Maple Leaf Rag"— boom-chuck-chuck, boom-chuck-chuck. The sound requires the left hand to grab a low octave and then hop quickly to midregister to find a three-note chord. It's difficult. While the left hand executes that, the right hand plays a lilting little tune in the upper register. Side by side, the piano piece and the two songs— perfectly suited to Jane's vocal style—represented an impressive lineup for a twelve-year-old girl with only one year of study.

Annie's multiple jobs made it impossible for her to sew Jane's evening dress for the recital, so she commissioned a neighborhood seamstress. The gown, of a rich yellow satin, was simple and elegant, with a scoop neck, princess lines, and cap sleeves. The cut and the color emphasized Jane's glowing skin.

You have one chance to do this right, Jane told herself as she took stage. *Don't blow it.* When her turn came, she played the piano like it was Monday night and her mother was sitting right behind her in the rocking chair. When she sang, she pretended she was standing on the woodpile announcing to the chickens: *I can't begin to tell you how much you mean to me.*

Chambersville discovered a new darling that night, clapping till their hands stung. They sought her out backstage. Miss Frances stood at her side, beaming like a fairy godmother. A member of the local Methodist church, who helped with the music, invited Jane to sing a special for the Sunday morning services.

Jane took every opportunity to showcase her music. But 1940s small-town Texas offered few stages other than at church and school. There was no consistent system of music education to develop the talents of the children in the community.

Singing with the Methodists was fun for Jane; she was assigned a duet with her good friend, Alma Jo. But the songs didn't suit her nearly as well as the ones she'd performed in the recital.

By the end of the year, kind and delicate Miss Francis was worn down by the workload and could not continue to perform her magic as a teacher.

That year with Miss Francis was Jane's only opportunity for structured musical studies. How good it had felt to sit beside a musical counselor who knew her, who chose styles wisely, who understood the importance of capturing the fleeting moments in the blossoming life of a young lady! But it was over too soon. That night in the gym, in a yellow satin dress, Jane played and sang the first and last recital of her life.

Leona Harris—patron, Madie Francis—teacher, and, most important, Annie Moses—mother: each did what she could with what she was given. As in the story of the widow's mite, God honored the sacrifice and began to give the increase.

I wish Annie Moses could have lived to see it. By the time she reached forty-nine years of age, the lovely face of her childhood had disappeared, and cancer was destroying her body.

The hard life drove her to an early grave. Yet, as hard as her short life was, she did not shrink from her earthly tasks or toy with thoughts of escape. Her relentless faithfulness, her work ethic, her strength of character, and her sensitivity to the Spirit of God left a legacy, a foundation, upon which every subsequent generation would build. She planted all these qualities in her daughter, Jane, who grew up with visions of how life should be: how a home should be run, how music should reach into every life. They were visions that would profoundly affect my destiny, both musically and spiritually.

A quarter of a century after her birth in the clapboard house, with my two older sisters at her knee and me in her belly, Jane would announce to my father— with all the demure reticence of a she-bear with cubs—that her children *were* going to have the best music teacher she could find. Daddy placed his cowboy hat over his heart, rubbed his eyes, and chuckled.

He was willing, even eager, but it would not be easy.

907 Port Arthur

I told Eddie…

LELA N. JOHNSON

Our family had settled into what would become a lifetime of missionary work in the Kiamichi Mountains. The Kiamichis are dark and rugged, hidden deep in the southeastern corner of Oklahoma like a terrible family secret. When we were growing up, the dense, brushy woods were peppered with tarpaper shacks inhabited by the great-grandchildren of outlaws and gunfighters who, in the late 1800s, had escaped into Indian territory to evade white man's law and the bloody noose of the Fort Smith gallows, where Hangin' Judge Isaac Parker presided.

Our own family had tasted violence. Daddy's father, William Valentine Donica, was murdered, shot behind the right ear at almost point-blank range by a mean, moonshine-guzzling scoundrel. Years later, Daddy's stepfather, a one-time law enforcement officer known as "Tex" was also murdered—gut-shot in a midnight confrontation with pig thieves.

Daddy had become a Christian in his teens, and he'd left the Kiamichi Mountains for a season to gain a degree in pastoral ministry from Dallas Christian College. It was a brand-new college—he was the first student to enroll—and he had only preached a few sermons. But his professors thought his natural speaking skills and his study habits to be worthy of a job, and they sent him on the weekends to minister to a small, new congregation in McKinney. He didn't have a car, so he took the bus on Saturday morning and walked from the bus station to his boarding house, choosing a different route each week so that he could knock on every door he passed and invite the family to church. One of those houses belonged to Jane's Aunt Alva, Annie Moses' sister and one of Daddy's first converts.

"You should meet our preacher," Aunt Alva said to Jane. "His name is Riley Donica. Isn't that a handsome name? A handsome name for a handsome man. Tall too. I just love the way he preaches. His sermons are full of stories, not boring at all."

Jane agreed with her aunt's assessment: Riley was handsome, and an eloquent speaker. But he also had big feet, she thought.

Riley was smitten by Jane's beauty. One day, when they were sitting alone on the sofa at Aunt Alva's house, he leaned in close, touched her hair, and whispered, "You would be so easy to love." Jane enjoyed the tenderness, but it took her a while to absorb what he meant.

Annie Moses loved Riley instantly, soaking up his witty, colorful conversation. When Jane brought him home for Sunday lunch, Annie hid the magazines so he would talk instead of reading—Riley was a voracious reader. His eloquence inspired faith in Annie, and she bought a new family Bible, making payments of a dollar a week for twelve weeks. (I cherish both the Bible and the stub detailing the payment history; my father's influence clearly brought Annie closer to God as she neared the end of her life.)

Grandmother Fortner, however, stayed true to her romance-thwarting self. One weekend after Sunday dinner at her house, Riley needed to leave early so he could do some work at the church before evening services. He went out to warm the car, while Jane collected her purse. Grandmother Fortner, scowling on the porch, grabbed Jane's arm as she passed. "Whatever you do," she said, "don't marry a preacher!"

"Don't worry," Jane said, patting her grandmother's hand. Then she took a deep breath and ran to join Riley.

One quiet Saturday evening, Jane sat, vibrant and youthful in her white shorts, playing hymns on her precious piano. Riley sat at a desk beside her, his dark head bent over the sermon he was preparing for the next day. In the magic of the moment, a realization swept over Jane that this was the way it should always be.

They were only nineteen when the vows were spoken, and sturdy vows they were too: for richer or for poorer, for better or for worse, in sickness and in health. Riley returned to the mountains soon after graduation, where he and Jane worked side by side for a lifetime.

It wasn't always easy.

Riley had a dual mission: to preach the gospel and to declare war on crime in the mountains. He received the rank of deputy sheriff, and from the pulpit of grisly personal experience—the murders of his father and stepfather—he delivered sermons with equal punch from either the truth of the Bible or the butt of a shotgun.

When Mama issued her edict that her children *were* going to study music, Daddy reminded her that music teachers were not around every corner—and missionaries, in case she had forgotten, made very little money.

The Donica family. Back row, left to right: Riley, Cindy, Jane. Front row, left to right: Robin, Sherry, David.

Mama crossed her arms and smiled, her pretty white teeth sparkling. No, it would not be easy, but she didn't pick cotton for nothing. When my oldest sister, Cindy, was eight, Mama packed her purse with Merle Norman lipstick she'd brought from McKinney and revved up the pickup. Then she loaded her protégées—Sherry and I were allowed to tag along with Cindy—and bounced the rig twenty miles east down the rutted dirt roads, through the cow pies, across the state line, and over the Mountain Fork River to the small town of Mena, Arkansas, to the piano studio of Mrs. Lela N. Johnson.

The city kids called her "Deedee," but Mama testily insisted we refer to our new piano teacher as "Mrs. Johnson." Whatever the label, Mrs. Johnson's energy amazed us all. Built like a baseball diamond, her figure began on home plate, where her small feet bulged out of even smaller shoes. As her head stretched toward center field, her torso rounded first base, heaved up toward second, and bounced past third, disappearing back into the bulging shoes for a home run. Her ear baubles swung in countermotion to her shaking head as she sympathized with Mama.

"I have a sob right here." Mama pounded her chest with her fist. "I know in my heart that I was born to play the piano and sing, and my mother tried, but the money, the opportunity to educate myself, was just not there."

Mrs. Johnson pressed her lips together and attempted to blink. Her chronic cream eye shadow—royal blue—tugged the eyelid upward as it peeled away from her brow bone. *"Mm-hmm,"* she said, in heartfelt commiseration.

"But I've determined that my children *will* have every musical opportunity I can give them. Not fun and games, you see, but a serious line of intensive musical instruction. That is why I have come to *you*."

Mrs. Johnson's pink lips pouted with pleasure. The deal was sealed.

Mrs. Johnson's piano studio occupied a corner of her lavender house at 907 Port Arthur Avenue, a street lined with Cape Cod cottages and an occasional Victorian dollhouse. She looked thirty-something when she came into our lives, and she looked thirty-something when she passed away forty years later. She cut a swath as broad as her bodice through the haze of the small-town music scene.

Early every Saturday for the remainder of our natural youth, Mama hustled us out of bed to wander bleary-eyed through our small, cold house, scrounging for shoes and music books. Rain, snow, sleet, hail, floods, or herds of cattle— nothing could stop us. We piled into our used 1950 Chevrolet truck and jounced to piano lessons with all the flair of the Beverly Hillbillies.

Mrs. Johnson met us at the door, perfectly groomed, the air around her dangerously spiced with Tabu perfume, her hair swept up into a frustrated French twist, the initial bend of which hung glued in midair like a frozen ocean wave that never completed its curl. She was a wonderful teacher. She had sass and brass, and we loved her with all our hearts.

She would clinch her beloved baton and click hard time on the edge of the piano or lead our eyes down the notes of the page. God help you if you couldn't keep up. Mrs. Johnson paid money for the most pieces memorized (a reward I won many times) and gave gold and red stars for attendance and progress. But if you had a bad lesson, she would, with irate deliberateness, sprawl your sorry name on a small white card and paperclip it on to "The Black Ribbon": Facts were facts. My sisters and I lived in fearful anticipation of one of our siblings tattling, should one of us end up on the Black Ribbon: It was a crime punishable by death-looks from Mama, who just might tell Daddy.

Between pieces, Mrs. Johnson would tug at the hem of her skirt, trying unsuccessfully to cover the knees that peeked rebelliously out when she sat down, her flesh spilling over like yeast dough. She never, ever wore pants and complained of tight pantyhose almost as often as she complained of the high school band, whose schedule conflicted irksomely with her agenda: recitals, adjudications, musicals, and competitions.

But dread of her disapprobation or dismay at her doughy knees faded in comparison to the opportunity each lesson offered to read the comic books piled on the coffee table that sat in front of the sofa where we waited our turn. *Betty and Veronica* and *Archie and Jughead* served as our musical colleagues. We thrilled to the spin of *Spiderman,* to the adventures of *Batman and Robin,* and to the crusades of *Superman.* Being the youngest, I got to play first and could then breathe easy, reading for a full hour while my sisters struggled to exhibit their keyboard prowess. When my baby brother, David, began his brief and frustrated musical excursion, it spoiled my Saturday luxury. I no longer had my pick of comic books. To avoid fights, I was told to give him whatever book he wanted.

Every December brought the Christmas recital, held proudly at the grand piano in Mrs. Johnson's gilded parlor instead of the upright in the small studio where she held our lessons. Every May brought the spring recital, a formal event she held across the street at her Methodist church. Mrs. Johnson approached these two extravaganzas with the ferocity of a world war, threatening to die of high blood pressure and arthritis, insisting that our lack of preparation would send her to an early grave. By the second year, we were inoculated, and turned a deaf ear to the drama.

Unlike us, Mrs. Johnson's hero-husband, Eddie, was never inoculated. Dapper in pleated, cuffed slacks and fraternity cardigans, Eddie swept to the rescue. He would frown at us and call the doctor, who would prescribe more medicine. Eddie adored his plump bride. The beads, the blue eye shadow, the bulging knees, and the bodacious style were a scalloped shell around the pearl of his life. The Johnsons had no biological children but two counties full of musical children they fussed over incessantly.

From the early days, my proclivity for music seemed to emerge naturally. But as an aural learner, I lagged at note reading. Unfortunately, Mrs. Johnson played for me each new piece she assigned, never knowing her preview would enable me to play it by ear at home. I didn't even need the notes! When Mrs. Johnson discovered my delinquency, my name decorated the Black Ribbon until I exhibited full repentance. She was not impressed with "playing by ear," and rightfully so.

The students of Mrs. Johnson's piano studio danced in musicals, sang Broadway hits, sweated through recitals, participated in local and state competitions, and ended each school year with a ten-piece adjudication under the auspices of the National Guild of Piano Teacher Auditions.

Jane Moses Donica with her Acrosonic piano.

For a monthly payment of twelve dollars at the Union Bank of Mena, Daddy had financed a spinet piano that would prove to become a sturdy member of the family. The petite beauty sat proudly in the living room, spilling music into every corner of the house. Victory for Mama! She would never again countenance music being locked away in a lonely room, as it had been at Grandmother Fortner's. No one would yell, as her own father had—"Get off that noisy thing!"—when the music began. This piano was open for business, and children of all ages were welcome to her keys.

Acrosonic was her brand name, and she sat like a short, stout nanny with a doily on her head, surviving spills, wax build-up, termite swarms, sunning cats, and baby mice, which suckled their mama in her inner chambers. The mice some-how grew immune to the boxes of dCON hidden behind her sound board—poison that my sister, Sherry, once ingested, compelling Mama to make a hyster-ical drive over the dirt roads for help. At some point in our musical development, the Acrosonic grew a hole in her metal sustain pedal, worn through from sheer miles, her only concession of fatigue.

When I was five years old, Mama sat down at the piano and began her own musical entrepreneurship; she gathered my sisters and me around the keys and played for us while we sang, giving birth to what might be likened to a fusion of the Andrews Sisters and the Chipmunks. She would not waste time.

As an adult, I attempted once to assemble my own infantile trio. After only one session, I realized what an amazing musical accomplishment my mother had achieved with our sibling ensemble. The fact that my sisters and I could hear and sing three-part harmony at the ages of five, seven, and nine is extraordinary. But that is what Mama expected of us, and that is what we did.

While we learned to play the piano and sing, Daddy learned to fly. He finally obtained a pilot's license, and his skill in the skies was impressive. He traded our Volkswagen Bug for an Aeronca Chief, a lightweight, high-winged, single-engine aircraft, and garnered two hundred hours of flight in a year. He then acquired a Funk, a rare and beautiful little plane built in Coffeyville, Kansas, where the Dalton Gang, those sweet boys who once frequented the Kiamichis, met their demise.

After seven hundred more hours of flying, the Funk was followed by a Cessna 180, a fairly fast, haul-anything tail-dragger favored by bush pilots around the world. In this versatile plane—call number 4581 Bravo—he flew more than 1,100 hours, many of which were medical emergencies. When an eight-penny nail flew like a bullet into a local cowboy's right eye, Daddy and the Cessna carried him out of the mountains. When two teenage boys were lost on the Mountain Fork River, Daddy flew his Cessna below the tree line, while an eagle-eyed ol' timer sat beside him, searching the water.

As Daddy's preaching reputation grew, he began to evangelize by air, flying our family across the forested mountains and the fruited plains. We landed in cow pastures, beside cornfields, and on empty back roads. Our singing, Mama's piano playing, and Daddy's preaching made us a team. David brought along a toy pistol and cowboy hat to pass the time while his sisters sang "Just a Closer Walk," "The Ballad of the Green Beret," and "It's Not an Easy Road." We learned to enjoy people, to own a stage, and to speak and perform. Looking back, I realize that the stage of the small, rural church is one of the most powerful grooming grounds on earth.

When I entered fifth grade, the public schools were consolidated. The educational powers that be closed the beautiful one-room schoolhouse that stood a mile from our door, where learning had been natural and easy. Overnight, we had to ride a yellow bus—three hours a day—over dusty mountain roads and rutted lanes, picking up scruffy youngsters who struggled to keep themselves healthy, clean, and warm. I figure, mathematically speaking, I sacrificed approximately a fourth of my childhood's waking hours on that bus, shuttling back and forth.

God rescued me through the music made in the corner room of Mrs. Johnson's lavender house, Mama's artistic nurturing, through the high flight of a Cessna 180, and through the ministry our family practiced in cracker-box church houses sitting demurely in midwestern cornfields. The travel, the musical goals, the performances— these were the mentors that shaped my horizon and gave me a heart of concern for the world of a child who has no music.

Still, my artistic orb pulsed weakly, shrouded under the isolated dome of the mountains. I excelled in navigating the musical route mapped by Mrs. Johnson and Mama, but I sensed that my path, like the mountain roads I traveled daily, was rutted and narrow and led to no place of importance. Although unwarranted, as is the case for many teenagers growing up in rural places, a sense of inadequacy grew, an unarticulated fear that, should opportunity ever come my way, I lacked that mysterious, innate capacity for greatness with which others were, somehow, magically imbued. Once in a while, a truly fine artistic display came our way, mostly through the Cinema in Mena—*The Sound of Music, Mary Poppins, My Fair Lady*—light but substantive fare that triggered hope in me. But even as I watched, an ugly voice whispered, *"Don't get your hopes up. You could never do that. It's for other people who live outside these mountains—people who were born greater than you."*

It would take quite some time to realize that these thoughts are the consuming lie, told by the Enemy. When we begin to believe, to go along with all the misguided praise about "natural talent"—praise that renders the investment in discipline, structured practice, and hard work impotent—we leave true artistic possibilities unexplored.

During my sophomore year of high school, Mrs. Johnson and I worked up pieces for a special adjudication—where you are judged according to a grading system—which was called the "Federation." The rules required that two pieces be performed for a judge. A grade of superior would usher the student from first tier to second tier, and those who received a superior on the second tier would perform in an honor recital.

Happily, I made it all the way to the recital, held at the University of Arkansas at Little Rock. After the performance, I wandered around the music building, and curiosity called me into a big auditorium.

On stage, a college-age girl with long, bushy, Carole King hair and a loose-fitting dress opened her mouth to sing. I couldn't believe my ears. An enormous, velvety voice took effortless hold of a difficult melody and reached for the stratosphere. I was on the edge of my seat, my mouth gaping. Although I couldn't catch the words, the emotion of the piece flooded my heart. I bet she could sing the socks off "Love Is a Many Splendored Thing," and "Born Free," I said to myself. The song softened to an intimate passage, and the singer stepped forward. She closed her eyes and moved her head slowly from side to side, singing of a tragedy I couldn't understand. It finally dawned on me that the words were in a foreign language, but her expression drew me in irresistibly. I could empathize with her broken heart.

As she performed, an older woman moved toward her, interrupting in a high clear voice. "No, no, Dear. Even though this section has a decrescendo, the range is still very high. The breath stream must not become limp, it must become smaller—but even more powerful and from a deeper source." She placed her lower leg next to the singer's, touching her calf. "In your mind's eye, you must picture the breath coming from all the way down here," she said.

The girl nodded and began the section again, closing her eyes and moving her head from side to side, mourning along with the song.

"Yes, that is much better," the older woman interrupted. "That sound will carry the *pianissimo,* the very softest notes, to the back of even the largest room, over the orchestra. You mustn't forget that noisy, bossy orchestra." She laughed, a twinkling, soprano laugh.

The girl nodded, her eyes glassy from concentration.

"One other thing," the older woman said. "Your eyes must reflect the emotion you are struggling to communicate. The eyes are one of a performer's greatest tools of communication. Closing them randomly for long periods is irritating and distracting to the audience."

The girl nodded her ascent.

"Try it again, keeping your eyes open," the older woman said. "And remember, a small, energized breath stream."

The singer stood still, looking straight ahead. The accompanist began, and as the girl began to sing, articulating the strange words with even more compelling emotion, I felt unexpected tears. The high notes of the melody shot to the back wall like a stream of pure, clear water, powerful but controlled, with focused, spinning tone that, if heightened, could have broken glass, but, as it were, broke my heart instead. The "eyes open" instruction had made a difference; the sadness mounted in the singer's gaze. I could see it even from a distance. She completed the piece, and the audience applauded vigorously.

Wow! That was good, I said to myself. That voice teacher sure knows her stuff. I looked around the auditorium, trying not to cry. My heart ached to sing like that too. In my naive, country-girl mind, I thought, *Oh well, Robin, ol' gal, you can't speak foreign. That kind of singing is for rich, city people who are a lot smarter than you, people who know foreign languages. You have to start that type of thing when you are real, real little.*

I looked at the program to see who the older woman was. "Inez Silberg, Guest Vocal Instructor." I stood up and stretched, hoping to ease my longing by dismissing the girl's performance from my mind. But God notices even dubious dreams. From the vantage point of my "Federation" trip to Little Rock, I couldn't see it, but my path and Inez Silberg's were converging.

After a short break, a competition began for college-age piano students. By this time, the other students from Mrs. Johnson's studio had joined me. The prescribed piece was Grieg's Concerto in A Minor, whose opening octaves run all the way from the top of the piano to the bottom. Student after student played the first movement, plus a piece of his or her own choosing. One young man was exceptionally good, playing a Chopin étude that consisted of nothing but running thirds.

On the drive home, I contemplated the situation, feeling lonely and inadequate. These people played with a skill that put them on a different planet. Musical pursuits had given me broader horizons than my hardscrabble hometown normally offered, but a low ceiling still pressed me down. "You have to be born with it," I told Mama, "to have what it takes to play and sing like that."

She reached for my hand and held it tightly. "I know how you feel," she said. "I feel so inadequate myself. I'm doing the best I can. That's all anybody can do. That's all my mother could do for me."

Little by little, new opportunities like the ones I had witnessed in Little Rock were being unveiled, raising the bar of personal expectation. Exposure to greatness is the inspiration that forces the bloom of opportunity. How can one shoot for the stars if one has never seen the sky?

I had attended the National Guild of Piano Teachers adjudication for nine consecutive years, since the third grade, memorizing ten or more pieces that met the criteria for composers and musical eras. Each year, I had earned a score of Superior or Superior Plus, the equivalent of an A or an A+. If I succeeded in accomplishing this for one more year, I would win the Paderewski Award, along with a small college scholarship.

My senior year of high school, however, was a time of confusion and instability. I didn't have a clue where I would go to college, though I was expected to go and to choose piano as my line of study. High accolades were within reach, yet I slouched along with all the enthusiasm of an organ donor.

Mrs. Johnson bellowed her frustration. "My blood pressure is sky high! I told Eddie yesterday, I said, 'These kids are going to be the death of me.' And it's all because *somebody* I know refuses to practice."

Then came the noose.

"Dr. Clarence C. Burg from Oklahoma City University will be your Guild judge this year. Let me tell you"—her head jerked, underscoring each word—"he is *tough*. He has written several books, you know—that's books, b-o-o-k-s, books—on piano pedagogy. Another thing"—a pinch of pleading entered her tone—"if you play well, he might invite you to perform at the workshop he teaches during the summer, and coach you while the participants observe."

The noose tightened.

"I have written to tell him that you are undecided about the college you'll attend. So you can look at the Guild as a double audition. Wouldn't it be exciting to be accepted into the studio of someone of his stature? And, if you make Superior, you'll have that great scholarship, as well."

I was hanged.

Dr. Clarence C. Burg weighed heavy on my mind, but not heavy enough to propel me to the piano bench for any sort of regular practice. The day before my audition, Mrs. Johnson heard my ten pieces, and when I finished, she cocked her head, eyed me with her dominant eye, and crossed her arms, which seemed an amazing feat, across her vast unibosom. Her triceps bounced like giant water balloons. "Dr. Clarence C. Burg judged Missy Pritts yesterday," she said. "Missy has a full, tuition-paid scholarship to Ouachita Baptist University! She's very good." The water balloons jiggled, affirming Missy. "Guess what score Dr. Clarence C. Burg gave her?" I slumped in despair. "Good plus, the same as a C on a report card. Missy was crushed and came home crying. I said it once, and I'll say it again. Dr. Clarence C. Burg is *tough*!" On the word *tough*, Mrs. Johnson threw her arms in the air. I jumped back as the water balloons slapped the unibosom again, applauding their agreement.

That night I dreamed I was in a huge auditorium, peeping from behind a red velvet curtain at a vast expanse of audience. At any moment, someone would pull the ropes, the curtain would rise, and I would be compelled by hearty applause to walk onto the stage and perform. There were, however, three problems in the dream. First, I had to play an instrument I had never played. Second, I had to perform a piece I had never learned. Third—and this was the most serious—I was naked.

The next morning, as I drove forty miles south to DeQueen, Arkansas, for the auditions, I offered every Christian promise I could muster. "Lord, I'm casting my cares on you, just like you said." I imagined tossing my repertoire, one piece at a time, toward the oncoming traffic. "And I'm humble, Lord, trust me on this. I am not proud of myself, so You can feel good about giving me grace." I rebuked the world, the flesh, and the devil, promising to do better. "I can do all things through Christ who strengthens me." I gripped the wheel: "Philippians 4:13 always works, *right*? Even if you haven't practiced?" The highway fled beneath my wheels, and my desperate pleas subsided into the humming of funeral hymns.

The road sat shiny and wet from an April rain, and the passing dogwoods gleamed, iridescent from the bath, but nothing could brighten my heart. As DeQueen drew near and the panic thickened, I began to strategize. Traditionally, a student is asked to select the first piece to be played, while the judge selects the second; then the two alternate back and forth for the remainder of the audition. I had monkeyed around with the first movement of my sonata quite a bit. But the second and third movements were gorillas in the mist; I could barely recognize them. If I played the first movement first, Dr. Clarence C. Burg would likely not ask to hear the second or third movements. *That works!* If, by some cruel joke, he asked for a subsequent movement, I would smile like Barbie and play my Bach instead. "What? You said Beethoven? I am *so* sorry. Their names sound similar, with those *B's*."

I pulled into the studio parking lot and looked down to make sure I was fully clothed, then opened the car door and shuffled reluctantly into the musical court of Dr. Clarence C. Burg, who is *tough*.

Oklahoma City University

There she is. Miss America!

as sung by Bert Parks

Mama cried when I told her OCU would be my alma mater. "Oh, how my heart yearned to go to a school like this when I was your age, and now God has opened the opportunity for you. I wish Buddy and Annie were here to see it. They would be so proud."

To decorate my dorm room, we went to Sears and bought a pink-and-white comforter and downy pillows with pink shams, plus pink sheers, pink towels, pink rugs, and brand-new underwear.

Mama and I crafted my daily schedule, including time for practice and study, and hung it on the bulletin board. At 5:30 AM, my feet would hit the floor. I would splash my face with water and put my hoe in the ground.

At the time, Oklahoma City University placed fifth in the nation for music schools, offering an extraordinary level of individualized instruction and performance opportunities. The Fine Arts department produced two operas and two Broadway-style musicals every year, enabling students to build an impressive résumé on the stage of Lyric Theater, a lovely, 1,100-seat facility. Later, during my family's time at the Juilliard School, I saw that the Broadway stages of New York are inundated with OCU graduates, including such Tony Award-winning performers as Kristin Chenoweth.

In addition to performers, OCU is known for its beautiful women, talented girls who vie regularly for a title and a crown. In the University's beauty-queen hall of fame, visitors view a wall of gorgeous photographs:

twenty-seven state pageant winners, three of whom went on to become Miss America.

My two older sisters, Cindy and Sherry, attended Dallas Christian College, Daddy's alma mater. DCC felt like family, but I was venturing into the world of the wicked university tree of knowledge, set to trap a rising generation like bugs. Daddy preached about it relentlessly. To him, going to any college but a Bible college ranked right up there with wallowing in an outhouse pit for four years. The stench might never wash off.

"Robin, you got a brain like a bear trap. Use it. I don't care how many PhDs a teacher has, if he don't know God he don't know much," Daddy said.

On the day I started classes, he handed me the keys to a blue-and-white 1965 Chevy Impala, a burly, boatlike automobile that floated on air at eighty miles an hour, started without a key, and would be stolen three times during my college tenure.

Loneliness washed over me like hot wax as I watched my parents drive away. I missed the mountains—already—and the little rock church house too. I missed shooting hoops with David when we were supposed to be carrying in wood. I missed Lullabelle and Cleopatra, our pet heifers, and I missed our donkey, Bunny, and her baby girls, Bernadine and Bernadette. I missed Jinks and Johnnie-Go, our valiant steeds. I missed Rusty, our arthritic boxer, and George, our baseball-playing hound, and Helen of Mena, our brilliant kitty-cat, who had cleverly deduced that every morning when the school bus honked, the front door would open, providing her a chance to dash indoors.

Mrs. Johnson and 907 Port Arthur seemed a million miles away.

I sank into my new pink comforter and cried. Just a few short weeks ago, I hadn't even known that Oklahoma City University existed. How did I get here?

It had started when I took that dreadful drive to DeQueen, where I'd been totally unprepared to play for Dr. Clarence C. Burg. My performance seemed to have flopped like a bass in the grass. Could this ancient man, whose face was freckled with age spots, even hear? He seemed to vacillate in and out of consciousness. He took no notes, made no check marks on the score sheet, nothing.

For my final piece, I performed my own interpretation of Chopin's *Fantaisie-Impromptu,* glancing at Dr. Burg during memory slips. He looked bleary. Perhaps he was stunned. Or was he unconscious? Hard to tell. I emoted all over the keys during the "I'm Always Chasing Rainbows" interlude, one of my favorite melodies, and one I knew fairly well. This was my last chance to gain desperately needed points. Yet I could see my "Superior" drifting out to sea as I gasped for air, drowning in an ocean of notes.

I played my last chord, took a deep breath, and waited. Dr. Burg stood up— as best he could. He tottered toward the piano, patted my hair, and spoke through a soft spray of mist.

"Well done, dear. Now, I am going to give you a score of…Superior-Plus. Let's see. What do I need to mark in order to accomplish this?"

He hobbled back to his chair to calculate the score, making my Superior-Plus a reality with a stroke of his pen and *because he said so.*

"Now," he continued, "I would also like to invite you to come to my piano pedagogy workshop this summer at Oklahoma City University, to play for my class. I will coach you while the participants observe." Then he did something he would continue doing during every lesson we shared. He pulled a chair up to the piano, gripped my upper arm with a trembling hand, and began to reminisce.

Slowly, it dawned on me. This old man wasn't tough. Like a well-aged steak, he had grown tender with time.

"I'll bet you didn't know this, dear," he said, "but I was raised right here in DeQueen." He closed his eyes and clutched my arm with his fingers, as if to prevent my escape. Then he sank back through the corridors of long ago—so far back that I wondered if he remembered I was in the room. He spoke of his childhood, his family, and his music with a wistful, end-of-life sort of remembering; the kind of remembering that pulls joy into the lap of sorrow and hugs too tightly. If I had not been having a nervous breakdown, I would have absorbed his melancholy. But the strain of it all had been too great. I gave up and wilted with laughter. This startled and pleased Dr. Burg, who awakened from his reverie, supposing my merriment stemmed from the charm and wit he'd exuded during his mosey down DeQueen's memory lane.

When the hour ended, I stumbled out into the sunshine like a prisoner of war set free from a firing squad. What happened in there? A miracle? No doubt. But how?

I drove straight to Mena to tell Mrs. Johnson. She clapped her hands, jiggling like warm Jell-O. "I knew it all the time! You sure can turn it on when you want to."

My sister, Cindy, a textbook oldest sister to my textbook youngest, drove me to OCU to perform for Dr. Burg's summer workshop. We would stay in the girl's dorm, Walker Hall, just across the small campus from the music building. I had a vague awareness that I'd have to accomplish my scheduled performance. But I yearned to get to know Oklahoma City: to watch movies, explore restaurants, and try on cute clothes, simple activities not readily available in my native territory.

On the morning of my performance, I dressed well and played well, then tiptoed out the door and roared off to shop and see a movie. When I returned to Walker Hall, Cindy met me at the door. "Robin, where have you been? Listen, Dr. Burg told me to tell you he wants to see you in his office tonight. He said he will wait until you come, so you'd better hurry up and go see what he wants."

My heart jumped. What could he want? It was after eight o'clock, probably hours past his bedtime. Was he mad at me? Maybe he didn't think I'd done as well for his class as I thought I had. Reluctantly, I approached the door of his studio, wiped my sweaty palms on my skirt, took a deep breath, and knocked briskly. At first, nothing. Then, slowly and evenly, the heavy door opened.

Dr. Burg bobbed slightly. "One-two-three-four," he said percussively, imitating the rhythm of my knock. "Come in, dear, and have a seat. I have been waiting for you." He walked back to his desk. "You played very well today, you know. Such talent." Then, in the same insouciant style he'd used to issue my Superior-Plus, he took up his pen: "Now, dear, let me see, what classes will you be taking this fall? You'll need Theory I and Music Survey and...." His voice faded as he assigned my classes.

I had applied to OCU late, dragging along in a doubtful cynicism, unsure of two things: whether I wanted to go and whether they wanted me to come. And yet, here I was, walking out of an old man's office with a slip in my hand that said I was a college student majoring in piano and minoring in voice.

It took no time at all to figure out Dr. Burg's plight. He was assuredly a great pedagogue, but the natural effects of age had left him with a dangerously diminished supply of students. Ouachita Baptist University had already snatched Missy Pritts. Through Mrs. Johnson's letter, Dr. Burg had learned that I was both available and aimless. He needed students, and I needed a teacher. It was a match made in heaven.

And I mean that sincerely, for God was directing the play. He is the divine strategist Who structures multilayered plots, broad and sweeping and love-filled. His plans went beyond OCU, beyond Dr. Burg, and beyond me. Strange things were happening, but I didn't understand how brilliant, how important, how miraculous my enrollment at OCU would turn out to be. I love God so much for offering kindness to me during those difficult days, and not only to me, but to a fine, elderly gentleman who struggled with purpose in the winter of his life.

The swirl of energy exhibited by the students around me eventually lured me from the security of my pink comforter. I dried my tears, and went to scout the music building, curious to locate the classrooms where my classes would be held and to see where I would spend the next few years of my life. As I walked up the steps, a slender young man with a headful of beautiful auburn hair was walking down. The radiant August sun reflected off his golden highlights, catching my eye. As he bounced past me, I paused, turned around, and said, "Hey."

He stopped and turned around to look at me.

"You sure do have pretty hair."

"Why, thanks," he said with a smile.

There he stood—my future husband. Reason number one why God activated Dr. Burg to assign my undeserved, destiny-filled Superior-Plus and drag me to OCU. Of course, I didn't know it at the time.

Only two weeks later, Bill called to ask me for a date. I refused. I didn't think he was my type. After all, a country girl needs a rugged country boy, right?

In retrospect, that refusal was the best thing that could have happened. Instead of becoming romantically involved, we became friends, studying together, going to movies, and writing songs.

To say Bill plays piano is like saying fish swim or sugar sweetens. His technique flows like a summer breeze, without restriction, a genius that comes from deep inside; music oozes from his soul like buttercream, a smorgasbord of succulent jazz and honeyed harmonies. On our honeymoon, I would awake with a jolt to hear him shouting altered chords in his sleep—"C7#9, G13, Ab9#11"!

Bill is 100 percent fluent on keyboard. OCU soaked him up and wrung him out. He accompanied the Keshena Kids, the Surrey Singers, musical theater productions, rehearsals, auditions, and master classes. He composed, arranged, and performed for Promise, a contemporary Christian band consisting of him and five of his buddies; their music featured brass that echoed the top forty hits of Bill's favorite seventies group, Chicago. Between the cracks, he played for church on Sundays and Furrs Cafeteria on weeknights, and still, he managed to practice four hours a day and graduate near the top of his class.

I once careered into one of Bill's recitals, entering the auditorium just as the doors closed, quickly snatching a seat beside Greg, a pianist and mutual friend. Greg leaned over to me. "Hi, Robin," he whispered. "Why are you here? You want to be depressed too?"

We all had to face it. Bill drop-kicked our royal piano-playing highnesses into the next galaxy. And all the time, he was so nice about it—his Eagle Scout badges resting humbly on their sash, his GPA halo hovering like the sunbeam I had admired on his red hair. While other students labored and lagged or swaggered and bragged, Bill was steady-on, with an unconscious humility that remains the hallmark of his character to this day.

Bill's piano-teacher mother, Dorothy, began teaching him at the age of eight. After studying piano for two years, he decided to try his hand at guitar instead. Only one semester later, he abandoned guitar and was down to nothing much musical. After spending an evening listening to students from his mother's piano studio perform in recital, he went to bed. A while later, Dorothy heard his urgent calling. *"Muh-ther! Muhhhhh-ther!"*

She hurried into his room to find him sitting up, looking alarmed. "Mom, I *have* to start playing the piano again. Right away. I just *have* to."

Bill's words struck heavy, like the chisel of God blasting His will into reality. This was no childish whim, but a heart-cry born of God's inspiration. Dorothy remembers it as a Mount Sinai moment, a prophetic proclamation of divine will in her son's life.

Bill was vastly more prepared for the rigors of music school than I was. My first semester at OCU, I suffered culture shock. Mario Lanza, Jane Morgan, Stamps Baxter, our chipmunk sisters' trio, and all the classical composers of piano music that Mrs. Johnson had nobly assigned for me to play hadn't prepared me for the elite classical-music world that OCU presented.

Dr. Burg and I plunged into piano repertoire full splash, practicing thumb preparation, form, and analysis. During lessons, he loved to pull his chair up beside me, take my upper arm in his hand, and squeeze lightly as he talked. "Most of my students really struggle with tension in their hands, dear," he'd say. "But you have the opposite problem; your fingers are too limber." He'd flop his hand loosely in the air. "I think that's why you can play so many difficult passages so easily. We just need to tighten those fingers up a bit."

I practiced hard, and Mrs. Johnson loved every letter I sent, updating her on my progress. Within a few weeks, however, I began to acknowledge a repressed fact: My strongest desire in music was singing, not playing the piano. But I wasn't ready for the job. Other than singing in small churches across America with my sisters, I had scant experience. I had taken only one formal voice lesson when I was younger: Mrs. Johnson, who knew less than most about singing, had once decided I should sing at the spring recital. She'd hummed under her breath as she fingered through layers of possible repertoire.

"Here's a cute one," she'd said, pulling out "Just Whistle While You Work." "Now, when you sing this, you'll need to be sure and get it out of your nose. No country music here. This is Disney."

Getting it "out of my nose" evaded me. Didn't she realize that nasal reverberations give a country twang its focus and create finely pressed harmony? My sister,

Sherry, suggested that I might just whistle through my nose; allergies made that possible for me.

As if that wasn't enough, I was also told to put certain word endings "in my nose." Every time I sang a word that ended with "ng," Mrs. Johnson flapped her arms with such vigor that it took a moment for the waves to subside. "No, no, no," she'd say. "A final 'ng' is not a 'guh' as in 'goat.' You finish the word by closing the back of the tongue against the soft palate. Put it in your nose; it is a nasal 'ng, ng, ng.'"

At the recital, I decided to forget the nasal problem and rely on brute talent. Folks clapped heartily in spite of my "ng's." The nasal reverberations gave me the pipes to make sure that everybody could hear me real good.

I liked singing. Singing was fun.

My choice of an OCU voice teacher had happened during Dr. Burg's summer piano workshop. I stepped onto the balcony of the Lyric Theater to feel the air and to imagine singing onstage. When I emerged from the stage through the swinging door, I almost collided with a pretty blonde who looked a bit older than an undergraduate. She smiled, her startling, pearly-white teeth stirring in me a flush of jealously. Her speech was without accent, and the polish made my backwoods vernacular feel extreme by comparison.

"Hi," she said. "You're new, aren't you?"

I nodded and gave her my name. "I'm a freshman."

"I'm Mary Hart," she said. "Where are you from, Robin?"

"Zafra, Oklahoma, out in the Kiamichi Mountains, southeastern corner of the state," I said, waving my hand in the air as if Zafra was an alien planet.

"Oh," she said. "I've never heard of it."

"Most folks haven't. I'm comin' to college here, though. Do you know Dr. Clarence C. Burg? He signed me up just last night." I smiled narrowly, my teeth, which were more the color of the oyster than the pearl, felt the competition.

"So, you play piano?"

I nodded. "I play piano, but I'm plannin' on singin' too."

"Who is your voice teacher?" Mary said, smiling kindly.

"I don't know yet. Haven't been assigned one."

"If I may make a recommendation?" She laid her hand lightly on my arm. "Most students who come here want to study with Inez Silberg, but her studio is awfully busy. I would highly recommend Mrs. Daray. She is a former student of Mrs. Silberg and teaches the same vocal technique. She is younger, however, and has more time to spend with beginning students."

It sunk in slowly that the "Inez Silberg" Mary mentioned was the same Inez Silberg I had seen coaching the opera singer at the "Federation" in Little Rock. I'd had no idea that she'd been teaching voice at OCU for more than thirty years.

Ever since that time, I had longed to study with Mrs. Silberg. But now that I knew she was within reach, I supposed my lack of training meant she wouldn't accept me as a student. So I heeded the advice of Mary Hart, the same Mary Hart who went on to host *Entertainment Tonight*.

During my freshman year, Mary performed occasionally in Master Class, although she was mostly absent, handling her blossoming career as a talk-show host. Always the epitome of charm, she had a singing voice that sounded exactly like her speaking voice, a sort of Broadway belt with a hint of helium stirred in.

I took her recommendation to heart, and I'm sure she meant to be helpful. But here's a tip to pencil in the back of your Bible: Never choose a beautician, a physician, or a voice teacher because they have plenty of time on their hands.

Mrs. Daray accepted me as a vocal student, though I was only pursuing it as a minor. *Land o' Goshen,* I thought, using a phrase I had heard many times from the old ladies in the mountains. *I am going to be really, truly learning to sing.* On my initial visit to Mrs. Daray's studio, she assigned me a lesson time and my first piece of opera, an aria and recitative called "De Vieni Non Tarder," from *Le Nozze de Figaro*, by Mozart.

"I can't speak foreign," I said to her, "but I have played Moh-zart on the piano."

Mrs. Daray's owl eyes, always etched with black liner, opened extrawide, as if awaiting drops. "What do you mean, Moh-zart?"

I stared, nonplussed. *Hadn't she heard of Moh-zart?*

"Oh my," she sniffed. "I guess we'll begin at the beginning. The composer's name is Moa*t*-zar*t*." She overarticulated the "t" at both the middle and the end of the name as if I had a hearing impediment. "A 'tee'—tut-tut-tut—as in the word "pete-zuh," precedes the 'zee.'"

Pizza, I understood.

"*Le Nozze de Figaro* is an opera, written in Italian, by Wolfgang Amadeus Moa*t*-zar*t*," she said. "Now please do not make that mistake again. Someone might think you are uneducated. Learn the piece in English, as you have had no Italian diction. And in English, we absolutely *must* correct your accent."

You cannot imagine the happiness I felt, clutching my new music, rushing to the practice room, determined to impress Mrs. Daray by having *De Vieni Non Tarder—Beloved, Don't Delay*—memorized in just a day. As I sang, I pounded out the melody on the piano with my right hand and slapped my knee with my left hand to keep the beat. The rhythm felt awkward and unnatural, though, and I fought to understand the confusing layout of eighth and sixteenth notes.

By lesson time the next morning, the song was mine. I knocked on Mrs. Daray's door, my face on high-beam from the overnight accomplishment. After a bit of warm-up, she took out the song.

"All right," she said. "Let's work on the Mozart."

Tapping my hand on my thigh, I began like a good gospel singer,

> *"This at laaa-st is the moe-mint.*
> *So dee-viiiine and so cherished*
> *I longingly awayee-tid."*

She furrowed her forehead and flagged me down. "What are you doing?"

"Did I learn it wrong?" My beam dimmed, and I moved to glance at the music. "That rhythm is tricky."

"This is *rrrecitativo*," she said, rolling the "r" like a high-brow. "You must not keep a strict rhythm. You must sing it as you would speak it, but without the country accent."

I smiled nervously and began again.

> *"This at laaa-st is the moe-mint."*

"No, no, *no!*" She waved her hand. "Lah-st, as in the word 'fall,' not laaa-st, as in the word 'sad.' Your vowel must be longer, narrower."

Eliza Doolittle came to mind.

"Have you ever sung *rrrrecitativo*?" she asked, articulating the *"rrrretch"* with operatic grandeur.

"Sounds like a stomach bug," I joked.

Mrs. Daray did not crack a smile, but stiffened her spine. "Have you ever sung an aria?"

I was out of words; I shook my head.

"In the future, when I assign a task that is unfamiliar to you, you must say to me, 'Mrs. Daray, I have never sung a recitative and aria before. I do not even understand what you mean by recitative and aria.'"

My beam faded to black.

As I left my first voice lesson, I ran into one of Dr. Burg's students, Cheryl Byrd, an upperclassman with glossy, dark-brown hair and a sweet disposition.

"Robin, will you be auditioning for *Man of La Mancha*?"

"Man of what?" Of my two high school English teachers, one had encouraged us to read the classics and the other had championed shallow, modern titles like *Love Story* and *Go Ask Alice*. I'd read some impressive works, like *Vanity Fair* and *Uncle Tom's Cabin,* but *Don Quixote* had fallen through the cracks.

Cheryl raised her eyebrows and lifted the corners of her lips in a patient smile. *Man of La Mancha*, you know, the Broadway musical based on *Don Quixote*."

"Donkey who?"

"No, not donkey. *Don Quixote*, the book. Anyway, the auditions are tonight."

I had just been told to ask when I didn't know; I decided to be bold. "What exactly is 'auditioning'?"

Cheryl's personality palette didn't include haughtiness. She stood in the hall for a full twenty minutes explaining the plot of *Man of La Mancha*, the female role available, and the protocol of an audition.

"A woman from New York City is coming in as guest director of the musical," she said. "It's a great opportunity."

"What do you think about 'Jesus Hold My Hand,' or 'The Ballad of the Green Beret?'" I said. "I know those songs really good."

Cheryl's smile looked fatigued. "It might be better to choose something from a Broadway musical, I believe."

So someone lent me a book of Broadway hits, and I thumbed through it as I traveled to the crummy spinet piano in the basement of Walker Hall, the girl's dorm. I recognized one of the songs in the book from a movie of the musical: In fact, I had been feeling a kind of kindred spirit with Eliza Doolittle, the character who sang it. The last note went a couple of shots higher than comfort allowed, but familiarity trumped range. I could do this.

I slipped on my finest brown-and-white sundress and my favorite platform heels. I fluffed my hair and applied my make-up with excessive precision. Those beauty queens weren't gonna beat me, not if I could help it.

Cheryl accompanied me while I ran through the piece in a practice room for the last couple of times. Besides the fact that I had to tighten my *gluteus maximus* to screech the final note, I thought it was pretty good.

In the theater, I peeped through the heavy black curtains. The New York City lady and the OCU director sat in the center of the auditorium. I was glad for my sleeveless sundress; they wouldn't see me sweat. "Robin, ol' gal," I told myself. "You're huntin' with the big hounds now. You better sniff like you smell something."

When the director, whom I will refer to as, "Mr. Director," called my name, I walked onstage with all the flounce I could muster. This impressed the New York City lady. She sat up on the edge of her chair and called loudly, "Do you dance?"

"No, Ma'am, I don't," I hollered back, brutally aware of my accent.

"All right." She sat back. "And what will you be singing today?"

I saw it coming: "I Could Have Danced All Night."

Mr. Director threw up his hands with a snort of laughter, and the New York City lady joined him.

Sweet Cheryl, undaunted, plowed into the introduction, forcing me to sing. *"I could have danced all night. I could have danced all night."* The words jeered like a mean little brother. The two directors tried to mask their laughter, but the harder they tried, the greater the guttural combustions. As I lunged toward that last wobbly note, they gave up altogether and whooped.

I slunk offstage, feeling like George, our baseball-playing hound who stealthily tiptoed into church services when hot weather dictated the door should stay open. Daddy would stop his sermon and growl, "Get-outta-here," and George would hunker down and slip slowly back down the aisle, thumping his tail against the floor, squinting his eyes as he glanced at the congregation—left, then right—lifting his upper lip to show teeth in an embarrassed, human sort of smile.

If I was going to hunt with the big hounds, I had a lot to learn.

Musical inferiority wasn't the only hurdle I jumped during those early days at OCU. Every night, for the first two weeks of college, one of my suitemates would come in drunk—very drunk. When she regurgitated or hyperventilated, her soon-to-be sorority sisters would pull her into a cold shower—clothes and all—jerking her hair back to direct spray into her face. When that didn't work, an ambulance came roaring. Her tenure at OCU ended before the first semester.

My mother came to my rescue, once again. She ordered a private room—forget the costs—and rented a small refrigerator, which she stocked with fruits and puddings. Now there was an extra twin bed, just waiting for her to visit, and no Joe College or swinging sorority sister could top Mama's company when it came to having a good time.

I realize now, having inspected dorms while scouting educational possibilities for my children, that Walker Hall, the girl's dorm at OCU, was vastly superior to most dormitory settings. The rules allowed no guys past the first-floor lobby, and the security guard locked the door at ten o'clock, requiring a resident to hit a buzzer to gain entrance.

Most evenings, the girls migrated to the central lobby on each floor to watch TV, play games, study, and visit. There was Susan, a future Miss America from the floor below me, who, in the wee hours of the morning, would gather a group to feast on crackers, cheese, olives, pickles, chips, and jalapeños. There was Becky, a bubbly mezzo who ironed her blouses every morning and, according to the grapevine, could bench-press two hundred pounds. And there was Lisa, a beauty queen who regaled us with stand-up comedy from the pageants. Once she had denounced the other contestants for their prissy charade at the Miss Oklahoma pool party—their refusal to muss hair or suits by playing in the pool while the press hovered 'round. Lisa had posed flagrantly on the diving board and taken a leap of grandeur into the pool. As her head emerged from the water, she was horrified to find that her foam-rubber falsies had not participated in the plunge, but surfed defiantly on the waves.

And then there was Joy, with the amazingly high coloratura range. Like me, the once jovial Joy had begun her jaunt at OCU as a student of Mrs. Daray. Gradually, she had become frustrated, even depressed, from the emotional toll of the political environment. She'd switched her vocal studies to Mrs. Silberg's studio, but her struggles persisted. A few weeks into her senior year, Joy had had it. Susan and I were startled to find the hall stacked with her belongings. She packed, returned home, and I never heard from her again. I pray she found an outlet for her remarkable talent.

These musicians, and others like them, kept the OCU community vibrant and energized. Every now and then, New York and the Juilliard School would surface in conversation.

"I hear they make you practice four hours a day at Juilliard."

"Whew, I bet you'd have bleeding vocal chords after that."

"I hear they have cameras in the practice rooms."

"Really?"

"They monitor to see that you have done the time."

"Sounds like prison to me."

The Juilliard School began to hang like a Christmas ornament in my thoughts, a curiosity dangling just out of reach. I felt the challenge rising, improbable, but no longer impossible.

OCU was difficult musically, emotionally, and spiritually, but the Lord, always faithful, interjected pivotal points, seeds planted in a harvest I could not yet see. One bright morning, sitting next to Bill in Music Survey class, miserable with sleepiness, I shut my eyes for a moment, then forced my lids open to watch the teacher, Mr. Phillips, pace the floor. Back and forth he went, like a hypnotist's watch. Mr. Phillips certainly lit no torch of inspiration. The only gleam came from his bald head. His lectures strayed early into boredom. In the flatline of college routines, how was I to know that this day would hold a moment of miracle for me? Not a clamoring miracle that claps its hands and demands attention, this was a private miracle that tiptoed quietly to whisper in my ear and—slowly—change my life.

Mr. Phillips paused and looked at his watch, and another man appeared at the classroom door. "Are you ready for us?" the man asked.

Mr. Phillips looked up, as pleased as we were to be freed from the lecture. "Absolutely!" he said. "Bring them in."

A group of five children entered the classroom, all of them carrying violins. A small Asian girl took the lead, no more than five years of age, a china doll of a child with straight, cropped black hair that reflected the light. I smiled, feeling the boredom lift. Her tiny legs jutted from the skirt of her shirtwaist dress, disappearing quickly into lacy anklets that disappeared into black patent-leather Mary Jane shoes, buckled primly. She stopped at her place in the lineup and stood without fear, straight and serious, carefully circling the forearm and elbow of her right arm around the bridge and fine-tuners of a tiny violin, a toy of an instrument, so little it looked like it had dropped from a fairy-tale drawing of the cat and the fiddle.

Can this be real? I thought.

Bill leaned toward me. "Cute, aren't they?" he whispered.

"Too cute!"

Bill smiled, a nice smile. When I once said, years later, that our days of sitting together in Music Survey class were "before we were interested in each other," he corrected me with a wink, saying, "Speak for yourself." Bill is nice. So nice that to be in his presence is to feel your own niceness sag with inferiority.

Mr. Phillips made the introductions. "Class, please welcome Mr. Lacy McLarry, concert master of the Oklahoma Symphony Orchestra. Mr. McLarry teaches very young children to play the violin using a somewhat new method codified by Dr. Shinichi Suzuki of Japan. I've been impressed with Mr. McLarry's achievements and wanted you to see some of his students perform."

Following Mr. McLarry's lead, violins nestled onto tiny shoulders and bows were raised. I sat transfixed, wondering how children this young could be playing the violin. Brian Bailey, one of my best friends from the mountains, had played a bit of fiddle, self-taught bluegrass tunes like "Bile Them Cabbage Down" and

"Orange Blossom Special," but I had never seen anything like this. I sat back in awe. The china doll turned her chin precisely to one side, lifted the violin, and placed it underneath, then set her bow on the strings. My heart buoyed up as she lit into "Go Tell Aunt Rhody."

After a few numbers, Mr. McLarry enlightened us on the philosophy of the Suzuki method, or what is sometimes called the "mother-tongue" method, of learning to play the violin. Dr. Suzuki had observed the way very young children not only learn to talk effortlessly by imitating the speech of their parents but learn the minutia of speech: the particular accent, the vernacular, the inflection and timbre. Why not learn the language of music in the same manner? "Even if a three-year-old can only focus for five or ten minutes, at the end of that time she knows more about the violin than she did before," Mr. McLarry said.

His students played their final piece, and as they played, I heard an inner voice say: *When you have a little girl, she should do that.* The words struck deeply, clearly articulated within my spirit. I sat back and confirmed that I had heard them. Then I tucked them away until the appointed season, and I never forgot.

I believe God gives everyone divine moments of impact, when His plans route the energies of our lives. It is our job to seize those moments, to make them our own, to watch patiently for His timing. The moment when that little girl played "Go Tell Aunt Rhody" in Music Survey class was to have a monumental impact on my life—and for generations to come.

The Force

Life's but a walking shadow, a poor player,
That struts and frets his hour upon the stage,
And then is heard no more. It is a tale
Told by an idiot, full of sound and fury,
Signifying nothing.

WILLIAM SHAKESPEARE, *MACBETH*, ACT V, SCENE V

By the end of my first year at OCU, I gave in completely to my love of singing and changed my major to voice and my minor to piano. When I heard pianists like Bill, well, who could compete? Besides, a chronic fear of memory slips leeched the life out of my piano performing.

That summer, Six Flags over Texas offered me a job singing, and I declined, going instead to Inspiration Point Fine Arts Colony in Eureka Springs, Arkansas, to study opera. The Ozark Mountains, like the Kiamichis, crawl with copperheads, and the caretaker of the campgrounds warned us to walk on the walkways and watch out. The dressing rooms were at ground level, underneath the stage, and the girls once did a group dance with a copperhead that slithered in without a backstage pass.

Our little troupe performed *Carmen* and *Lakmé*. I especially enjoyed the *Bell Song* aria, from Lakmé, complete with high E's, and the popular, lovely, *a cappella* opening cadenza. A cadenza is a virtuosic solo moment in which a performer is encouraged to show off; I'd had no idea that some sopranos could sing that high. A familiar yearning came to me as I listened: *One day, I hope to sing that song.*

God logged my prayer.

In addition to *Carmen* and *Lakmé,* we performed a couple of smaller operas written by the camp director, who might have been Dr. Burg's elder brother. Dr. Van Grove had Albert Einstein hair that stood up, gray and wizardly, to state the obvious: "I am very, very old!" When a heavy-set soprano heaved a horrible high note, Dr. Van Grove's head bobbed down, down, down to sag in despair on his collapsed chest, and his palsied hand rose slowly to cover his milky eyes. "Don't scream, honey, don't scream," he said.

At lunch, Dr. Van Grove gave motivational speeches from another century, encouraging girls to be ladies and boys to be gallant—and to stay out of each other's cabins. His words were met by the *artistes du jour* with a smirk. The arrogance of the *artistes,* strutting the parameters of their imaginary kingdoms, defied comprehension. I gained the insight that certain artistic genres carry a great capacity for conceit. Consider: how many snooty tuba players do you know? But singers: they're the worst.

At summer's end, I returned to OCU and the stage of the Lyric Theater. As a freshman and sophomore, I played several small roles: a lay sister in Puccini's *Soir Angelica,* a snowflake in *Gypsy,* and a chorister in *The Magic Flute.* During the quirky musical, *Candide,* I sat in the dressing room for what seemed like hours, waiting for my part. To pass the time, I admired how white my teeth looked against the dark, pancake makeup I was obliged to apply. I clicked my tongue and sighed. The makeup, the costume changes, the backstage boredom, waiting for entrances, the monotonous repetition night after night, all combined to turn off the Broadway lights for me.

Mr. Director—the same one who had guffawed at my failed first audition— enjoyed telling us about a friend who had played a Russian soldier in the original cast of *Fiddler on the Roof.* "My friend," he said, "dressed in full costume and waited backstage to dramatize one single line of dialogue, five nights a week for years."

Poor Feller! Ethel Merman—and Mr. Director's Russian friend—could have it. I preferred to perform concerts, singing songs born from the inspiration of my heart. My friend, Betsy, a soprano with Greta Garbo lips and a buzz-saw vibrato, confided that Mr. Director possessed special powers that enabled him to read a person's "aura."

"Isn't that some kind of toilet paper?" I asked.

"Are you from Earth? An aura is a beam of color that circles your head." Betsy cupped her fingers around the air above her head, then leaned in to whisper. "Only those with special spiritual powers can see it."

I felt nervous about my aura. What did Mr. Director see when he looked at me? So far, he had seemed to like my work; he had cast me in every production the school had performed, with the exception of *Man of La Mancha*. Not huge parts, but good for a novice.

Mr. Director was the husband of Mrs. Daray, who enjoyed knowing her students were being cast by her husband. No doubt, my auditions found favor because of this arrangement. Though I had come to feel that I did not enjoy Broadway or the opera, I knew I needed stage experience, plus credit for a required acting class, to graduate.

During my sophomore year, I took the class in acting, taught by Mr. Director himself. At first, the class met in the small auditorium. Mr. Director called everyone up on stage, dimmed the lights, and had the upperclassmen do "rhythm studies." Toward the end of the hour, a large tenor got down on all fours and, with hairy front paws, beat out the "body rhythm" of Mr. Director. As the rhythm grew in passion and complexity, the tenor began to sweat, his double chin jiggling wildly.

This was getting just a tad scary! Eyebrows raised, I looked around. The other students watched with a variety of emotions: surprise, embarrassment, discomfort, curiosity. As the percussion reached its climax, Mr. Director threw back his head and laughed a perfect horror-movie laugh. "Whoooooo-ahhhhhhhhh-ah-ah-ah."

Where I came from, "body rhythms" would have been easy to drum—cowpoke slow and quilt-stitch steady—except, of course, for the annual brush-arbor revival, when certain excitable ladies took off their glasses and fainted dead away onto the dirt floor, while a transient preacher jumped up and down on the rough benches, hollerin' "Yip, yip, yip."

This class reminded me of a tent revival. In fact, "Yip, yip, yip" seemed the perfect words for the setting.

The next week, acting class moved into the basement—to the ballet room. I loved the ballet room. As a little girl, I had longed—yes, yearned—to be a feather-bedecked ballerina, fanning my arms in the air, dying slowly and passionately, like a swan, the way the girl in the Miss America Pageant once did. I had seen her on TV, down the hill at Raymond and Thelma Owens' house.

During the dark walk home after watching the ballerina that night, I had somehow managed to watch out for copperheads with one eye while studying the thousands of stars pulsing against the blue-black sky with the other. The story-book wonder of the pageant sat heavy, like melted chocolate, in my throat. But that dream was for other girls, who got up every morning and dressed in satin gowns and lived far, far away, somewhere close to those stars.

At home, I got a couple of books on ballet from the Bookmobile and tried learning the positions, twisting my feet out awkwardly. Alas, the harder I "turned out" the more my hips "stuck out"—a big no-no, the book said. Yet when I tucked my hips in, my feet swung in as well.

One dreary day, the mean wife of one of Daddy's visiting friends regarded my struggle and drove a stake through my heart. "You'll never be a ballet dancer," she said. "You're too heavy here." She patted my hips.

I managed to hide the tears until I reached the barn, where the dam burst and I cried, nestled in the burlap feed sacks. George, our hound dog, comforted me with his embarrassed smile, flapping his tail on the straw floor and nuzzling my cheek with his nose.

At the next opportunity, I returned my ballet books to the Bookmobile, which offered no sympathy, but lumbered off, a wobbly red wiener on wheels, smothering my ballerina dreams in a cloud of dust.

In college, the required course in ballet had offered only humiliation, as I obeyed the instructor and leapt across the floor, praying for at least as much lift as a Brahman heifer. Yet I loved the shiny mirrors and smooth wooden floors of the ballet room. They stirred the happy memories of childhood dreams, as well as the reality checks.

The students in the acting class filed in and found places to sit on the floor. Mr. Director, it seemed, had plans other than dancing for the windowless room.

At first, we sat in front of the mirrors as he spoke on the place of the "spirit" in acting. He said that summoning the "spirit" of a character is the essence of acting, and that some people have the ability to send their "real spirit" on trips outside their bodies. *Star Wars* was all the rage, and Mr. Director concluded with a reference to the "force," then instructed a plump, older girl named Debbie to sit on the floor in the middle of the room. Happy to be chosen, Debbie hurried to her place. Mr. Director then nonchalantly instructed his favorite male protégé, Lance, to "take all of Debbie's energy."

Lance stood up and began slowly to circle Debbie, staring at her fiercely. Suddenly, from behind, he ran up and caught her head between his hands in a vice grip. With growing malice, he twisted her face, his lips snarling. Debbie struggled and tried to push his hands away; he clamped even tighter. Debbie weakened and began to sink, and as she descended, Lance swung around to the front and straddled her. He took his hands from her face and used them to pin her hands to the floor. His breath blew out with a raspy sound as he lay down on top of Debbie and, with his eyes opened extra wide, pressed his forehead into hers, pressing her head onto the hardwood floor.

Debbie grew weaker and weaker, her groans diminishing into whimpers, her whimpers becoming voiceless gasps. Then she died, at least that's what it looked like to me. Her puffy white remains puddled on the floor like a melted marshmallow.

Lance got up and circled her again, staring darkly around the room. The air felt charged and oppressive.

I pined for Zafra—or one of Daddy's six-shooters—just in case somebody tried to take *my* energy. But I would have been shooting wild because, at that moment, Mr. Director turned off the lights. Tom Sawyer's cave, in its absolute blackness, couldn't have been darker than that windowless room. Images came to mind of a headless chicken, going berserk in the barnyard as its last few heartbeats ebbed away.

Game over! I lunged for the door, ran up the hall, took the stairs two at a time, and burst out into the sunshine. Shaky legs carried me toward my room, and the cheery sunlight helped me gain some perspective. Somehow, the study of acting had become tangled up with dark mind games. The students had no clue of the invisible dangers of their little shenanigans. I would not go back to that class. But drop it? So be it. I clenched my jaw, contemplating the confrontation. Back at the dorm, I called Daddy.

"Sounds like he's into some sorta oddball occult-type thing," Daddy said. "Seems to me an acting class should be about the study of human nature, you know, facial expressions and natural ways of sayin' the lines. I think you're right to drop it, and let the chips fall where they may."

The dean was surprised when I told him. "I can't believe you're doing this. That acting class is one of the most popular courses in the music school."

"Yes, I know," I said, not wanting to get into the spiritual details.

"Oh well," the dean said, "Why don't you take an acting course through the drama department instead."

That was that—the beginning and end of my acting career. But my decision to drop Mr. Director's class would affect my OCU experience *dramatically*. Before—as a novice—I was in every show produced except *Man of La Mancha*. Afterward—as a skilled upperclassman—I was never again cast in a production on the stage of the Lyric Theater.

In addition, Mrs. Daray, already bent toward negativity, allowed her attitude toward me to digress into open hostility. Although I progressed rapidly that semester, advancing to the semi-finals in NATS (National Association of Teachers of Singing) and learning repertoire in excess of the required pieces, she issued a *C* for the semester—the only *C* in an otherwise perfect string of *A*'s in voice on my transcript. I had scorned her husband's acting class, and by doing so had lit a slow burning fuse on an explosive saga of malevolence that was far from over. I expected consequences, but the breadth of her intent came to me like a cancer, invisibly at first, then with increasing toxicity.

Three blessings came to me out of the ordeal. First, although I didn't take the course until my junior year, I excelled in the drama department's acting class and enjoyed a focused and intelligent study of the art form. "Won't you come back next year, Robin?" the teacher, Mrs. Davenport, said, when she took me aside at the end. "We could use you."

God bless her!

Secondly, my classmate and friend, Ellen Wight, by far the most beautiful Miss Oklahoma ever and a voice student of Mrs. Daray, said, "Robin, I heard what you did, dropping Mr. Director's acting class. Oh! I wish I were spunky like you. I just prayed and prayed during that class, that God would protect me. Thank you for taking a stand."

A devoted Christian, Ellen exemplified grace and poise. She was an inspiration to me, both artistically and spiritually. A few years later, she died tragically in a hotel fire in Vienna. I know she is happy in the home of the Father, but I still miss her. Her kind affirmation is forever embedded in my heart.

My third blessing was none other than Inez Silberg, the guest vocal coach I had observed teaching at the college in Little Rock. I had noticed the superior vocal skill of Mrs. Silberg's students but felt shy about asking to be included in her studio. When I finally summoned the courage to speak to her, I realized how wise she was—her wisdom gained from fifteen years as head of the vocal department.

She listened to my problem with sober attention and pulled no punches. She said that she knew Mrs. Daray well, had taught her in years past, and understood completely my predicament. She had heard it before. I would later realize this was vintage Mrs. Silberg; she did not downgrade her co-teachers, nor did she defend them.

"Mrs. Daray is young," she said.

And mean, I thought.

"When a student is just beginning to learn technique, the teacher must wait patiently for the lessons to take hold. It is very, very difficult to be so patient. But I must say, dear, you seem very sweet. I am sorry you have had this experience."

Tears brimmed. I had gone to Mrs. Silberg's studio to ask for recommendations for transferal to another university, and her next words came as a lovely surprise. "Why don't you come study with me, dear? Sometimes, when students like you have come to me in this situation, I have seen, after a while, that some of the problems lie within the student. I won't know if this is the case with you for a while, but we shall see."

Like Dr. Burg and Dr. Van Grove, Mrs. Silberg was seasoned, classy, and intelligent, and used the word "dear" as a favored endearment. She held her head high and carried her slim figure with regal posture. Her studio housed furnishings from a gilded age, and antique books and stacks of old music manuscripts seemed to cuddle contentedly on the shelves. A photocopy of a fat pig, sitting upright on his haunches with a stupid look on his face, hung on the side of a filing cabinet over the caption, "Never try to teach a pig to sing. It wastes your time, and it annoys the pig."

Mrs. Silberg loved to teach and insisted a student stay in her studio until the lesson was learned, which caused a massive and continual traffic jam at her door. One might wait days for a lesson.

Fragile health weighed her down, and I often glanced at the top of the scar that ran down the center of her chest, curious about the story behind it. Still, the crème de la crème of the vocal crop came from all over the country, seeking her musical wisdom. Her graduates worked the stages of such opera houses as the Metropolitan Opera and the New York City Opera, and many gained starring roles.

Mrs. Silberg also coached many of OCU's beauty queens. I had recently joined their ranks by winning the title of Miss McAlester, or "Miss Oklahoma State Penitentiary," as my friends liked to joke. My only fan mail came from a young car thief doing time in the prison near McAlester. *Wonder if he's ever stolen a blue, 1965 Chevy Impala?* I mused.

God's grace visited me through Mrs. Silberg. A brilliant diagnostician, she knew what to fix and how to fix it, which is the fundamental job of any teacher. She soon had my upper register working beautifully, and my vocal studies began to carry hope and excitement. I worked hard, performing in churches wherever opportunity lay.

I loved to sing. Singing felt natural, much more comfortable than the piano. How happy I felt to express thoughts and ideas with words set to pitch and rhythm. I never had a memory slip with words. In high school, I had won awards in both speaking and writing. On the long bus rides, I'd memorized great works of timeless poets: "The Highwayman," "The Raven," "If," "How Do I Love

Thee," "The Great Colossus," "Oh, Captain, My Captain," "Trees," "Stopping by Woods on a Snowy Evening," "Columbus," along with speeches from Shakespeare and chapters from the Bible. Even now, I can quote verse much longer than my family wants to hear.

Like a kitten pounces on a toy or swipes at a string, I chewed on classical poetry because I couldn't help it and developed personal life skills God had prepared in advance for me. A love for the puzzles of wordplay, rhythm, rhyme, and tone captured my imagination. This, coupled with a lifetime of hearing Daddy's intelligent and vivid sermons—his Twain-style knack for storytelling—delivered me to the power and beauty of painting images with words.

My new vocal setting heightened my happiness. Mrs. Silberg's Master Classes, our lessons together, injected something akin to brilliance into my quest for vocal chops, and the semester ticked by steady-on, swinging like a pendulum clock.

To nod in passing sufficed for Mrs. Daray. Forgive and forget, right?

Finals drew near, and with them my first vocal jury as a student of Mrs. Silberg's. The "jury," a semester-by-semester grading process, would force me, once again, to face a panel of five voice teachers. In music school, a jury is a group of instructors compiled from a specific musical category—say, voice, piano, or violin—who gather to gauge the progress a student has made at the close of each term. Each juror issues a "level," a number-letter grade. These are tallied and issued to the student as an average. As usual, the judges would include Mrs. Daray and a woman I came to refer to as her "comrade," a young master's student who taught voice part-time and understood the power structure behind the Lyric Theater.

My level had climbed admirably when I was a student of Mrs. Daray. But this time, for some reason, I felt like I was reliving that woeful audition for *Man of La Mancha*, two years before. I took the stage with forced enthusiasm. "Robin, ol' gal," I told myself, "don't be afraid of a cat scratch." I set my eyes above the fray, lifted my ribcage, lowered my diaphragm, and prepared to sing. An irritated voice interrupted, scolding from the back of the auditorium. "Robin!"

I jumped, startled.

Mrs. Daray's owl eyes glared. "When you change teachers, you should indicate that you have done so at the top of your jury sheet."

Brandishing her pen in the air, and with a frown of deep disapproval, Mrs. Daray crossed out her name from underneath the caption *Teacher*, and, using a series of short, blunt lines, wrote in large capital letters, INEZ SILBERG. The comrade added her scowl of disapproval. A suspicious frown furrowed the faces of the other two panel members. Mrs. Silberg ignored them all and smiled as if we were gathered for a recital in a patron's parlor. "What will you sing first, dear?"

A Perfect Proposal

Barkis is willin'!

CHARLES DICKENS IN *DAVID COPPERFIELD*

I tried my hand at songwriting during my junior year at OCU. When I presented my first set of lyrics to Mama, she didn't laugh, as I do when I remember them. She looked me straight in the eye, threw the notebook onto the table for emphasis, and said, "All I've got to say is, keep on. Just keep on writing."

Perfect advice for a beginning songwriter.

As my last years of undergraduate school passed, it became obvious that Mr. Director would never cast me again, not even in a chorus. Midway through my senior year, I quit auditioning. Mrs. Daray's rudeness raised its head only during juries. "Just twice a year," I told myself. "You can handle that." *But what about your level?* I pushed the words into the back of my mind. Some way, somehow, getting a passing level would happen; it all would work out.

The summer following our senior year at OCU, Bill asked me, once again, to date him. "I don't mind going out some," I said. "But I'm not interested in anything serious right now."

Bill smiled patiently. "Okay. We'll keep it on the back burner."

The month of July burned fiery hot, and Bill's protocol for relationship development defied anything I had ever experienced. He pulled out friendly courtship assignments: sermon tapes on godly dating by Josh McDowell and Elizabeth Elliott, followed by tender moments doing Navigator Scripture memory drills.

Bill devoted himself to prayer, prompting me to pray with him every time we met. We never, ever got into the car to go out that he did not, very kindly and humbly, begin the journey with these words: "Robin, let's pray."

My girlfriends teased, "If you marry Bill, he'll probably carry you over the threshold, throw you onto the bed, and say, 'Robin, let's pray.'"

But weddings, specifically, my wedding, had been the theme of recurring night-mares since my early teens. In them, I stood at the altar, all wispy in white. I puckered up for a kiss, but as my beloved leaned in, lo and behold, he was not the man I was supposed to marry. It was Jacob and Leah in reverse. In the dream, I writhed under the realization that there was no way out of the marriage without breaking the vows I had made to God. My stomach churned, and I broke out in a clammy sweat. I was trapped—for the rest of my life. You cannot imagine the relief when I awakened, traumatized and teary, to realize it was only a dream.

Daddy had strong feelings on the subject of weddings. He had heard more than one testimony from brides who, during the engagement period, secretly wanted to call off the wedding but felt embarrassed; the preparations had gone too far. "If you girls, when you are engaged, ever, *ever* have any second thought about going through with the marriage," he told each of us, in a surge of fatherly protection, "all you have to do is let *me* know. I don't care if the gifts are in and the flowers are bought and the caterers are paid. I don't care if you are all dressed up and walking down the aisle and have already kissed your mama good-bye. All you have to do is *let me know* and *I'll* handle it. You don't even have to show your face. Listen to me now. Once the 'I do's' have been said, there's no turning back."

I appreciated his caring. I really did.

In one particular dream, I stood at the altar beside my beau, but my hands were tangled in the veil. As I fought the fluff, the minister turned my groom and me to face the congregation. "Ladies and Gentlemen," he said, "I'd like to intro-duce to you, Mr. and Mrs....."

"What?" I quit wrestling my veil and stared in disbelief at my groom's face. Wrong again! Oblivious to my turmoil, the groom took my arm and proceeded down the aisle, out the back door and into the waiting limo, somehow not notic-ing that I had broken his grip at the second pew and run to Daddy.

"Daddy," I whispered, "I have married the wrong man." I wrung my hands, wadding my veil. "Oh, Daddy, the 'I do's' have been said, and there's no turning back. What can we do?" Daddy ducked his face to the side, thinking…thinking. Then, an inspiration:

"Let's kill him," he said. Together, we marched down the aisle and out the door to descend the church steps. My numbskull groom had finally noticed that I was not at his side. He emerged from the limo to greet me. Daddy pulled out his pistol and, like a cowboy Corleone, shot unshelled peanuts from his Smith & Wesson. My groom danced around, dodging the nutty bullets, which bounced like Nerf balls off his tuxedo.

The Lord used these episodes—in fact, I believe He gave me these goofy but horrifying dreams—to instill in me the serious nature of a covenant relationship and to encourage me to wait for His man in His time.

As an outgoing, vivacious girl, I had gone on my share of dates. Some suitors beat their hairy chests, testosterone seeping from under a blanket of English Leather and Certs, as they brandished their bankroll over lobster tails and garlic butter.

Others had a pitiful concept of a night on the town. Jerome, a law student from New York City who nurtured a secondary ambition in radio announcing, had no car, so he ushered me across the street from Walker Hall to the Roy Rogers Restaurant. We settled onto the unfriendly coils of a red vinyl booth to eat a burger. For entertainment, we played "Name That Tune." Jerome's rather large mouth never really closed, and his sonorous bass voice bounced like a racquetball around the greasy room, smacking Roy's other dinner guests right in the head. Even now, I sometimes unexpectedly gasp for air, feeling myself in that booth with Jerome, trying to decipher "Climb Every Mountain" from three notes.

Don Juan or Don Yawn—Superman or Stuporman—it made no difference. The morning light always brought a frown of distaste at the thought of continuing the relationship. I love the morning, when nightmares are over, mercies are new, and answers are clear. "One thing's for sure, Robin, ol' gal," I'd tell myself. "You'll know love is true when you're in love in the morning!"

I was officially in my fifth year of study when I accepted a job teaching voice at Ozark Christian College, which would require a move to Joplin, Missouri, three-and-a-half hours from Oklahoma City. Joplin, a town of about 45,000, would later gain fame when it was devastated by a tornado, but in 1980 it was just an old-fashioned town, chirping along at a less-than-modern pace. My classmates, including Bill, had already graduated, and I had just two classes, math and religion, to complete. I tried to be optimistic about it. The classes would be easily accomplished, even if I had to take them a little later at some school other than OCU. More daunting were my junior and senior recitals. I would need to knock out that junior recital soon. Then, in the course of the two juries performed at the end of each semester, I could secure the vocal level necessary to perform my senior recital right after graduation. It was a solid plan.

Throughout the week, I taught voice lessons at OBC, grabbing every available minute in between to practice. On weekends I traveled from Joplin back to Oklahoma City to work with Mrs. Silberg in the parlor of her pink house.

Mrs. Daray haunted the periphery of my mind. I had begun to fear that if she had her way, I would never graduate. The only way in which she still held sway over me academically was as a juror at the end of each semester. To earn a Bachelor of Music degree in Vocal Performance from Oklahoma City University, a student must attain the level 8B. If, say, three of the jurors graded in a conservative and judicious manner, while two consistently issued an inordinately low score, it skewed the average, necessitating another semester, and another, and another. That's what happened to me.

My level, which had climbed impressively prior to the acting-class debacle midterm of my sophomore year, had plateaued at 7B. I was sinking, semester after semester, into a quagmire of music-school politics.

An ominous tone droned at the back of my mind, something akin to the buzz of a faulty florescent light that crazes your brain. How many thousands of dollars spent? How many hours in the practice room? How many years of my life devoted to a title on a piece of paper, only to be denied my goal by the wicked whims of a resentful diva?

Bill brought the sunshine, laughing, praying, taking me out to dinner, and playing the piano for my lessons. Accompanying had been his profession since his graduation from OCU, earning him a mere trickle of cash, a problem he reckoned to solve. A well-known composer of church music for Word, Kurt Kaiser, came to Bill's church one Sunday to perform. Cautiously, Bill approached him. "Mr. Kaiser, I am a pianist and a composer." Bill handed him the piano/vocal notations for a couple of songs he had written. "Would you be so kind as to consider these for publication?"

"I don't do that end of things," Kurt replied. "You should send them to Ken Barker. He's the one who reviews new material."

The next day, Bill and I went out to the post office and sent to Mr. Barker a listening cassette, handwritten manuscripts of the songs on it, and a cover letter. In the letter, Bill inquired about job opportunities.

Ken wrote him right back. "I only do reviewing once a month," he wrote, "so that will have to wait. However, I did notice your neat manuscript notations. We're set to hire another editor. If you're interested, I've enclosed a song by one of our artists, David Meece. Please transcribe it for voice and piano and send it back to me."

Praying for the Lord's will, Bill transcribed the song and sent the manuscript back to Ken. Then, while he waited for a reply, he returned to his work as an accompanist, patiently playing Mozart's *Alleluia* and *Le Papillon* for my lessons in Mrs. Silberg's pink parlor. My admiration for both his musical skill and his character swelled.

On the days when I was in Oklahoma City for my voice lessons, Bill's parents kindly offered me a room in their home, Bill's old bedroom, to be exact. He was living at home until he landed a job, but when I came to town, he pulled an antique, wedding-ring-patterned quilt out of the linen closet and dragged it upstairs to the game room sofa to sleep. His mother told me Bill had won the quilt at the Piedmont Methodist Church his grandmother attended; when the church held a raffle, his grandmother bought each of her grandchildren a ticket. Billy, as they called him, won, which came as no surprise to me; I already saw him as a natural winner.

During my time as a guest at his folks' home, we rifled through his cabinet full of Christian albums, playing recordings of a young, curly-haired fellow named Keith Green; a husband-wife team called "Farrell and Farrell"; and the newest album from the Imperials. Bill especially lauded the production skill of a pianist named Michael Omartian, producer of the latest Imperials project. "I tell you, Robin," he said, "Michael Omartian is an incredible keyboard player. He has taken the Christian record industry to a higher level of production than ever before. This is a great time to be in Christian music!"

My mother, who had become acquainted with Bill during her visits to OCU, loved him dearly. When I told her we were courting, she pouted her lips. "Oh, Robin, don't hurt Bill!"

"What can I do about it?" I said. "I'm going to give it a chance, but beyond that, I can't promise anything." Wedding scenes from my bad dreams haunted me. "Besides," I said, "if Bill and I don't fall in love and get married, I'm gonna owe his parents about ten thousand dollars in rent!"

I began to pray with passionate honesty for the Lord's will to be done in my relationship with Bill. "God," I prayed, "you can see that I don't know how to love. I cannot play games with my feelings. I cannot summon love, or pretend it is there if it is not. I am horrified at the thought of being trapped in an unhappy marriage for my entire earthly life. So, I take no responsibility for this relationship. It is *all Yours!* If you want me to marry Bill, You will have to give me love for him."

The days passed, as summer segued into autumn. Bill continued to lead me in prayer. We discussed our failures and weaknesses, our hopes and likes, our theological differences. When we drove to concerts, he brought along his beloved box of Navigator Scripture Memory review cards, and we learned together. At first, it felt a bit corny and square. Bill made no pretense of trying to sweep me off my feet. He seemed to hold no regard whatsoever for the romantic precedent set by Hollywood and the glamour magazines. His easy sense of humor and his respect for me more than made up for that, though, and I enjoyed his company.

Little by little, the truth was told; there is no intimacy like that born of prayer. I began to find completion and fulfillment in our relationship—a satisfied sense that something winged and beautiful was being coaxed out of its cocoon.

One luminous October day, we drove to the mountains to visit my parents. We walked through the woods, beneath oaks and maples, the leaves glittering in shimmery golds and fiery reds. I realized—rationally, softly, and peacefully—that I was in love with Bill. I say "in" love, because it seemed as though I had walked through a door into a particular place, a sphere of grace and affirmation specially designed for us by the Lord. We'd had three years of friendship and about three months of earnestly seeking God about our relationship. My fear of being trapped and smothered was melting into a strong confidence that this uncomplicated man, so plainly called Bill, might as well be called Faithful and True, like the rider of the white horse in Revelation.

In that way, Bill became my knight in shining armor—but the knowledge of my love was still mine alone.

One Saturday afternoon, Bill and I drove to OCU to pick up some music. As I visited the powder room, Kaye, one of my favorite girlfriends, entered. Her face, always glowing and happy, lit up when she saw me.

"Hi, Robin," she said. "Are you still dating Bill?"

"Yes, I am." I smiled as I finished washing my hands and took a towel to dry them.

"Well?" she said, her eyes curious. "Tell me more."

"Oh, Kaye, I am so in love." The words flowed from my mouth and smacked me like the Aqua Velva Man. Articulating what my heart already knew shocked my ears.

Kaye giggled, ecstatic. "Really! Are you going to marry him, if he asks you?"

I thought for a moment and felt an assurance well up. "Yes, yes I am."

Such preludes are helpful for when the real crossroad comes. That very night, and quite as a matter of fact, Bill and I, for the first time, confessed our love for each other. Early the next morning, around six o'clock, a soft knock awakened me.

"Come in." I propped myself up on my elbow, wondering what was up.

Gingerly, Bill entered, his pajamas puffed like a parachute on his thin frame, his beautiful hair standing straight up on top of his head like a bright-red turkey crown. He knelt beside my pillow, swallowed three or four times, and said,

"Robin, I couldn't sleep last night. I once made a promise to God that I would never tell you I loved you without being prepared to back up such a declaration with an offer of commitment.

"Robin, will you marry me?"

No diamond ring flickering in candlelight at an expensive dinner; no rhymed query planted in a fortune cookie; no moonlit stroll or oceanfront kiss could have topped this proposal setting. No extravagant foolishness messed with my sensibilities; no Roy-Roger burgers blocked my brain. Here, in the light of an early morning, despite my greasy nose and bleary eyes, I felt the full force of a bright sunny reality shining in my face. Bill had popped the question, and I was—undoubtedly, contentedly, blissfully—still in love. For me, it was the perfect proposal.

The answer was easy, having already been rehearsed. "Yes!"

Within two weeks of our engagement, Bill received a call from John Purifoy, Ken Barker's associate at Word, asking if he could come to Waco, Texas, for an interview. Within another two weeks, Bill had secured the job as music transcriber and editor; it was God's hand of blessing on our commitment. He would move to Waco, where Word was located, and begin the job in January. I would join him after our wedding in June.

In light of the approaching nuptials, Mrs. Silberg redoubled her efforts to secure my graduation. She watched with compassion and, I believe, admiration for my tenacity, as I taught at Ozark Christian College, commuted from Joplin to Oklahoma City for lessons, performed on weekends, and prepared for a wedding. She became my encourager, marching me toward graduation day. "This semester, dear, let's pull out some of your favorite pieces from former semesters and begin really polishing your junior recital. We should have put that behind us long ago."

"Will it lower my level to present previously offered repertoire at my jury?" I asked.

"No, I am the one to determine what your repertoire will be. This is your fifth year of study. You have more than fulfilled the required four years of repertoire." Presenting familiar material for my end-of-semester jury would give me good options, she argued, both for my junior recital and for my senior recital soon after.

Perhaps I should have kept my mouth shut, but I wanted to be sure she was right. Leaving her studio, I walked directly to the music office. The music-school secretary, a slim martinet, patted her ratted, freeze-sprayed hair as I explained my question.

"I don't know about that," she said. "I think you need to perform brand-new repertoire every time you sing for a jury."

"This is my fifth year," I said. "Mrs. Silberg believes I have fulfilled the repertoire requirements dictated by my degree."

"Well, I don't know." She patted her hair nervously.

I was worried as I descended to the basement practice rooms. I shouldn't have questioned Mrs. Silberg's judgment, but she was up in years, and I knew she could have been mistaken about departmental policies. I became aware, on the tiled stairs, that someone was following me. Tap, tap, tap, tap, tap.

Someone was racing after me in the isolated building.

I hurried faster. Mrs. Silberg had recently advised me to "carry a hatpin into the practice rooms if no one is around." Strange episodes involving theft and harassment had been reported by some of the female students. A hatpin? I'd tried to visualize the moves necessary to defend myself with a hatpin. *"En Garde!"* I'd brandish my hatpin like a sword. Or should I wait until the attacker came close and drive the hatpin into something? What? Where? In any case, I had no hatpin.

I ran into a practice room and hurried to close the door behind me. Too late. My pursuer pushed open the door. My heart lurched as I turned.

It was Beverly, a wealthy, middle-aged opera lover who volunteered her time at the music office and took voice lessons from Mrs. Daray. She had witnessed my conversation with the secretary and followed me. The rumor mill had it that she wanted the secretary's job.

I was weak with relief, and sank onto a piano bench to hear her out.

Beverly looked around the practice room nervously. "Robin, don't listen to her." She jerked her head toward the office above us. "She doesn't know what she's talking about. Your teacher decides what your repertoire will be."

My fifth-year jury probably would have proceeded without incident had I kept the whole thing to myself, but Beverly, as well-intentioned as she might have been, took voice lessons on the side from Mrs. Daray. My choice of repertoire leaked out, and at the end of the semester, Mrs. Daray came to my fifth-year jury loaded for bear.

I sang the last note of the last song, quite pleased with my performance, and Mrs. Silberg called out, "Thank you, dear. Excellent!" I'd nearly forgotten department politics as I walked down the aisle to retrieve my papers.

To my shock, Mrs. Daray snatched them up angrily as they were handed down the row. She fumbled furiously through the files, comparing titles as if she was only now figuring something out.

"How much new material do you have?" The fumbling stopped, and her blazing eyes met mine.

She already knew the answer.

Where does one buy a hatpin?

Mrs. Silberg instinctively put out her arm, as though to restrain Mrs. Daray, and turned to me with a thin smile. "Dear, why don't you share with us what you are doing with your voice, your job, and your travels."

I was trembling inside, but I kept my voice steady. "I am commuting here from Joplin, Missouri, where I have been teaching voice and music history. I am also doing concert performances on the weekends. I will be giving my junior recital February 1st, and Mrs. Silberg wanted me to spend this fall semester polishing my pieces for it."

Mrs. Silberg turned to the others, certain the information would mean to them what it meant to her. "See? She has already presented the required repertoire. So we're concentrating on finishing up her recitals. I just think it's wonderful, all she is doing."

"No new music!" Mrs. Daray fumed. With feigned shock and outrage, she scrawled her dissent across my jury sheet. Her comrade shook her head in disgust, and the other two teachers looked puzzled and doubtful.

With my degree held hostage, Bill and I set the date and began to prepare for our life together. In January, he moved to Waco to work as a music editor with Word. Shortly thereafter, I gave my junior recital, then finished out the spring semester, teaching at OBC and studying voice at OCU. Bill and I married in June—an uptown affair with classical guitar, cello, piano, and no nightmares. God delivered the right man at the right time, and in the process, He shaped me into the right woman at the right time.

In our new home in Waco, Bill's piano performance degree hung crisp and fresh on the wall; I still had an ordeal ahead.

Three White Sisters, Two Good Twins, One Bad Pig

Jessie Mae says [hymns] are goin' out of style . . . I disagree.

MAMA WATTS IN *THE TRIP TO BOUNTIFUL* BY HORTON FOOTE

As my vocal technique improved in college, so did my desire to pursue Christian music as an opportunity for ministry. However, this desire presented a troubling question, a dilemma to which every Christian artist in those days of the 1970s struggled to find an answer.

A new and more rhythmic style, a sort of frenzied artistry, was entering the Christian music world, replacing the simple style of the White Sisters, the Good Twins, and other recording artists our family had listened to in the sixties. Many church leaders had a scratchy, woolen discomfort with the new music, and so did I.

Some say it all started in the fifties when Elvis gyrated onto the nation's stage. Women screamed and fainted, sales rocketed, and the *ka-ching* changed music forever. But mountain folk are uninspired by gyrations and dreadfully slow to change. Elvis and his audience could get "All Shook Up," but not us. Take Mrs. Lucy Shepherd, a fine old southern belle with a body as soft and round as a jelly doughnut and a wit as pungent as her sour pickles. She lived just down the road from the church house, and we stopped in to visit one Sunday, after she had seen Elvis on TV. She clucked her tongue. "Why I hear-ed some lady a-sayin' she loved Elvis mor-n her own husband! Tut, tut, tut." I had heard the same remark, relegating it to the "surely-she-doesn't-mean-that" file. But straight shooters like Mrs. Lucy take folks at their word. If you say it, you mean it. Likewise, in 1963, four young men with bowl haircuts and funny accents had rocked their way, via the *Ed Sullivan Show*, into the living rooms of most Americans. The Beatles created even more furor than Elvis. Rock 'n' Roll was here to stay. Suspicions that the new style was spiritually dangerous were confirmed for us when John Lennon announced that the Beatles were said to be more popular than Jesus. Daddy and Mama deduced that one could not love the Beatles and Jesus simultaneously. So we prayed for Beatles fans, since they probably, most likely, very well could be going you-know-where. Even the long-haired, drum-beating music spawned by the Jesus movement of the sixties smacked, to Daddy and Mama, of Beatles in sheep's clothing.

But the wheel of change had gained momentum by the time I went to college. Christian rocker Larry Norman had roared the question, "Why should the devil have all the good music?" and Norman's words had popped the cork on new musical wine. Like-minded longhairs were nodding and thumping their agreement. The early seventies saw Love Song, The Second Chapter of Acts, Nancy Honeytree, Resurrection Band, Randy Stonehill, and others bubble over and spill out as lead musicians from the unseasoned wineskin of artistic change.

While the musical cold war raged, I bounced back and forth. Without a doubt, church music had been stale, perpetually old-fashioned, a beat behind. Just because a cultural norm is old doesn't mean it is godly or, more important, *more* godly than something new.

Yet the music of the Jesus movement sprang, in part, from the bitter water of the hippie era—acid trips, sexual promiscuity, Woodstock—it was an angry fist shaking in the face of all authority. Perhaps the materialistic mindset of many Americans deserved a fist-shaking. But sifting the gold from the grime required spiritual stability, maturity, and discernment.

It is a task that still challenges church leaders today.

During my first year of college, a friend invited me to accompany her to a Christian coffeehouse concert. The rock band took up more than half of the tiny space and busted our sinuses with sound. In between songs, the lead singer softly chanted a dreamy-eyed portrait of his favorite hippie, Jesus. Then the roar of the electric guitar resumed.

I leaned in, yelling into my friend's ear, "If this is 'Christian Music,' I'm Billy Graham."

She shrugged, and I sat back. Nebulous biblical definitions of "godly" versus "ungodly" music flapped through my scriptural memory file. My ears felt cottony, rebelling against the glut of sound. I leaned in again. "Take me home," I said.

She sighed, gathered her purse, and silently drove me back to the dorm. As I got ready for bed, I thought about that lead singer screaming indecipherable lyrics, then morphing into a hey-dude vibe between songs. My education as a Christian and as a musician had been founded on Spirit-led logic: Bible reading, prayer, study, fellowship, practice, obedience, and learning the theology of the Scriptures along with the theory of music. How did that singer's performance fit with anything I'd learned?

I told myself not to be ignorant and narrow. Yet the debate raged in my mind: What defines music as "godly?" The sincerity of the performer? The instrumentation? The beat? The wardrobe? I called Daddy. "I can't say a specific drum beat, or the volume, or the soggy talk is blatantly ungodly," I told him. "But something is wrong. What is it?"

Daddy's answer provided a defining moment in my life. "Here's the problem," he said. "The band is attempting to literally 'drum up' an emotion. This reflects their belief that faith comes from feeling. But faith doesn't come from feeling. 'Faith comes by hearing the Word of God.'"

Daddy's dislike of "modern" church music stemmed from an intense opposition to the worldview that birthed it, not to the music itself. He philosophized that cultural trends in music are often initiated by ungodly or rebellious attitudes and that anything springing from them must be fully examined and cleansed at the source. Daddy's sense of what was right and wrong in music was bound up with what was right and wrong in the culture.

The summer following my sophomore year, I teamed up with a childhood friend, Melanie Glover, an easygoing brunette and fellow pianist who hailed from Mrs. Johnson's studio. Together, we toured the Midwest, presenting concerts at churches that financially supported my family's Kiamichi Mountain missionary work. We'd sing for the congregants and give an account of all the Lord was doing through our ministry.

As Melanie and I prepared to leave on the tour, Daddy tugged the brim of his Stetson low over his eyes. The extra-large and well-used toothpick that he'd stuck in the snakeskin hatband pointed at my face like a finger.

"Now," he said, "on this trip, I don't want you to be singing any of that modern stuff. The folks who provide the funds for our mission work don't like it, and neither do I."

That was it, in a nutshell.

Melanie and I launched our tour of the Bible Belt with a full set of familiar gospel songs ready for rendering, but we also began to seek fresh, new music to perform. I felt a bit guilty at first: Daddy's opining made some sense. But I also felt compelled to avoid allowing musical rigor mortis to stiffen me into one style, proclaiming all else as unholy. While browsing in the Christian bookstore in St. Louis, Melanie and I discovered a recording of a cute little blonde named Evie Tornquist. My voice sounded a lot like Evie's, Melanie said, and I agreed. Her music was not weighed down with underlying attitudes and ungodly beliefs, we felt. Young and old alike would enjoy her happy songs.

When I returned to OCU for my junior year, I was excited about the new direction of contemporary Christian music. The harshness of the initial pendulum-swing from the mid- to the late-seventies had softened into something I could stomach. I decided to dig further into new music.

One autumn weekend, with the red and gold of the mountains blazing overhead, I traveled back home to find my parents away and the house empty. I got back into my VW Bug and drove myself over the muddy roads to Mena to browse through the album section in the Fancher's Bible Book Store. The Fancher family, who owned the store, worked hard to offer the small, isolated community cutting-edge books and music. I had heard enthusiastic reports about a new folk/pop artist named Amy Grant, and hoped to hear her recordings. She had grown up in Nashville, Tennessee, and attended Belmont Church, a noninstrumental Church of Christ. Daddy always referred to the Church of Christ as our "nonfiddlin' brethren" because they forbade musical instruments and solo performances during worship services. In Amy's case, something powerful had moved the stone at Belmont: Church leadership had acquiesced and allowed her to accompany herself on the guitar as she sang a solo during a Sunday evening service. I snatched up Amy's new album, along with a hymns album by Cynthia Clawson and a collection of pathos-filled tunes by Reba Rambo, daughter of veteran gospel song-writer, Dottie Rambo.

The house was quiet as I lay on the sofa and listened. Outside the breeze blew soft and balmy after an evening rain, and the mountains hovered as if they too hoped to hear. I laid the needle onto Reba's album. I liked the emotion, and her capacity for lyrical twist.

Then came Cynthia. She sang beautifully, I thought, especially on "It Is Well with My Soul."

When I'd listened to all of Cynthia's hymns, I put Amy's album on and lay back down to shut my eyes. The lyrics were stunning, Amy's alto voice tender.

Just like my Father's eyes. My Father's eyes. My Father's eyes.

It put a painful sort of cramp in my heart, and I knew at that moment: I wanted to make music like this, music that could inspire both your heart and your mind in a whole new way.

But how did an isolated mountain girl get there?

I got up off the sofa, knelt down on the floor, and prayed, "Father, if there is a place for me in the world of Christian music, I pray you will take me there." The words hovered heavily in the humid air, then, like carrier pigeons bound for destiny, began to ascend. A sense of pregnancy entered my spirit. I claimed the nod from heaven and began the watch, wondering what God would do.

My journey through the musical maze of tastes and styles—the wild, undulating waves of contemporary fashions—has kept me wide awake since college days. Christians from different generations, nations, ethnicities, and cultures create different artistic offerings. Like a diamond, the result is multifaceted, sparkling and beautiful. Those who are commissioned to communicate truth through music have an important and sacred assignment, a rigorous one, accomplished only by continual communion with the Lord. They must discern His specific Word for each era, occasion, setting, and people-group.

It's a challenging discernment. Without God's Spirit as the divine guide, without the Word that created all things directing our artistic endeavors, we lose our creative compass.

How often do Christian music conglomerates simply shake out a fresh sheet of tracing paper, stick out their tongues like first graders, and attempt a "Christian" copy of every financially successful musical venture, regardless of the trappings associated with it?

I once sat in the Nashville office of such a conglomerate, chatting with a publishing executive about Christian music. She lauded the creativity of a Christian thrash group called One Bad Pig.

I laughed. "How far we've come since The White Sisters and The Good Twins."

"Who?"

"Never mind," I said. "You were telling me about One Bad Pig."

"Oh, they reach young people who cannot be reached any other way," she said. "One Bad Pig plays heavy metal music. They go wild on stage and bust up guitars and other instruments. It's very dramatic and crazy. I love it!"

I stared in astonishment. Not on your life, sister! Hand me the Sharpie. I need to draw a line. Everyone draws a line, you know.

But where should the line be drawn?

I have a friend who loves taking the youth group he mentors, which includes his sons, to concerts of Christian bands. "It's loud," he told me, "but I just take my earplugs." He smiled, but then his expression grew sober, introspective. "The last concert we went to, the kids down in front started a mosh pit. All these guys had a pretty young girl up in the air, you know, riding the wave. They were passing her along the front of the stage. She disappeared down the line, and when she came back, her shirt was gone. And this was a major Christian act! It was way out of line."

So there is a line.

And it's not just a line between earsplitting heavy metal and old-fashioned gospel or between stuffy pipe organs and rock bands. It's a line between sloppy spectacles and disciplined musicianship. It's a line between selfish ambition and humble ministry. It's a line between God's glory and vain conceit. Music the Holy

Spirit can use is a consummation of a wise head, a pure heart, and practiced skill, dedicated to God's glory.

At college, I saw firsthand, in Dr. Burg and Mrs. Silberg, the work of the old school versus the new school of thought. They believed in cultivating skill first. They believed that technical excellence gives an artist the toolbox from which to display both mind and emotion. To them, the stage wasn't a free-for-all. A performer was expected to know his craft.

Mrs. Silberg once told me, "Technique allows performers to get beyond themselves, to communicate the heart of a piece of music. A pianist, for example, may *feel* the emotion in a Chopin nocturne but until she has the *technical skill* to play the piece well, she will just...." here she quit speaking and made a pounding motion with her hands, "...the heart of the listener will not be moved."

On the flip side, elite conservatories, with their ever-pressing demand for increased technical skill, can sometimes drive a conscientious student to lose the expression of the heart, to play like a machine, pristinely doling out musical data that leaves the listener cold.

Head and heart. Heart and head. Two horns on the same steer.

When I contemplate the struggle for balance, I am carried back to memories of our annual high-school rodeo. The smell of the animals, the oats and hay and manure, the popcorn, the cheeseburgers, the colorful trailers jumbled haphazardly across the grounds, the voice of the announcer bouncing over the cheery crowd, the clowns, the flags, the rodeo queen—once my sister, Cindy, eye-catching in her glittery western-style blouse—all blend together in a sweet perfume. We joined in the opening parade of horseback riders, processing with cowboys in Wrangler jeans and Justin boots, Copenhagen snuff stuffed like cow pies into lower lips. Later, those same cowboys would pull their hats down over their ears and ride buckin' broncs and bulls, rope calves, and wrestle steers. I nurtured a love-hate relationship with steer-wrestling. It seemed mean to the steer, but I enjoyed watching brawny wrestlers with arms like tree trunks.

They worked in teams, a wrestler on his pony riding the left side of the steer while his assistant rode the right. When the gate opened, the trio bolted out, side by side, into the arena. The assistant pressed the steer close into his partner, who slid off the pony onto the back of the steer, reaching big, rough hands up to grab both horns. Then he dug his heels into the ground, violently pulled the horns toward him and, twisting the animal's neck, flipped it onto the ground and sometimes all the way over onto its other side. This noble deed accomplished, the cowboy would jump up and throw up his stout arms in victory. The steer would jump up too, shaking its head in a puzzled way, in desperate need of a chiropractor. Or so I imagined. Did the same steer have to go through this night after night?

That image of the steer wrestler has cowgirled me up for many a battle. Head and heart, skill and spirit: As I confronted the rigors of college, I'd summon a stern resolve to grab both horns of the musical beast and wrestle it to the ground, then throw my hands up in victory, like a steer-wrestling cowboy.

But there's another image, too, that sticks with me from those rodeos. Somewhere in the middle of the line-up, we kids would enter the arena to chase a greased piglet. We'd scramble every which way, and if we got close enough, we'd flop on the slick, squirming beast, which more often than not, would squirt from our arms and go squealing off to evade the next pursuer. As a young woman grappling with the music world, I often felt more like a kid in a greased piglet chase than a triumphant steer-wrestler. My artistic answers were hard to hold on to, and like those little pink squealers, they'd slip out of my hands just as soon as I tightened my grip.

Like the writer of Ecclesiastes, I finally arrived at "the end of the matter," which is this: *There is no end of the matter.* I surrendered to the task of examining each artistic offering by the light of God's Word, by the Spirit's discernment, and by the fruit it bore, praying each time for the strong love that humbles the mind to see clearly. I began to seek, exploring what the Lord required of me artistically, committing to do my best to prepare myself for the call.

Those early years of searching—at college and on tour—gave me an acute sensitivity to the demographics of ministry, the necessity of excellence in all things, the importance of remaining pliable, and the art of honoring the old while creating and enjoying the new. They gave me the forbearance I would require to set aside personal taste and tailor each moment of ministry to best fit the imminent needs of people.

A Matter of Degrees

Or being hated, don't give way to hating.

RUDYARD KIPLING IN *IF*

To spin straw into gold one must first possess straw. Word paid music editors a mere pittance, and in our frantic days of financial despair, Bill supplied me with solid advice. As he hurried out the door to work, he kissed me and said, "Robin, pray! And call your mother."

Mama, often broke herself, mercifully supplemented our coffers when ends refused to meet. Bill and I lived in a lower-class neighborhood because we were decidedly lower class. Our monthly salary hardly paid the utilities and groceries.

We once asked our church elders to help us draw up a budget, and a plump, friendly couple came over to drop advice like a trail of crumbs, a path out of our dark financial forest. After an initial interview, the husband sat down at our rickety kitchen table to study the facts. He furrowed his forehead, wrote down every bill on a tablet, and after a long silence, declared, "Well, on paper you're sunk." Then he ripped the sheet out of the notebook and jostled it high in the air. "But praise the Lord! He's bigger than paper."

Bill's mother wisely advised us to avoid becoming accustomed to two salaries, which would demand a big financial adjustment when babies came. It had taken only a few months of marriage for it to dawn on me that babies were now sanctioned. I anticipated their arrival with delight.

My vocal performance degree still demanded a couple of basic courses: math and religion, to be specific. I had deliberately procrastinated, regarding both: the first, because my brain rejects numbers as my stomach might reject, say, toilet water or Drano; the second, because I dreaded sitting in on a verbal gutting of all I believed, as religion professors sometimes delighted in delivering.

I took both courses at the local college in Waco, where Bill and I were living. Math was math. But the religion course was exactly what I'd feared it would be. The simple, community-based, academic setting did not shield me from being compelled, twice a week for an hour and a half, to listen to a wiry religion professor whose single educational ambition seemed to reside in squelching any spark of faith his students might possess.

"Were any of you *there* when Moses saw the burning bush?" His Brillo-pad eyebrows lifted, daring us to answer. "*Hmm?*" He pressed his lips together, and his long brittle mustache reached over his lower lip to touch his chin. "Because if any of you say you were *there*, I'll call the men in white coats, and they'll carry you away." He assumed an amused air as his eyes darted, challenging the upturned faces.

I raised my hand. "No," I said, "we were not *there*. But neither were you. So instead of using our absence to disprove the story, why can't we just study what the record states and believe it or not? You are only speculating."

His aim, however, was not to *inform* the class about Christianity but to *disprove* Christianity. I readied for my verbal debates with hard studying, and I aced each test to procure his respect for my academic discipline. His dogged determination to destroy the validity of Scripture outraged me. I knew my arguments would not change *his* mind, but perhaps they would lessen the spiritual slaughter of the vulnerable students around me—students whose lack of sound doctrinal apologetics betrayed the paltry instruction received in their youth.

Once, after class, a freshman classmate found me. "Thank you so much for taking a stand," he said. "I just cringe when I hear his lies, but I'm not very good at arguing."

My willingness to argue may arise from an oddity in my brain: I remember specific interactions with sharp clarity, as if someone had stuck a thumbtack into the wall-map of my life and said, "Remember this!" Once, I was eating dinner in the OCU cafeteria with Ross, a law student from New York City with a disagreeable, overly aggressive, personality. When someone at the table brought up

Christianity and the pursuit thereof, Ross waved his fork. "I used to believe in that crap," he said, "until I went to undergrad and found out it was all just b—s—."

To underscore his disgust, Ross got up, kicked his chair back, and stalked away.

His words were infuriating. How different his life might have been had the teacher of his religion class in undergraduate studies sought to build Ross's faith rather than impugn it. Thinking of such moments, I'd look around at my Waco classmates. The religion professor might have seen only notebooks, pencils, and pimple-faced kids as he spouted his faithless lectures. But had he looked into the heavenly realm, he would have seen blood on the ground as he wielded doubt like a machete and mowed down every bloom of faith.

"I do not understand what drives him," I said to Bill. "But one thing's for sure. It's not human."

I started to feel quite maternal toward the younger students in the religion class in Waco, and for good reason. At the beginning of the second semester, Bill and I learned we were expecting our first child.

What can top the expectation of a new baby? We scraped and painted the second bedroom in our tiny, wood-frame, circa-1950 home. Bill's dad, a gifted builder and architect, crafted the first of many cherished heirlooms he has given us: a beautiful cradle and bright wooden toys. I cross-stitched, sewed balloon shades, and dressed the crib and cradle with bumper pads, dust ruffles, and comforters. Bill's mother sewed tiny clothes and soft cotton blankets. Bill stood on the cracked, sunken, almost-red, concrete slab we called a patio, wiping sweat from his forehead with one hand, while wiping stain and polyurethane on baby furniture with the other.

Our nursery beamed with hand-hewn charm. When my folks came for a prebaby visit, I turned on the lamplight to reveal a celestial glow. "Isn't it pretty?"

"Lovely," Mama murmured.

Daddy took in the baby-blue pastel, the puffy balloon shades, and the finely stitched wall hangings, and opined: "Looks like a little sissy boy to me."

During the first year of marriage, I took the math class and came out with a *B*, for Beautiful. During the second year of marriage, I survived two semesters of religion class with straight *A*'s. During both years, I continued to travel to Oklahoma City for voice lessons and the dreaded juries, my nemesis. Graduation plans became a tense topic, deliberated in subdued tones. Twice more, Mrs. Silberg felt I'd sailed through the adjudication, but Mrs. Daray shot me down with a stroke of her jurist's pen. Daddy entertained ideas of taking legal action, but how does one convince a legal entity of something as arbitrary and subjective as singing at a certain level? Round and round, the trips to Oklahoma for voice lessons made me feel like a mouse on a wheel. The emotional stress swelled with my belly. I had dropped Mr. Director's acting class years ago, and still, I was caught in the clutch of the pooh-bah. What kind of mind carries a grudge for so long over something so insignificant? Frustrated tears came with the realization that there was nothing I could do but "keep on keeping on," as Daddy loved to say.

"Keep on keeping on!" That's it! The battle should be fought, I realized, in the style of Mr. James Fob. A silent chuckle used to ripple Daddy's muscled shoulders as he told the story of Mr. Fob. He'd shake his head in amazement, trimming his fingernails with his pocketknife:

"Fred Johnson, the high school principal, knew quite a bit about boxing, so he gave me and several of the Nashoba boys a brief tutorial in the basics," he'd begin. Daddy's father bought him a cheap pair of gloves, and he and the boys got good enough that when the nearby town of Moyers held a boxing tournament, Mr. Johnson sent them, a de facto boxing team. Daddy weighed in at 147 pounds, the top for a welterweight, but the school only had five boxers, half as many as the other schools, so the boys would each have to fight two matches.

"The Fob boys, from Moyers, were famous for gettin' in a brawl," Daddy explained. James Fob was a middleweight—tall, good looking, well built, probably half-Choctaw—weighing in at around 160 pounds. Since Daddy was only a pound away and they were short on middleweights, he got paired with James.

The first round was a slugfest, and Daddy got hammered, but in the second round, he had James hanging on the ropes. The ref would pull Daddy off, and he'd back up and wait for James to go down, but he never did. Instead of falling like everybody expected, James rebounded off the ropes, put up his guard, and started dancin'. "Again and again, that's what he did," Daddy said, "comin' back and back and back." When the bell sounded for the final round, Daddy was exhausted.

But not Fob.

He just kept on fighting. "Someone told me later that when you fight those Fob boys, you have to be ready to stay a while," Daddy said. "They just get up one more time than you can swing."

The referee gave the fight to Daddy, but the two judges, both from Moyers, were split. One called it a draw, the other gave the fight to Fob, by a substantial margin. So the fight went to Fob, in a split decision. "If I had won that match, our team, if you could call it that, would have taken home the trophy," Daddy said. He closed his knife and sheathed it. "Let me tell you something, an individual can overcome a lot in life by fightin' like a Fob."

Mr. Fob: my hero. I kept coming back and back and back, performing jury after jury, struggling under the lion's paw: *7B. 7B. 7B.* My level sat there stubbornly, finally edging up a minuscule increment, to *7B+.*

By this time, my vocal skill was quite advanced, and yet I had watched moderately skilled singers who had enrolled in the vocal degree program years after me go on to graduate. I looked back at the years—five, six, seven—slugging along on a path to graduation. I had taught voice at Ozark Christian College, performed across the United States, married, moved to Waco, Texas, completed two elective courses, and begun a family.

Mrs. Silberg observed my dilemma quietly. I had grown to love her, and here's why: My success was her goal. A great teacher understands that her distinction builds indirectly, a byproduct of her students' achievements.

I studied Mrs. Silberg's face as she talked to me of breath streams, pure vowel sounds, and placement. The fragile skin around her eyes only thinly covered the tiny blue vessels networked underneath, lending a sorrowful, lavender hue to her countenance. She once spoke to me of tragedy in her life, and her eyes filled with tears. She wasn't accustomed to confession, and I struggled to intuit her meaning. It was as though she desired to express a fathomless emotion without really telling the tale. It would be years before I knew her full story.

Robin with Dr. Inez Silberg

Margaret Inez Scott was the last to be born of thirteen children. No one knew the year. She'd fibbed about her age to obtain some long-ago teaching position and was infamous for never really squaring up—but she would admit to April—a flower-filled month that suited her. Several great voice teachers invested in the development of Inez, endowing her with a wealth of understanding of the fine conventions of singing. While singing for the Kansas City Opera, Inez fell in love with and married William Fredrick Lunsford, a veteran of World War I and a physician who worked for the military. She gave birth to a son, William, and began to settle into Kansas City society as a singer of opera, a wife, and a mother. Late one Fourth of July, her husband, who had been visiting his parents in Arkansas, hurried homeward, having made big plans with William Jr. for a spectacular fireworks demonstration.

No one knows with certainty what caused the accident. Perhaps Inez's husband fell asleep behind the wheel, or an oncoming car forced him off the road, or he took that segment of highway, which is dangerously narrow, too fast. The sharp curve led to a bridge abutment, and he hit it.

Inez was called to his bedside, and they spent his last few hours together. On that Fourth of July, as Americans geared up to celebrate a nation's birth in explosions of light, Margaret Inez Scott Lunsford, not yet thirty years old, became a widow. Her husband had no life-insurance policy. To make a living for herself and her young boy, she quit the insecure pursuit of performing and devoted herself to teaching.

Through her tragedy, the world of singing gained an amazing instructor of voice. The stories of her students' successes quickly spread.

Somewhere in her busy schedule, Inez met and married Max Silberg and moved to Oklahoma City University. She taught there for forty years, serving fifteen of those as head of the voice department. Her visual, cerebral approach to vocal technique ultimately became known as the "Silberg Technique," and she went on to become the second woman inducted into the Oklahoma Hall of Fame. Her students have performed in more than two hundred major opera houses and concert halls across the globe.

Mrs. Silberg grew more pensive upon learning I was expecting a baby. Unbeknownst to me, she began to strategize. Perhaps she had a penchant for stealth. Perhaps, behind the facade of innocent teacher of voice, she schemed covert international operations for the CIA. Whatever it was, I look back now with a keen appreciation of the fact that folks from her generation were *survivors*. Like Dr. Clarence C. Burg, they were *tough*!

In a fit of optimism, we scheduled my senior recital the same weekend as graduation, as though everything would work out as it should. Then one day in her special month of April, when we had just finished a lesson, Mrs. Silberg and I were walking together in the hall of the music building, the perfect place to disclose secret missions. "Dear, since you are sometimes required to fly in for your lessons, I have arranged a special time for your jury this semester. Not every teacher can be there." She reached into her purse for some powder, "but I'm sure that will be okay." She dusted her nose, clicked the compact shut, smiled innocently through the pale ivory dust floating in the air, and turned and walked away.

Mrs. Daray, it seemed, would not be present.

Because of his work, Bill couldn't come with me for the special jury Mrs. Silberg had arranged. Instead of the stage of the Lyric Theater, the performance was to convene in the room where master classes were held—a smaller, more intimate setting. I stayed at Bill's parents' house. Lying on his bed, I gazed up at the holes in the ceiling where he had tacked his Chicago poster, and their hit song came to mind. *Does anybody really know what time it is? Does anybody really care?* Fun music. Isn't that what music should be? Fun and enjoyable?

Time passed in slow motion as I dressed and walked early to the music building to warm up. I took my place in the practice room, realizing this was my last hope. I could not continue to travel with a baby in tow. What would the comrade do without Mrs. Daray at her side? To have enough jury members, Mrs. Silberg had drawn in one of the choral conductors as a sub. Did he have any experience? Had Mrs. Silberg told him of my dilemma? How would he apply a level out of thin air, with no frame of reference?

Anger and fear merged as I walked to the master classroom. The injustice of the situation was unsettling. I glanced at the jurors as they walked in and found their places. The comrade's resolve seemed tepid in the absence of Mrs. Daray. Funny, how easily a chord of one strand unravels. Like Mrs. Daray, the comrade had once been a student of Mrs. Silberg. In fact, Mrs. Silberg had, at one time or another, taught everyone in the room except the choral conductor who was subbing for Mrs. Daray. The most flamboyant teacher on the jury had once lost her voice completely, and Mrs. Silberg had helped her regain it.

When Mrs. Silberg entered the room, I could see that her authority still held—a fact the others did not necessarily like. Some surely squirmed under the pressure, as her clout bore down. But bear down it did.

"Now," Mrs. Silberg smiled knowingly, "we all know why we are here, don't we?" She looked down to straighten her scarf as she spoke, then lifted her eyes to look at each member of the panel. The comrade's eyes shifted to the left, away from Mrs. Silberg's gaze.

I went to stand in the crook of the grand piano, as I had been taught, and Mrs. Silberg took a seat with the others. "Okay, dear. What would you like to sing for us today?"

The music school secretary sat at the piano to accompany me. She patted her hair and opened the music to the song. Outside, the spring blossoms beckoned me away from it all. Why did it have to be this way? Couldn't music, especially singing, pull people together with its beauty and joy?

I did my best. An aria; an oratorio; French folk songs; Shubert Lieder; American art songs: my voice seemed to shrug off the panic. Song by song, with daredevil courage, I met each phrase and wrestled it into submission. Patience and concentration saw me through, though I felt my trauma building, to climax with the last note. Yet the note hung in the air, clear and full. I felt weak.

I looked cautiously around.

Madame Secretary sat patiently at the piano as the jury wrote. When they had finished, she briskly collected the papers and headed out to her office. Mrs. Silberg jumped up and followed, a step behind her.

I brought up the rear.

8B. 8B. 8B. Dear God, let it be an 8B, I prayed. Mr. Fob was about to go down for the last time. How could I add the expense of a lawsuit to seven years of private-school tuition? How could I juggle a new baby and this silly, expensive game? How could I live, knowing I had missed a college degree by one level because of infighting and politics?

In the office, Mrs. Silberg caught up with Madame Secretary. "May I see the adjudication sheets, please?" she said, holding out her hand. Instead of handing them over, Madame Secretary held up the compilation sheet for Mrs. Silberg to examine. I looked over her shoulder: *8B. 8B. 8B. 8B-*. My heart pounded. Tears stung. How unfair! Foiled by one tiny dash.

"Oh dear, see that?" Madame Secretary shook her head, pointing to the minus with glee.

The image of what Mrs. Silberg did next will forever play in my mind as one of life's great heroic moments. She reached up, grabbed the paper out of Madame Secretary's hand, took her pen, and, with trembling hands, marked a plus sign beside her own 8B.

"There 'tis!" she said brightly between gritted teeth, her eyes shooting nails at Madame Secretary. "That," she said pointing at the plus sign, "balances that out!" She pointed at the minus sign.

Madame Secretary, surrogate detractor, sagged in surrender. She lifted her hands like white flags—then dropped them to half-mast to pat her hair.

Like Jacob, who worked seven years to win his beloved Rachel, I had worked seven years to obtain my degree. Finally, thanks to God and Mrs. Silberg, I held it in my hands. It would take a while for God to heal the wound, but I was soon to see the miracle behind the madness.

In preparation for my senior recital, scheduled for graduation weekend late in May, my Beverly Sills albums blared, and I sang along, high and loud. It was opera, morning, noon, and night. I cleaned house singing

Bill and Robin on graduation day. Finally!

opera, cooked dinner singing opera, and sewed for the new nursery singing opera. When Bill came home at night, he accompanied me on the piano as I sang opera.

The recital was held at the old Methodist church that adjoined the OCU campus. I decorated it with a large spray of maroon-colored flowers to match my dress. Mrs. Silberg inquired about the color—she wanted her outfit to match mine—and wore a coordinating suit. The vivid shade suited the triumphant occasion, and I felt radiant in my formal dress, sewn by Bill's mother to accommodate my baby bump. Husband, family, and friends applauded, and happy hands succumbed to the irresistible urge to pat my burgeoning belly. I thought back to that first voice lesson with Mrs. Daray, her eyes bulging as I belted my aria and recitative, "This at laaaaa-st is the moe-mint." How far I had come since 907 Port Arthur! I owed a lot to OCU, "warts and all," as Daddy would say.

God instigates all sorts of secret schemes that can be seen only in the rearview mirror. While I had been fighting a War of Degrees, He had reached into the "secret place" and begun to weave together the ears of a tiny baby girl. I didn't know it at the time, but hearing is one of the earliest senses to function in an unborn child.

As I had battled hostile jury members, clawing up the slippery music-school slopes toward higher vocal levels—and as I had sung opera night and day in preparation for my senior recital—the captive audience that was our unborn baby had matured, listening. God had conducted His own purposes on a parallel plane, collecting the injustice, cupping it in His healing hands, and pouring it out as a blessing in the life of our child.

In my mind's eye, I could still see that little Asian girl with her tiny violin playing *Go Tell Aunt Rhody.* As I prepared for the task of training up a child, I could still hear the divine directive: "When you have a little girl, she should do that." Mrs. Daray had no idea, but her malevolence had become a core component of a divinely beautiful gift to our family.

Our child's giftedness, developed in the womb from hearing my relentless singing of opera as I struggled for a degree, would draw our family onto a musical platform that would affect the lives of thousands of children, inspiring them to take up a violin bow and "Make His Praise Glorious."

Summertime and Grace Kelly

Thou didst make me hope when I was upon my mother's breasts.

PSALM 22:9 (KJV)

Born in the infamous city of Waco, Texas, Annie, upon arrival, took a deep breath and cried on pitch, A-440. She enjoyed the sound of her voice so much, she continued to cry for three weeks before settling into life as a charming child, one who cried deliberately only in predetermined spots, like the car seat. The only endeavor capable of pacifying the lament? High, loud singing; the opening lines of George Gershwin's "Summertime" were her favorite.

Once, and only once, did I deposit Annie in the church nursery. When I returned to reclaim her, the nursery director gave me the glare of the gods, stabbing her thumb toward Annie's bawling face. "Is this your baby?" she said. "Don't bring this baby back!"

I tried to tell her about "Summertime."

Undaunted, we attempted to introduce fresh repertoire. I sucked in as big a breath as permitted by my pummeled, postpartum diaphragm and howled, "Born free, as free as the wind blows...." Or, for old time's sake, and to secure Annie's roots, I'd croon "Love Is a Many Splendored Thing." But nothing less than "Summertime" suited her psyche. When I pinched off "Chug-a-Lug, Chug-a-Lug," she spit up; upon hearing "Blood on the Saddle," she grew red in the face, highly offended. Two Bachelor of Music degrees in the family, and we had birthed a highbrow.

Music became our pacifier, and I do not exaggerate in saying that just one note of "Summertime," sung high and loud, caused our screaming daughter to shut her mouth instantly, turn her head to the side, and close her eyes to listen, in a comfort known from the womb. The deliberate nature of her response still amazes me.

So we sang "Summertime," even during wintertime, changing the lines to reflect our personal reality:

> *Oh, your Daddy ain't rich*
> *But your Mammy's good lookin'.*

I liked that, and the second verse pulsated with prophecy:

> *One of these mornin's, you're gonna rise up singin'*
> *And you'll spread your wings and take to the sky....*

My prayer.

The birth of a child unpacks a plethora of puzzles in the psyche of a parent. Bill and I felt the urgency to keep our baby healthy, to give her the best education, to see that she, like Jesus, grew "in wisdom, stature, and in favor with God and man." Annie's birth ushered in a time of remarkable transformation in both my life and my way of thinking.

When I gave birth to Annie, I ignorantly imagined that perhaps I couldn't breast-feed successfully. The whole process, in my mind, was a hodgepodge of racy tidbits passed down from the women with whom I'd grown up. I learned of inverted nipples, sore nipples, breast infections, and weak milk. I knew of a neighbor who "couldn't feed her boy, so she raised him on potato juice." I believed it; with his swarthy, mottled skin and his odd build—narrower at the top and bottom, but wide and round in the middle—he looked exactly like a jumbo Idaho baking potato.

There were also, however, examples of dedicated nursers. One mountain mama would sit proudly in the church pew, unbutton her dress, peel down a bucket-sized flap, and plug in her seedling, or anybody's seedling who needed a nip. Daddy had seen it all, and thought so little of it that he neglected to warn a visiting evangelist about the prolific nurser in his flock. The modest young man turned beet red at the sight. He lost his train of thought and frantically searched the room for a place to rest his eyes; not easy to find in such a tiny building. His revival-meetin' sermon could not be revived.

And then there was the visiting daughter of a foreign missionary who told me she hadn't known what "those" were for until she went to Africa.

What are those for?

For sexual pleasure, certainly. But have we overdone it? Plastic surgeons are busier than ever implanting and augmenting, impairing a young girls' ability to nurse potential future children. We've lost touch with the most noble purpose of the breast: to give health, nourishment, comfort, attachment, and verbal fluency to a new generation.

When I became pregnant with Annie, Bill and I had to choose which influences to heed. As Bill's mother testified, "Nobody breast-fed when my children were little. Nobody!" Yet while my mother spoke of "not having enough milk for her first two children," she was a cotton-patch girl. Even as breast-feeding in America hit an all-time low, she'd persevered and successfully breast-fed my brother and me.

I wanted to breast-feed, despite the tall tales. I instinctively knew that it mattered deeply. After all, God had designed the equipment and the process.

My friend, Debra, who was also pregnant, told me about La Leche League. "A lot of women don't like it," she said. "But I do. The information is fascinating, and it's fun to be with the moms, all sitting around talking and nursing their babies."

"La Leche League—what does that mean?"

"Leche is the Spanish word for milk," she said. "Do you know Grace Kelly, the movie star? She's a member."

Ooooh, Grace Kelly. The most beautiful woman ever born. "May I go with you to the next meeting?"

La Leche League plucked me from my cauldron of misinformation and doubt. *The Womanly Art of Breastfeeding,* the League's book, was a giant tome of knowledge for me, and began the flow of books I would consume on the subject as I rocked and suckled Annie.

Breast-feeding is not just "feeding the baby." It is God's way of jump-starting a relationship of disciple and disciple-maker. It is a time of relational bonding through language development, with and without words. Breast-feeding secures the strongest bonds of love and communication possible between a mother and her child. These bonds grow stronger through the years, but the first three years are a critical formative time.

That magical moment when a mother receives her newborn into her arms teems with potential. Oxytocin, the hormone of connectedness, cascades through the mother's body, and the fiercest of all bonds is forged. The newborn's eyesight is developed to focus remarkably well at eight to ten inches, the distance from a mother's breast to her face. How thoughtful of our Designer! Looking into my eyes, Annie could feel the warmth of my body and drink deep of my love and nourishment. Humanity is set apart from much of the animal kingdom in this; most animals do not have the luxury of eye contact while suckling.

Humans who nurse not only make eye contact, we have special hormones that make it meaningful. As the milk flows, the hormones flow with it: An exchange of oxytocin floods the mind of both mother and baby. As our eyes meet, we mothers reach to stroke our baby's face, and our child learns to return the favor. The bonding that begins with nursing will transfer to a lifetime of commitments to friends, to churches, to social groups, and most importantly, to a spouse.

Could the neglect of this magical time, I wondered, *be a root cause of the fragmentation of the family?*

Nursing became a passion for me, as I learned its amazing benefits. Not only was I bonding with my new baby girl, I was equipping her to secure lasting relationships all-around and throughout her lifetime. The hormones exchanged between us were enabling us both to look into the eyes of others and to sense their state of emotion, to empathize and understand.

As I gave myself to the bliss of young motherhood, I studied how mothers teach. We talk. We raise our eyebrows and smile. The timbre of our voice lifts from midregister to upper register as we coo, innately emphasizing and extending our words in a sing-song manner. "How's my little lamb today? Are you hungry? I have just the thing for you!" All these components—the oxytocin, the speech, the eye contact, the tone of voice, the cuddling—play into an important phenomenon. From birth to two years old, the right hemisphere of the brain, the part that oversees nonverbal communication, is experiencing a huge surge in development.

As Annie nursed, she was learning to read my eyes, the movement of my brows, the position of my mouth and jaw, and the tone of my voice, as clues to meaning and relationship. She was assessing, through facial expression, body language, pitch, timbre, and musical nuance, the message derived from speech apart from the words. It's not just what you say, it's how you say it: the most important kind of communication.

This mother-child symphony was the beginning of my discipleship of Annie. It was softening both our personalities, making us more patient and kind, assuring us of our love for each other, and preparing us to work together harmoniously. We would both appreciate these benefits when the practice sessions associated with formal music lessons began. As breast-feeding and other life-affirming interactions with me continued, Annie would be learning to regulate her emotions, and this, too, would contribute to her success not only in music and performance, but in every realm of life.

Artistic development is about fluency and the power of words. It's about the strength to develop extraordinary relationships through extraordinary communication skills. Breast-feeding, I realized, targets those processes specifically.

In spite of a brisk undercurrent of cultural disapproval, I became a pioneer for the cause of breast-feeding as I came to understand its vast importance in the healthy rearing of a child. I also became good at it. I could probe through layers of clothing and begin feeding as quick and slick as a magic trick. The person sitting beside me on a church pew or in a restaurant might have fainted to know something so primitive was occurring at his elbow. But my little girl's healthy development was more important than false piety. After all, this is *life*. And mothering is the most important job on earth.

The Yellow Bluebird

*. . . As I inched sluggishly along the treadmill of the Maycomb County school system,
I could not help receiving the impression that I was being cheated out of something.
Out of what I knew not, yet I did not believe that twelve years of unrelieved boredom
was exactly what the state had in mind for me*

Harper Lee in *To Kill a Mockingbird*

I began to think ahead, planning my daughter's educational development, and as I did so, I became aware of a vague discontent within my heart. In my school years, I had failed to cultivate a high regard for our educational systems. Now, with a child in my arms, I found it necessary to draw my thoughts and opinions to the surface, to examine them in the light of truth.

I cued the picture show of my youth, lying on a personal psychiatric sofa as the projector purred, unrolling reel-to-reel reruns of mostly... Mama.

Mama, I recalled, really didn't obsess much about our schooling, especially in the upper grades of middle school and high school. Nonetheless, we excelled as leaders and made good grades. She didn't know we made good grades. I don't remember Mama ever asking to see a report card. But after we wagged them in front of her nose to receive a nod or a pat or some gesture of affirmation, she would glance briefly, nod, and say:

"Have you practiced your piano?"

My girlfriend, Dana, who attended school across the state line in Arkansas, won awards for perfect attendance. Her mother cracked the whip, and Dana, a superbright and talented student, loved the prestige of those awards. What a mystery Dana was to me. Why would anyone care to pursue an award for perfect attendance? Did it serve any purpose?

When my friend Jimmy and I skipped out of high school on a sunny spring morning and drove all the way to Mena to go bowling, Jimmy nearly jumped out of his skin every time someone entered the alley. He'd jerk his head to scan the room, terrified his mother might find him. I, on the other hand, looked everywhere for my mother.

I needed cash.

Odd, I thought now, when I recalled Mama's laissez-faire take on education. *What was the source? How did it affect me? How was it spurring the unrest I felt in the educational planning for my newborn daughter?* I dug deeper.

Zafra's school, built of warm, brown and gray rock, sat narrow and long on a small acreage: three rooms—the first for grades one through four, the second for grades five through eight, and the third, and most important, our lunchroom. In first grade, I sat merrily in room one, working on reading with Michael, the lone male among four first-grade females. At recess, Michael and I, along with Karen, Roberta, Viola, and Judy, a second-grader, would race to our playhouses at one side of the softball clearing.

These Neverland dwellings sat under pines that punctured the clouds with shivering needles and softened the rocky ground with a natural carpet. Our makeshift families were structurally dysfunctional because Michael, the only possible candidate for a husband, insisted on being Superman, who could fly through walls, especially walls built of pine needles, while his many wives demanded hotly that he use the door.

We played with boundless imagination, cooking pretend meals in pretend kitchens, rocking our babies on rocking chairs configured from rocks, and tussling over Karen's doll, which had a soft cotton body and a box full of hand-stitched clothes.

When that game sagged, we waged pretend wars, building waist-high forts of yellow oak leaves gleaned from the majestic trees on the opposite side of the softball clearing. We tried to persuade Michael that Superman wasn't around when the cowboys fought the Indians. But it hardly mattered. Our real little Indians enjoyed playing cowboy, while our real little cowboys whooped it up like the Indians they'd seen on Daniel Boone. We never paused to ponder the politics.

At noon we hurried into the lunchroom, where Ada, the pinnacle of a pioneer woman—with a hairnet shaped like chicken wire and a pinch of snuff in her cheek—cooked fresh hot rolls every day. Sometimes, she'd shaped the dough into cinnamon rolls whose centers sagged with sweetness. The only thing Ada could not get us to eat and could find no culinary use for were the gallon cans of thumb-sized, pitted, gourmet black olives straight from Italy. The government shipped them to us by the carton. Daddy questioned the outlay: jumbo Italian olives—in Zafra?

We played basketball on a rutted, outdoor court and during our softball games we chased George, our baseball-playing hound. He trembled with delirious pleasure at the thought that he might grab a grounder and bolt away, bulleting through the schoolyard with the only softball on the premises clamped inside his slobbery smile. The entire student body chased him 'round and 'round the playground, while passersby stopped their log trucks to point and laugh. On impulse, George would make a sudden 180-degree turn and run back through his pursuers. At that point, baseball turned to football, as student after student lunged to tackle dirt. Skirts flew and pants ripped, but George, who could fancy-foot and fake like a furry Emmett Smith, scored touchdown after touchdown. When the bell rang, the whole gang would return to their desks, exhilarated and breathless, while George deposited the slimy ball by the door and sank into slumber on the porch, tongue lolling in pink bliss.

With our bellies full of sweet rolls and sunshine, we discovered that to learn is a pleasure. Reading came easily to me, and I perused the tiny cloakroom library for books. To encourage us first-graders to read, Mrs. Elder, who taught grades one through four, set a rule: She would call us to stand beside her desk and read out loud until we read a word incorrectly. We would then return to our seats for further study.

After I finished my beginning reader, Mrs. Elder gave me a "big-girl" reader, a thicker, hardcover book with glossy pages. I finished it by Christmas, except for the final poem. So I carried it home and sat on Daddy's lap as I labored, asking his help with the hard words on the final page, words like *lawn* and *scarcely*, *precious* and *cubit.* I studied so hard, I inadvertently memorized that final poem, and I still remember it as a beloved part of my poetry repertoire.

"Our House"
Our house is small
The lawn and all
Can scarcely hold the flowers
Yet every bit, the whole of it
Is precious for it's ours.
From door to door
From roof to floor
From wall to wall
We love it;
We wouldn't change
For something strange
One single corner of it.
The space complete
In cubit feet
From cellar door to rafter
Just measures right
And not too tight
For us, our friends, and laughter.
—Dorothy Brown Thompson

The next day, when I approached her desk, Mrs. Elder drew me into the circle of her arm as I read, a practice I later adopted when hearing my own children read. From that close vantage, I could see the silver in her smile echoing the silver in her hair, swept up in a casual bun. I read the whole book for her and, as a grand finale, quoted the poem. Mrs. Elder beamed, and I beamed back. I can still feel the light of God's pleasure, shining like a sunbeam through the dusty haze of the cramped schoolroom. "You,"

Mrs. Elder said, "may have a brand-new reader. Keep going, and you might read up everything we have!"

I planned on it.

On Monday mornings, Mr. Elder, who taught grades five through eight, invited all students into his classroom to sing. I already loved to sing. A few of our school songs would today be banned as politically incorrect, but we never thought about it. Our ignorance erupted in melody as we sang "The Yellow Rose of Texas," "Ol' Black Joe," "Long, Long Ago," "Way Down upon the Suwannee River," and "Ol' McDonald Had a Farm." I loved the turkey tongue twister:

… with a gobble gobble here and a gobble gobble there …

It would be three decades before I would come to understand the power of singing, but I sure felt it.

In my fourth-grade year, the experts landed in our rock schoolhouse to *gobble-gobble* up our way of life, persuading parents to consolidate the schools. Bigger, they said, is better. I wonder now why the otherwise no-nonsense men of the community didn't pull out their oily twelve gauges and declare war.

Somewhere along the way, it seems, they had subtly been sold a bill of goods: Experts know best. "Good parents," the experts implied, "will turn over responsibility to the government's chosen few. Experts *know*. *Parents* don't *know*."

Daddy and Mama smelled a rat but failed to pounce, never quite pinning down the government's agenda to examine it carefully. So the little rock schoolhouse closed, ending the golden era of my childhood. The new school, though only twelve miles away, demanded three hours a day on the yellow Bluebird bus, a real pickle in my pudding. The rutted dirt roads, the log trucks, and the brainless heifers lollygagging across our road from their shady mountain paths made the route endless. One felt a kinship with God; a day became a thousand years.

The government offered to pay off incrementally the accumulated college loans of a newly graduated teacher, loaded with debt, if the teacher would agree to come into the mountains and teach us.

Were we that repugnant?

Daddy's mother, Granny Dema, had taught school in the mountains since the early 1930s. She loved the ambience of one-room schoolhouses, every grade a single row. Reading out loud in her husky alto voice, she'd introduced young hillbillies and Choctaws to what I now know to be the bedrock of education: music, poetry, and literature—Henry Wadsworth Longfellow, Robert Louis Stevenson, and Sir Walter Scott. She loved to end each read-aloud session with a cliffhanger, and only the best behavior could persuade her to allow a sneak peek at what happened next. She hosted Christmas pageants, songfests, and special events. She took great pride in the fact that her presence eliminated ignorance and lifted a child from poverty. She loved her job. She loved her students and was once selected as teacher of the year in Pushmataha County.

Our high-school district employed a few teachers who understood the territory, loved the children, had a passion for learning, and ran a first-rate classroom. But there were those who neither knew nor appreciated the colorful history and unique cultural heritage of our mix. They simply marked time until their debts, like hemorrhoids, shrank. Some were forced to leave prematurely, after inappropriate behavior with female students.

This is a familiar scenario today, consistent with many public and private educational institutions. Some care. Some don't. But riding a bus three hours a day, five days a week, for the tutelage of even one lousy, lazy teacher is cruelty, a waste of a child's life. Going to school took nine hours of my day, yet I could make up a day of assignments in approximately forty-five minutes. This waste had its effect on me, and I knew it even as a child.

> *Tomorrow, and tomorrow, and tomorrow*
> *Creeps in this petty pace from day to day...*
> *Macbeth*, Act V, Scene V

Early every weekday morning, the yellow Bluebird beeped from the foot of the hill, the spring on the screen door uncoiled as we shoved it open, the cat dashed in as we dashed out, the spring convulsed, and the door slammed shut with a slap. We ran down the hill, books in swing, my baby brother, David, at six years old, trying his best to keep up.

Whenever I lacked the liver to face the drudgery of the yellow Bluebird or the painful grind of high school, Mama saved the day, picking up the receiver and dialing the school. "Ned," she'd say, "Robin is suffering from 'proud flesh' and will not be coming to school today." I never understood exactly what proud flesh was, and I think Ned related it to female problems. But if Mama ever needed a term to cover a hypothetical state of health, proud flesh sat at the top of her list. "It's that ol' proud flesh," she would say. I later learned that it is an old-fashioned term for scar tissue. Mama knew her illnesses, all right. The way she saw it, the whole yellow Bluebird situation was likely to leave us with the scars of proud flesh, and no rules applied.

American society exalts a "formal education" as a surrogate savior. Not Mama. In her book, smart and educated people were, first and foremost, cognizant of the necessity of love, the great conundrum that many grapple with but few pin down. Education was meant to serve and further the cause of love. I learned at her feet as a steady stream of characters, whose oddities deserve being written up in their own book, came to reside in my childhood home. They partook of Mama's love with relish, nourishing their souls and their stomachs around her table. Some came and went. Others remained for years.

Mama had her own school running on a parallel line. She taught us to practice hospitality, to entertain and converse with charm, to set an elegant table, and to serve a balanced meal. She taught us to store food from the garden, to play the piano and sing in harmony, to dress with feminine beauty, to welcome strangers, and to love children. She taught us to bring home the needy, to wash their hair and their clothes, to feed their bodies and their souls, to offer help in times of trouble, to stay the course, and to fear the Lord.

Her lessons were practical and persuasive: the proper use of toilet tissue, how much is enough—"Honey, a wad that big is not even effective." When bathing a baby, she taught us, be sure to thoroughly cleanse, rinse, and dry every crease, or a red, sore place will develop. Laughter is akin to crying, so don't be surprised if a baby begins to cry soon after a hard laugh. When sweeping, pull, don't push, the broom. Mopping is more than just wetting the floor: Press down hard for an effective scrubbing action. Change your cleaning water often; it should be kept fresh, hot, and soapy. After washing the dishes, thoroughly clean the sink, especially behind the faucet, and finish up by cleansing and wringing the dish cloth. Fold laundry just so, and place it carefully in the drawer; properly folded laundry shows love and respect for the person who will wear the garments. Fold towels with the edges rolled to the inside; they are more attractive that way. Iron thoroughly. When setting the table, use all pieces of flatware every time, even unnecessary ones. Pots and pans are an insult to those who will sit at your table, so use pretty serving dishes. Throw away old food; mixing old food with fresh just ruins the fresh. Beds are the most important pieces of furniture in the house; dress them cleanly and comfortably. When cleaning toilets, wipe the base and the floor around the base, as well as the bowl. Dust thoroughly, removing every knickknack and lamp. Furniture loves to be rearranged, and the change freshens the house.

Presalting softens steamed vegetables; do not salt vegetables intended for frying or they will be soggy. A flat, disc-shaped onion with no discoloring at the root will be sweet; thick onions will be hot, discolored onions foul. When baking bread, knead yeast dough thoroughly to develop the gluten. Avoid overhandling piecrust or biscuit batter lest they become tough; roll piecrust generously and trim with margin to spare to ensure beautiful fluting of the edge; carefully cut slices in the top crust to let the steam escape. Make sure biscuit dough is very wet with buttermilk before turning it out on a generously floured surface and patting it lightly into a circle. Do not overlap the cuts when cutting biscuits; they must be perfectly round. Dip them, front and back, in hot butter. Don't crowd biscuits in the pan or they will not be golden brown and crusty all 'round. Look for and gather all wild berries; make jellies and jams. Measure carefully, especially when baking a cake, because cakes are insecure, prone to falling, and need to be beautiful. Baking powder causes food to rise. Soda sweetens buttermilk. Never, never, *never* open an oven door without permission from the cook. When making iced tea, wash all containers thoroughly—Mama's favorite word, *thoroughly*—with hot soapy water; otherwise the tea will be cloudy and will not taste fresh. A beautiful table overflowing with healthy food communicates love.

Mama's teaching, learned at the feet of Annie Moses, has served me throughout my life.

Sunday dinner: Mama floating across the kitchen floor, her shiny hair wrapped around rollers, her face radiant with Merle Norman makeup, her chenille robe sashaying across slim ankles. She'd plop a heavy rump roast into the Dutch oven, and I'd hear the sizzle of hot grease sealing the flavor. The added onion, garlic, and spices would soak the air with the fragrance of peace and plenty. By the time we left for services, the rump would be basking in a slow oven, with carrots and potatoes ready to add, and pies would be cooling on the counter, sometimes filled with such wild fruits as huckleberry, or with coconut, my favorite.

At church, Mama taught Sunday school, played the piano, sang, and, with her strong hands, picked through the fleece of the flock, checking for suffering, sadness, or sores. Assured that everyone was all right, she'd hustle us home to help her augment the feast with a fruit salad, a plate of fresh tomatoes and onion, a pot of green beans, and a basket full of hot biscuits.

My sisters and I flowed through the kitchen like ballerinas on point as Mama's motor purred. "Robin, set the table, and use the good glasses. Cindy, don't put the bananas in the fruit salad until the last minute, I don't want them to be discolored. Girls, our guests will be here directly, so don't be slow. Sherry, take your daddy a glass of iced tea."

Scoffers may cry, "This isn't education. This is housekeeping. This is Ma Ingalls meets Martha Stewart. This is June Cleaver meets Aunt Bea. This is gag meets reflex."

But look closer. Mama ran an exceptional school. To her, brilliant people knew how to do one thing: create a sphere where love could activate. Priority one was to secure the basics; set straight the practical matters of heart, service, and relationship. With such foundations cemented, learning could proceed unimpeded, directed by prayer and a personal compass toward the singular destiny designed by the God Who created each one of us.

When I became a student at Oklahoma City University, I loved music, and OCU held top honors in teaching it. But Mama knew that life in the city wouldn't be easy for me. So she got going, smoothing the rough edges of college life like a 1960s girdle. When I was lonely, she visited me. When I needed solitude, she swung a private room. When I entered pageants or planned recitals, she bought dresses and jewelry. When I needed money, she did her best to send it. We honestly had no idea that the price of OCU, a private institution, would be

dramatically higher than that of a state college. We had had no experience whatsoever with universities. It was not until my younger brother David called home and
asked for $225.00 to cover the first semester's tuition at a small state school that
we understood the choice we'd made for me. Mama almost fainted from shock.
But even had we known the disparity in price, it would have made no difference.
Mama did what had to be done, God help her.

And He did. Always.

Such sepia-toned scenes segued through my head as I nursed my baby girl
and thought about her future.

Annie cried unless she could see and enjoy everything going on around her.
So as I prepared meals, I put her in a pouch that clipped over my shoulders. With
her back against my chest, she sat like a kangaroo, looking out on her new world
with rapt attention, her arms sticking out like Frankenstein's. Knives, heat, water,
oil: I worked around my infant spectator with great caution. When Bill and I sat
down to eat, we laughed about the salt and pepper in her hair, accumulated as I
opened bottles over her head.

One day as I washed the dishes, I tuned to a local radio station, unaware that
a pivotal moment in my life was approaching through the airwaves. The voice
of a nationally known talk show host entered my kitchen, and to my surprise, I
knew the special guest he introduced. Chris Hayward served as administrator at
the church our family attended. What were they talking about? Chris Hayward
almost went to *jail*? How could that be? Somehow, he'd always reminded me of
a real, live Winnie-the-Pooh, a tad soft, a tad chubby, and wholly good-hearted.

What was his crime?

I listened on. Seems Chris was pioneering a new way of education by removing his children from public school to teach them himself, at home. The concept
was so new that authorities had considered it truancy. After a boisterous legal battle, Chris had won the tug-of-war and had opened a new educational option. My
head spun, and the earth lurched under my feet. What a concept! Pooh Bear had
detonated a nuke in the secret chambers of America's educational power brokers.

Were parents qualified to educate their children at home? More to the point,
was *I* qualified to educate *my* child? Shouldn't the *experts* know better than I how

an education should proceed? But wasn't I a *product* of the *experts*? To say I wasn't qualified was to say they had failed. Then shouldn't the cycle be stopped? Perhaps these were the same *experts* who had decided I should spend my childhood riding that yellow Bluebird bus. Perhaps these were the same *experts* who had mown down the frail faith of every student in my religion class. Perhaps these were the same *experts* who held grudges and tried to keep hard-working voice students from gaining a degree.

Homeschooling…Maybe I could *learn* how to do it.

I felt a surge of independence, and tucked the tantalizing tidbit into my treasury-of-novel-ideas-to-be-prayed-about-and-implemented-when-the-time-is-right. It sat prettily alongside the directive God had whispered to me that freshman year at OCU, when I'd watched the little Asian girl play her violin. "When you have a little girl, she should do that."

I had my little girl. And I had the beginnings of an amazing plan filled with fresh ideas.

Make His Praise Glorious

Shout with joy to God, all the earth!
Sing the glory of his name;
make his praise glorious.

PSALM 66:1–2 (NIV)

"Hey Robin, want to hear some good news?" A week never went by that Bill did not say those words to me. His optimism saturated our lives, and blessings rolled down like gumballs. By the time our second child, Alex, was born, Bill and I had settled into a penniless bliss. Our neighborhood church, filled with families like ours, infused our lives with friendship and laughter.

The music-publishing department at Word grew rapidly, and Bill enjoyed his job as a music editor. John Purifoy, his boss, kept the pace at an easy gallop, while the senior editor, Ken Barker, turned out to be a jolly young fellow who inspired plenty of laughs.

After a couple of years, John left to start his own publishing company, and Word struggled a bit with hiring, firing, and reorganizing. When a new executive came to reorganize the department, he suggested Bill begin working on a self-employed status and offered him a contract guaranteeing right of first refusal on any transcription and editing jobs Word might offer.

Thus was born Living Stone Music Company, one of the greatest blessings of our lives. For more than two-and-a-half decades, Bill has generated the lion's share of print-product manuscripts offered by the Christian music industry, and all from the comfort of his home. With Bill available to monitor Annie and Alex a few hours a week, I found the freedom to enroll in Baylor University and begin a Master's degree program in vocal performance.

Dr. Joyce Farwell accepted me as a voice student, and I immensely enjoyed both her teaching and her company. Music-school politics at Baylor were placid when compared to OCU, and the steady nature of life with Bill pulled me into a smooth stride. A new concept occurred to me—how narrow-sighted it is that so many parents deem it necessary for their kids to finish college and graduate school before marrying. For the first time, I felt truly settled, mature, and ready for the challenges of higher learning.

During the week, I bustled around the house, singing along with Beverly Sills as I wiped tops and bottoms and everything in between. My two babies loved both the music and their mama. As Beverly roared up and down the scale on *"Una Voce Poco Fa,"* I roared along, and four-year-old Annie chimed in. Tin Pan Alley had nothing on us.

Dr. Farwell encouraged me. In one lesson, she took me by the chin to adjust the position of my jaw on a particular note. Then, continuing to hold her hand softly on my face, she looked at me and said to Bill, who sat at the piano, "I think her voice has an unusually pretty tone, don't you?" Bill almost broke his neck, agreeing.

Amazing energy proceeds from a timely line of prescient praise, "a word fitly spoken" (Proverbs 25:11, KJV). When a perceptive, visionary leader—a teacher, a parent, a pastor, a friend—assesses the gifts in an individual and articulates a vision of what those gifts might become, there is nothing more powerful. It is the moment when the quixotic *glorious quest* begins. It peels back the thick skin of low self-esteem and overcomes lack of exposure. It dusts off the residue of harmful attitudes, such as I had experienced with Mrs. Daray.

When the National Association of Teachers of Singing held their annual competition, I roared through *"Una Voce Poco Fa"* without Beverly Sills's help and won first runner-up. I could speak foreign, after all. I could make the grade, after all. I could sing the big notes, after all! Just like the girl with the Carole King hair, back in Little Rock, *I* had potential. Good things would come *to me.*

God, in His godly way, walked beside me, gathering up the dubious dreams I had discarded, dusting them off and re-presenting them to me, as if to say, "Do you remember how you longed to do this? I do. Now I have made it possible."

Dr. Farwell once casually mentioned that my voice reminded her of Lily Pons, "high and light, but with that powerful spin that carries well over an orchestra."

Really? My spirit surfed on the energy of her words.

Dr. Farwell flipped through the pages of my book of arias to the "Bell Song" from the opera *Lakme.* "Oh," I said, "I have wanted to sing that for years. I know you might think it's too difficult, but I have those high E's." I sang a snippet—the fast-moving ornamental notes of the coloratura—to demonstrate.

She listened with eyebrows raised. "If you really want to do it, I believe you should." I ran my eyes over the notes, remembering the soprano at Inspiration Point Fine Arts Colony, where I studied during the summer between my freshman and sophomore years. That's where I'd first heard the aria. At the time, I had felt depressed because I believed that I lacked the talent to sing it.

I was surprised by how easily the piece came to me. It was as if I had been singing it in my heart for years. Dr. Farwell scheduled a performance of it at a convocation service in Roxy Grove Hall. The auditorium was packed with students as I walked onstage, poised and ready. I concentrated on the task at hand, steering my mind, which is the real center of vocal technique, through the opening *a cappella* cadenza, which is challenging, featuring multiple high C's and a few high E's thrown in for sport. I then proceeded to sing, in French, the tale of the young Indian girl, daughter of a pariah, who used her snake charmer's bells to save a handsome traveler from a jungle beast. My voice twinkled clear and bright, imitating the bells.

Had I been a mountain climber, I might have compared the experience to ascending Kiamichi Mountain to fly my flag. I trilled on the last high C, then, like a fireplace bellows, floated the final high E with all the exhaling of breath I could muster.

The audience is applauding rather enthusiastically, I thought as I bowed. I retreated to the backstage area and plopped down to wait for the end of the service.

After a few seconds, a stagehand demanded, "Hey! You gonna get back out there and bow again?"

"What?"

"You gonna get back out there and bow again? They're still clapping."

Shocked and pleased, I raced back to center stage for another bow. I exited, then had to return for another, and another; the applause brought me back for four curtain calls.

Before the Lord takes us onward in our destiny with Him, He often gives us a landmark moment, a souvenir of a season that has culminated in a celebration of victory. My performance of that beloved and difficult aria came one day after finding out that I was pregnant for the third time. I knew that my short, happy tenure at Baylor was over, and what's more, that my years of studying voice were over, as the growth of my family demanded more and more of my energies.

It was not to be a sad good-bye. That performance of the "Bell Song," the long applause, the curtain calls, healed my heart like a spring rain. For years, I had carried fears: of being musically inferior; of Mrs. Daray being right all along, if only I would admit it; of never measuring up, no matter how hard I worked.

I left the auditorium through a slew of compliments, and Dr. Farwell stood in the foyer, glowing with affirmation. "That was really, really good, Robin," she said. "I have never heard you sing so well."

"I just found out I'm pregnant," I blurted.

Her smile turned a bit purple. "Oh...well." She thought a moment. She was a mother of four herself. She smiled again, bigger this time. "Congratulations!" she said.

A chapter in my life closed, and a new one began, for God was about to play His trump card, one that would propel Bill and me into a whole new arena of music.

"Hey, Robin, want to hear some good news?" Bill came into the kitchen waving a brochure. "The Sunday school board is having an anthem contest. I think we should write something for it. In fact, I've already started. How do you like this? He sat down at the piano and began to sing, over percussive right-hand chords. "'Praise the Lord of Heaven, Praise the Lord of Earth'....Then I have the end of the chorus..." He began to play a syncopated rhythm, singing, "'Blessing and honor and glory and power be unto the

Lord. Come and let us make His praise glorious.' That's all I have," he said. "What do you think?"

"I like it," I said. "I wouldn't go to the tonic on the last note of the melody."

"Well, it ends on a G chord, so these are the notes that are available for the last note of the melody." He played the chord. "How about if it goes like this." He played E-D-D and sang, "Glo-ri-ous."

"Oh, I like that a lot better. Write out the melody for me and I'll work on the lyric. Are you thinking from the Psalms?"

"Yes, mostly. Let me know what you come up with."

I took the melody and laid it out to various passages from the Psalms, primarily using those that instruct us to "Praise the Lord with music."

Bill arranged the piece for choir and handed it off to Bruce Greer, a friend and former coworker at Word, to see if he had any suggestions.

Bruce called the next day. "Bill, look, I went through that song. In fact, I showed it to some of the others around here. We were wondering....Did you know that Sandi Patti is looking for material for her new album? I mean, you should have sent this song to her, like, yesterday."

We hurried to the local studio of a dear friend, one of those people with an ultracreative brain that never stops hyperventilating on possibilities, and made a demo. The song cut a fine figure by the time we stuffed it into the mailbox the next day, hurrying it off to the desk of Debbie Atkins, Word's Nashville song plugger, with a letter saying we thought it might suit Sandi Patti.

I put the whole episode out of my mind. I had learned that the songwriting industry is uncoordinated and fickle, that to stand around waiting for your latest creation to hit is to be paralyzed forever. Songs that should be stuffed deep inside a cinch-sack and hauled to the dump somehow rise to enjoy international familiarity, while truly beautiful music lies cruelly paper-clipped in a dusty, dormant file. So I adopted an "I'll-believe-it-when-I-see-it" posture and practiced my arias, quilted my quilts, and tended my babies.

I have observed that God neutralizes obsessions before He delivers the goods. When the dream has ceased to control us, to mean more than it deserves to mean, when it has been brought down to size, *then* He will act.

Only a few days after we sent the demo to Word in Nashville, Debbie called to say that Sandi and her producer, Greg Nelson, loved "Make His Praise Glorious." That night, Sandi's manager, Dan Johnson, called to tell us that Sandi and Greg thought the song was "an answer to prayer." It would be on her album.

"Vinyl is final, though. Right? Are you sure they will record it?" Bill asked.

"As sure as Jesus is coming again," Dan said.

I hung up the phone, cool as a card shark. Bill, however, was embarrassing. He hugged me, jumping around, giggling. "Aslan is on the move," he said, quoting C. S. Lewis. He punched the air. I found his boyish enthusiasm so funny that I gave up my cool and laughed along. Then I picked up the phone to share the news with Mama and Daddy.

"Hey, guess what! Bill and I got a cut on Sandi Patti's new album."

"That's wonderful, honey," Mama said. "I must say, I'm not surprised. What's it called?"

"Make His Praise Glorious." The words sounded regal to me now.

Daddy either didn't hear us right or didn't immediately catch the significance of placing a song on Sandi Patti's album. He launched into his own news: "LeRoy Blakenship has a song being sung at the Grand Ole Opry. It goes, *I've still got the garden, but someone stole my Rose.*'" I couldn't help but laugh. For Daddy, no musical news surpasses performing in the Grand Ole Opry. I'm sure Mama impressed on him the nature of his daughter's good news the minute they hung up.

Sandi's song selection process included many layers of screeners. From hundreds of tunes vying for a mere ten slots, *Make His Praise Glorious* not only came to be selected, it emerged as the title cut. A miracle! Don Cason, president of Word Music, a division of Word, Inc., called us into his office in Waco, in the same building as Bill's old Word office. "I've heard a lot of songs in my life," he said, "but this is really fresh and creative. I know you two will need to pray about this, but we want you to sign up with Word as songwriters. You might want to move to Nashville, to work with our song pluggers there."

Just two days before Don's invitation, Dan Rather had reported on the evening news that Waco, Texas, rated third from the bottom in real estate sales, nationwide. What did that ranking mean to God? Not a thing. We sold our beautiful, freshly painted love nest on Reuter Street, packed up our belongings, and waddled to Nashville, with only two weeks to go until the birth of our third child.

A Hard Row to Hoe

But your genuine Inner Ring exists for exclusion. There'd be no fun if there were no outsiders. The invisible line would have no meaning unless most people were on the wrong side of it. Exclusion is no accident; it is the essence.

C. S. Lewis in *The Inner Ring*

"My mama has told me a thousand times not to exaggerate," Brian Bailey used to quip. That joke still makes me smile. But I would not be exaggerating to say that every living creature in Nashville, Tennessee, is a songwriter. Look behind the white-haired man at the counter of the AAA Sewing and Vacuum. See his platinum album on the wall? His success is not measured by Hoover and Pfaff. That framed disc tells his real story, a tale of sweaty hours in cramped rooms pounding out hook after hook, as only country music songwriters can do, songs like "Is It Cold in Here, Or Is It Just You?" or "Thank God and a Greyhound You're Gone" or "If I Said You Had a Beautiful Body, Would You Hold It Against Me?"

Look out. If you should slip up and mention music while chatting with the pastor of the Baptist church at the T-ball game, he will babble on about his latest witty lyrics. He will let you know he's just preaching on the side, until he writes the big hit that's hiding around the corner.

Or if you should, in a fit of wit, pop a pun to a salesclerk in the men's department at Dillards, he'll pencil it down as a hook to remember. And don't worry. That policeman parked in the shade? He isn't nabbing speeders; he's writing country songs.

Nashville flexes such creative muscle, it thinks it can snap its fingers and order inspiration like a side of grits. "I've penciled you in for Thursday with Wanda and

Hank, 10:00 AM, down on Music Row." Songwriters strain their brains, collaborating to compile an impressive catalogue of compositions, a fraction of a fraction of which make it on to a recording.

Meanwhile, industry A&R professionals wade the water searching for that magical moment when a great artist, a great song, and a great producer converge to create a radio hit, a superstar, and a flood of cash. Hooking such moments, like a giant trout, is all that matters.

Nashville has served as the crusher of a great many dreams. There are endless tales of genius rejected, of powerful naysayers giving verbal backhands to incredible young talent, talent that sometimes—just sometimes—manages to sneak in through a side door to create a sensation anyway. Most would-be performers and songwriters grow disgusted with the whole mess and go into real estate, or preaching, or selling shoes.

It was a great blessing that "Make His Praise Glorious" hit the top of the Christian music charts just as we moved to Nashville—and that it stayed there a long time. Both ASCAP and the Nashville Songwriters Association awarded it Gospel Song of the Year, and the accolades helped carve a home for us as staff songwriters at Word. As a musician, it would have been dreary to move to Nashville with no musical frame of reference.

Music Row is a hard row to hoe.

But Nashville is more than Music Row. It is a city saturated in southern grandeur. Homes like the one gracing Tara, the plantation in *Gone with the Wind*, are scattered everywhere you look: the Belle Meade Mansion, the Belmont Mansion, Rippavilla, the Carnton Plantation, the Hermitage.

North and south, east and west, Nashville is a city of converging contradictions—sophisticated and simple, cosmopolitan and country. A brand-new subdivision of million-dollar houses was built recently near our home, and I enjoyed watching as blue-collar craftsmen created a pond, tested the spray of an elegant fountain, emplaced a wall of gray stones around a lovely gazebo, dressing it with wax begonias. But looky there, right across the road, just spittin' distance from all this finery: That's right, it's a farm, where Billy Goat Gruff plays king of the mountain, standing on a pile of wooden crates sprinkled with soft tuffs of hay, a contraption erected by the owner who sympathized with Billy's need for a throne. The old goat stands with a noble air, ignoring the fountain, ignoring the gazebo and the flowers, ignoring the growl of BMWs and Mercedes. Billy is not intimidated by city slickers and their fancy airs. Let them build their mansions. As far as he's concerned, they don't have a crate to stand on.

Nashville comes with a heaping spoonful of culture. Drive around, and you'll see a college on every corner. The educational bourgeoisie, led by Vanderbilt University, declare the city the "Athens of the South." Doubters may stop by Centennial Park, with its authentic reproductions of the Greek Parthenon and its statue of Athena.

"Authentic reproduction?" Daddy unplugged his toothpick and grinned when I told him about it. "Is that anything like a 'genuine imitation'?" Daddy, and patriots like him, believe Nashville is best described as the "Country Music Capital of the World"—not the whole wide world, just the world represented on the stage of the Ryman Auditorium, the historical home of the Grand Ole Opry, where the ghosts of Patsy Cline, Roy Acuff, Minnie Pearl, and Bob Wills reside, and where LeRoy Blankenship's song is sung.

Country music used to be known as country and western music, emphasis on the Western. More idiomatic than the country music of today, it brought us the favored musical style of two American icons: the Texas rancher and the Oklahoma cowboy. Country and western music spun the yarn of the Wild West. It was the music I grew up on in the mountains of Oklahoma: albums like *Gunfighter Ballads* and *More Gunfighter Ballads*, with songs like "Blood on the Saddle," "Chug-a-Lug" (until Mama nixed that), and Johnny Cash's *basso profundo* roaming the rails of Americana on "Ride This Train."

No more. The world has shrunk, and today, thousands of visitors from cultures across the globe bring their thick wallets to Nashville to line dance at the Wild Horse Saloon and shush their noisy neighbors when the music begins at the Bluebird Café. It must be an out-of-body experience for them, mouthing lyrics about a life they don't live but enjoy thinking about and hope actually exists somewhere. Wearing shiny belt buckles and lizard boots, they board tour buses and pay cash to see where the legends walked, to gawk at Dolly Parton's front porch and

RCA's Studio B, where so many hits were recorded. Such tours are not encouraged to take visitors to the neglected and controversial flag-waving memorial of Civil War General Nathan Bedford Forrest, but he has a share in the history.

Before leaving town, the tourists might drop by Centennial Park one more time to see the Parthenon and buy a postcard of Athena, the warrior goddess of wisdom, holding Nike, the goddess of victory, in her right hand. They might throw a fleeting kiss toward the Country Music Hall of Fame, wink at Hank Williams' former home, and almost crash their cars navigating *Musica*: the bronze statue of Dionysian revelers frolicking in the buff that sits on the grassy knoll inside the traffic circle on Music Row. Then they speed back onto I-40 and drive off into the blue, scratching their heads in bewilderment at the city's identity crisis, a riddle that might be reconciled if only Athena would put down Nike and pick up a spittoon.

Moving to Nashville as a songwriter and musician is difficult, and God had to work powerful new spiritual disciplines in Bill and me before we found the path to survival, productivity, and peace. Our first few months in town, we accepted invitations to two parties. The first, at the upscale apartment of a well-known writer and producer, thrust us into the circle of first-call players and singers. *First-call* is the term used to describe those who are first on the list to be called when a recording session contractor hires singers and players.

"I came from a family of first-call pickers!" I joked to Bill as we parked the car. "Cotton-pickers!"

It was true: Annie Moses and her two oldest children, George and Jane, enjoyed local celebrity as a cotton-pickin' trio who consistently delivered well above the daily quota of extra-clean cotton. Local farmers hired them first for their thorough and honest gleaning of the fields; some hired hands were known to deliberately pick leaves and sticks, along with the cotton, to add weight to their sacks. My family's pickin' legacy might have been legendary, but it wouldn't have impressed this Nashville crowd.

I swayed into the room wearing nine months of baby, and as I crossed the threshold, I stepped on a small rug that slipped like soap on the waxy hardwood floor. Had it not been for Bill, I would have taken a nasty fall. He caught me just in time. Some grand entrance! I felt embarrassed, awkward, and shy, and Bill, too, remained exceptionally quiet as we lumbered through the room, clumsily attempting to interact with people who never quit performing.

They seemed to see our new-kid-in-town status as a prime opportunity to exclude. They laughed too loudly and dropped names like ice cubes down the back, sending a chilly message: Who's who? Not you!

At the second gathering, a Christmas party, I had the chance to meet one of Nashville's premier session contractors, a big-boned gal with a determined air about her. A contractor is one who, for a percentage of the proceeds, schedules players and singers for studio recording sessions. With my performance of "The Bell Song" fresh in mind, I planned on breaking into vocal session work, and I'd prepared a package to introduce myself. As the party drew to a close, Bill and I happened to walk out to the parking lot alongside the contractor. Our turkey brown Mercury Marquis sat, wounded and precious, beside the contractor's golden Jaguar. What a lucky coincidence!

As she searched for her keys, I mentioned my educational background and asked if I could send her a demo and a list of recommendations. Her response stunned me. She flipped back her hair, refusing to make eye contact, then opened the door of the Jag and lowered herself into the front seat. "I don't care who you know or what they think about you," she said over her shoulder. "You can send me something if you want to." The door slammed, the Jag growled, and she was off.

I had to forgive her. Contractors carry a lot of responsibility. They do an important service and mustn't make mistakes. It is their job to know Nashville's talent pool, to hire musicians who are creative, fast, and accurate—not just mostly accurate but absolutely accurate. The clock at a recording studio scarfs the seconds, translating time into beaucoup bucks. Better to hire the best at top dollar than a novice who spends hours never getting it exactly right.

I cringe whenever I hear a parent or teacher let sloppy playing or singing slide by, knowing that they are closing the door for their students on this lucrative and artistically fulfilling slice of the music market. I once sat in a Nashville coffee shop listening with great sympathy to a young woman as she described to me the disappointment she felt, lacking the technique to obtain entrance into a prominent conservatory or to pursue a professional career in violin. "No one told me the truth when I was little, that my playing was lousy," she said. "Why couldn't they say, 'Ellie, your jingle-bell petticoat is cute, but you're off pitch and your bow hold stinks. Let's fix that, huh?' Instead, everyone just clapped and said, 'how adorable.' I guess they thought they were building my self-esteem or something. Well, nobody in this town gives a rip about my self-esteem."

After that conversation with Ellie, I began to pray that I would have the tenacity to lead my children into musical excellence and that I would learn to navigate the balance beam, speaking the truth "in love." It was another turning point for me.

Yet it was the "in love" part that Nashville was missing. I had expected stiff competition from a city glutted with musical ambition, but I had not expected a lack of kindness, especially among those who professed to follow Jesus. This new world of comparisons and one-upmanship was just plain ol' meanness, and I found myself shrinking from the fray. The newly minted confidence the Lord had polished in Waco began ebbing away.

Bill and I longed for prayer, for a listening and supportive community like the one we'd enjoyed in Waco. When we finally found a small, family-friendly church, it came with a bonus: Priest Lake Christian Fellowship had only one other attendee who made a living from music—Barbara Mandrell's drummer and band director—and he turned out to be an all-'round great guy and a wonderful praise leader. The position of church pianist lay vacant, so the addition of a player with Bill's expertise and unassuming nature delighted everyone.

Priest Lake was a fertile congregation, with toddlers peeping over every daddy's shoulder, and I enjoyed a robust flock of moms who truly loved their babies. Our burgeoning broods played together so contentedly that they'd beg, at the end of each gathering, to stay just a bit longer. I cannot tell you how impressed I was to find the pastor teaching in the toddlers class, which, for me, was the most important class of all. Keeping up with four-year-old Annie and two-year-old Alex, while tending newborn Benjamin, was keeping me skinny. Both Benjamin and Alex still nursed, and I could hardly consume enough food for the three of us. My continued reading on the subject had led me to believe that, instead of dictating when children should wean, it was best to allow them to indicate when they no longer needed the comfort of my breast or the nourishment of my milk. I had plenty of kindred spirits at Priest Lake. The moms there knew their stuff, nursing their babies right along beside me. It was one of the most nurturing settings of my life, this fellowship of young mothers who embraced the ways of nature and nature's God.

Benjamin, my newborn, was at the first stage of cerebral development: learning to read nonverbal clues, facial expressions, and body language, as an indicator of meaning and relationship. Annie's birth had brought me up to par on that phenomenon and how breast-feeding played into its success.

Alex, however, was at the second and most startling stage of development—one in which my milk continued to play an important role. Sometime between eighteen months and two years old, the left hemisphere of the brain begins to surge, and a child's emerging vocabulary enables him to put words to what he feels. A two-year-old child knows about three hundred words. A three-year-old child knows about three thousand words. That's more than seven brand-new words a day. Miraculous! By the age of six, a child will know approximately six thousand words. A hearty, intelligent Sunday school class is the perfect time to expose children to the superior word-power of Scripture. Not even the lofty texts of the Bible are too difficult when a child is processing every word as "new" and has never categorized a word as "difficult" or "big."

It's also a great time to begin a more in-depth form of interactive music, both at home and at church. Capturing a toddler's phenomenal season of cerebral growth is the foundation for Dr. Shinichi Suzuki's "mother-tongue" method of teaching music. If three-year-old children can learn language with ease, why not utilize their awesome brain power to teach music in the same way: by pattern, imitation, and repetition?

A supercharged brain network allows the three-year-old to process information at 2.5 times the speed of an adult. All those little Beethoven's and Mozart's running around our feet, imagining themselves to be Superman: as a matter of fact, they really are Superman, ready to fly.

I had placed Annie on the waiting list to study violin at Vanderbilt University's Blair School of Music. Having a music school in queue and a church that caught the important vision of children felt comforting.

Our dedication to the group, however, ran contrary to the advice of publishers, musicians, and writers, who encouraged us to look at every relationship as an opportunity to get ahead. "Being connected is imperative," they'd say. Or: "Most deals are made because of relationships. Find a church where the action is."

I was pulled in both directions, and began to wrestle with two mind-sets. Like a young boy's tree house, a getaway high in the clouds, Priest Lake offered a sort of shelter from the music scene. I hid out there on Sundays, then descended, Monday mornings, to pummel the air until a song fell from the sky. I wrote verses, choruses, bridges, climbs, and tags, skewing clichés, polishing phrases, and refining rhymes. Words became my pleasure; I hammered them the way a blacksmith hammers horseshoes. The poetry of my youth came into play—providential preparation. I morphed into Wanda and Hank, meeting other Wandas and Hanks in those sweaty cramped rooms in the basement of Word, rolling out hooks like a wringer-washer.

Bill, however, is a solitary fellow. He enjoys a quiet workplace for maximum productivity. He figures the words, "business meeting," are code for laziness and lead to nothing in particular. The group-writing scene held no allure for him, and he scurried away whenever it was suggested. I finally fell into the rhythm of handing him a finished lyric, which he would set to music, often with my collaboration. It's a system we enjoy to this day.

Slot machines in Vegas carry better odds than song slots on a Christian artist's album. Most songs recorded in the Christian music industry are born from personal testimony and thus are composed by the artists themselves. There's a big financial incentive for Christian recording artists to compose, too, as the niche is less profitable than other styles, and songwriters reap great royalties. This constricts the flow of songs from songwriter to artist, resulting in a fierce frustration for many talented folks. It also diminishes the quality of the songs that are aired. A great singer is not necessarily a great songwriter.

By contrast, country music artists who aren't in the Christian wing of the industry look for the best possible songs, living by a bottom-line principle: A great song is fundamental to a big hit. Most country artists review thousands of songs in the span of a career, and that compels great writers to keep on writing. An abundance of country-music radio stations renders hundreds of thousands of dollars for a big hit. Christian radio stations reap only a small fraction of that.

A few years after "Make His Praise Glorious" reached the top of the charts in Christian music, Billy Ray Cyrus' "Achy Break Heart" began to beat on country radio. I was surprised to hear buzz through the Nashville grapevine that Achy's first-quarter royalty check alone produced $250,000 for writer Don Von Tress. While I never confirmed the figure, I do know it's somewhere in the ballpark for such a hit in the country music industry, and the weary truth is that Don Von Tress's first-quarter $250,000 was a couple of zero's bigger than what "Make His Praise Glorious" made for us in the Christian music industry.

Cold-cash facts aside, I plowed on, as the revolving door spun on our determined group of composers. Song after song. Lyrics. Music. Demos. Hit and miss. I felt like I was at the county fair, playing the game where you stand back and try to spit into a bunch of pop bottles. Try long enough and you're bound to score, but the process will spit you dry.

A songwriting friend shared with me her prayer. "Every day, I ask the Lord to give me a sphere where I can write music and create artistic offerings in peace," she said. That prayer became a part of my family's petitions and remains so to this day.

In answer, the Lord turned Bill and me toward writing for church choirs, pianists, and ensembles; the revenue from such work is the best-kept secret in Christian music. Artists come and go, but choral music is the artistic center of church music, a faithful financial friend for musicians, as well as direct service to the body of Christ. We composed seasonal musicals, children's musicals, octavos and anthems, and Bill produced many compilations of piano arrangements. All the while, Living Stone Music Company served as our bread and butter.

Nashville is rife with opportunities for a musician and writer, and I found myself being pulled in more directions than I thought possible. Church, home, business: I grappled with the professional and emotional complexity of the city, struggling to find success and balance amid the roadblocks of industry infighting and indifference. I felt the Fob-style fight in me succumbing, sometimes, to angry frustration. I began to resent the intrusion of my children, whose needs made the process of building a career difficult. I started to shirk the once-in-a-lifetime privilege of mothering and of being a helpmate to the wonderful man I had married.

God was not about to let my attitude go without confrontation.

Barnyard Beginnings

Be not forgetful to entertain strangers:
for thereby some have entertained angels unawares.

HEBREWS 13:2 (KJV)

"We just need to get away from it all." My Eagle Scout husband grinned as he proudly displayed a brand-new tent and cooler. "We're going camping. It's family-friendly fun. I should know, I'm prepared!" He saluted with two fingers. He had matches, marshmallows, and most important, he said, he had a double sleeping bag. "I will personally put the babies to bed and build you the most romantic, Boy Scout campfire on the planet." He gave a wink. "I have searched the maps and selected a beautiful spot specializing in horseback rides for mountain girls from Oklahoma. I am proud to announce that we are off to *Land Between the Lakes*."

With Bill's help, I stocked the cooler and packed the clothes: three small suitcases and two big ones. The Blue Bomb, a used Chevy van we had purchased upon alighting in Nashville, opened her big mouth and swallowed it all. The van ranked among the wheels my hot-rodding older sister, Sherry, called "embarrassing." The floor-to-wall-to-ceiling carpet had been inaugurated when Alex, queasy from the smothering environment, had reissued a chocolate ice cream cone.

The Blue Bomb would have made a great title for my emotional state, and getting away from oneself is tricky. As Confucius said, "Wherever you go, that's where you are." But I was willing to try.

Land Between the Lakes nestles between two lakes in western Tennessee, a 170,000-acre camper's paradise of lush forests teaming with wildlife. With my familiar melancholy in tow, I meandered down the misty trails, flanked by romping toddlers who chased lizards and insisted on sharing their excitement at such incredible realities as dried leaves and brown rocks. "Look, Mommy, look!" I felt like a character in a first-grade reader.

Except ye become as a little child. God spoke the words curtly as I loitered along. "Yeah, I know," I replied. "But I'm a little bit mad at You."

My mind whirred with anxiety. Sandi Patti was once again in the process of selecting songs for a new album. Bill and I, along with the other writers at Word, had sent demos and were deep into Nashville's most prominent posture: waiting.

"God, why don't you help us out, here. I want to write, but there's hardly anybody to write *for* in Christian music. Who can win in this process?" I picked up my step, attempting to move ahead of Bill, who insisted on cheering me up by cracking corny jokes, one right after the other, like Christmas nuts. I was wound too tightly to let him get through to me, and dragged my blue mood right on up through the roasting of marshmallows and the singing of a few songs, the last one ending with "Have Thine Own Way, Lord."

The second day began with rain, and we moved our outdoor kitchen underneath the picnic canopy. The children, enthralled with the nature of nature, played silly games in the cramped, muddy space, dashing out into the wet, thrilled by their own daring. The Lord tapped me on the shoulder as I scrambled eggs. *The Kingdom of Heaven belongs to such as these.*

I answered Him by cracking a few more eggs. *Why don't they stop that laughing?* I frowned at the children. Their minds engaged unseen worlds filled with gladness and surprise. How irritating.

"You kids pipe down over there!" I yelled.

"Hey, Robin," Bill said. "Know what I think about eggs?"

I could tell another joke was coming; I ignored him and hit the next egg harder.

"They're not all they're cracked up to be." He laughed. "Awe, come on. Not even a smile? That was a good one."

"Why don't we just pack up and go home after breakfast?"

"Let's wait and see if this rain gives up." He put his arm around my shoulders. "All rain gives up eventually, you know." He hugged me gently. "Besides, it will be better in the long run to break camp after things have dried out."

By midmorning the clouds had parted and the sun was pushing out, slurping the excess water into a clammy humidity. As a premier attraction, *Land Between the Lakes* extends to its visitors an opportunity to view a working farm reminiscent of the 1800s, where young men and women, dressed in Ma and Pa Ingalls hand-me-downs, demonstrate foxfire-style procedures.

We watched in the farm kitchen as a flushed-faced woman stirred beef stew over the fireplace and paddled butter, informing us that real buttermilk is the last bit of milk removed when paddling the cream, a crucial step because any milk left in the butter will curdle it, while butter that is thoroughly paddled will keep without refrigeration. "And buttermilk is light and sweet, delicious to drink," she said, "not clabbered like the modern-day buttermilk."

"I already knew that," I grumbled to Bill.

We walked out to the pasture where a field hand worked and animals grazed, accustomed to intrusions. The landscape was luminous with that enhanced green that glows after a morning rain. Sturdy, gray outbuildings dotted the scene.

"Judy Owens could do better than this," I complained to nobody in particular. My childhood friend, Judy, still lived in our remote hometown of Zafra. Many of the Choctaw Indians the government had resettled during the early 1800s had wiped their final tears in Zafra. The place seemed to have freeze-framed their shock and never snapped out of it.

Judy, one of Daddy's converts, lived a real pioneer's childhood. One hundred and fifty years after the Trail of Tears, her family still had no electricity and no indoor plumbing. Judy's Choctaw mama drew water from the well, located just outside her kitchen door. Their farm consisted of multiple outbuildings, loosely woven of rough-cut planks. To me, they were rich in mystique. One antiquarian shed, built of native stone and roofed with hefty wooden beams, had served as a trading post when Oklahoma was Indian Territory.

"With a gal like Judy as a friend, I don't need anybody to impress me with old-fashioned ways," I complained, as we tromped through the pasture.

Bill looked at me with concern. "We've got to have faith, Robin. Don't fret. 'Tomorrow will take care of itself.' I feel the same frustration you do, but we have to look to God."

He gazed for another moment at my unhappy face, then sighed and held out his hands to the children. "Here, come on with me and let's go see the animals." The four of them scampered off, leaving me with a pang of guilt. I felt tired, wounded, and unable to respond as a "happy mother of children."

"Thank you, Bill," I called after him, across the distance. He smiled and waved. You'd better perk up, I berated myself.

An inner voice spoke: *The Noble Brutus hath told you that Caesar was ambitious. If it were so, it was a grievous fault and grievously hath Caesar answered it.* I had memorized the lines in middle-school English: Marc Antony, from Shakespeare's *Julius Caesar.* Not Scripture, but maybe an element of truth. I was ambitious. Constantly climbing. The realization loosed the tension in me, and I wilted, weary with the whole wadded Music Row mess. It had to change, and I knew it.

"You told us to come boldly before you, so I will be bold," I said out loud to the Lord, and I began walking briskly down the sloping pasture toward an old barn. "I refuse to live like this. I refuse to live any longer with this anxiety, this frustration and fatigue. God, You need to speak to me here. Tell me what to do. Do I keep writing? Do I quit? What is Your will?" As I prayed, I walked around the corner of the barn. The sunshine segued into shadow. The smell of hay and manure, damp in the shade of a lean-to, floated raw and pungent, a barnyard potpourri that transported me back to girlhood games in a grainy old cowshed and loft. I dropped my demanding prayer. My heart softened.

"Hello, there."

I started from my reverie. A man sat on a wooden barrel under the tin awning of the lean-to that sloped from the barn.

"I'm sorry," I said, "I didn't see you."

"I said, 'Hello there!'" he repeated.

"Oh . . . hello." I smiled wearily.

His old-fashioned clothing, well-worn, sagged comfortably on his wiry frame. A scruffy beard etched his cheeks and neck and, in his rough hands, he held a long piece of carved wood. Beside him hung a motley assortment of saws and chisels, with brown lines of rust where archaic metal sank into old wooden handles. Their sharp edges were ground down from years of good use.

"Didn't see me, did ya? Well, maybe you should look up!" He raised his eyebrows, questioning, then smiled and motioned me closer. "Bet you've never seen one of these in the making." He took up his blade to whittle. "What I'm carving here's a yoke. Do you know what a yoke is?"

"Sort of." I studied his work, the long, swooping curve his knife was creating.

"A yoke is an important thing," he said. "What most people don't know is that it has to be tailor-made to fit the neck of the ox exactly." He leaned forward and looked me in the eye. "If the yoke is not an exact fit, it will rub a sore on the back of the ox's neck. Sometimes, it'll even bleed. The ox won't pull into the yoke because it hurts, ya see, and he can't pull his load." He dropped his eyes and sat back, continuing to carve.

"Take my yoke upon you and learn from me, for I am gentle and humble in heart, and you will find rest for your souls. For my yoke is easy and my burden is light" (Matthew 11:29-30, NIV).

My soul grew quiet. I felt suspended in the moment, as if I were being given time to swallow medicine.

"Another thing!" His craggy eyebrows gathered in concentration. "I'm making this yoke for that young team of oxen right over there."

My eyes followed the point of his knife to where two young beasts ate from a trough. They swished their tails and chewed thoughtfully, standing side by side as if contemplating a unified pull.

"As that young team of oxen grows, I'll have to make them a brand-new yoke," the old man said. "You can't put yesterday's yoke on today's ox!"

You can't put yesterday's yoke on today's ox. The timing, the turn of phrase, the tone of voice, and the spark of the old man's eye recessed the tangible world and thrust me face-forward into the unseen. How many years had I paraded around, wearing my musical ambitions like a tight and tattered dress from a high-school prom? I felt a flush with embarrassment. The Lord stood before me, holding out a new yoke for a new season. A feathery joy billowed up, and I surrendered with an ease that surprised me.

Be not forgetful to entertain strangers: for thereby some have entertained angels unawares.

I looked around. God had talked to me in a barnyard through a country gentleman wearing a drop-shouldered muslin shirt from another era.

God knew me well. "Thank you," I said to the old man. "I really appreciate your words." Wasting no time, I strode off to tell Bill.

"That's powerful, Robin," he said. "It's definitely been hard to pull the load lately. I want you to know, I'm with you. Whatever the Lord is telling us to do, we'll do it."

"Mama, Mama!" Annie's voice came piping. "Benjamin is drinking the animal's water."

I scooped up Benjamin and smooched his fat pink cheek. He giggled and nestled into my shoulder, a cuddly cherub with curly blond hair. "Hey, buddy," I said, "are you thirsty?" My heart felt buoyant and free.

In the evening, we broke camp, loaded up the Blue Bomb, and drove home. Bill reached for my hand as the children slept. The peace and silence said it all: Everything had changed. The musical aspirations—songwriting, performing, making records, being somebody—had shrunk to their rightful size in the context of God's grace. Wanda and Hank would have to meet in the sweaty rooms without me.

I turned and glanced at the back seat, where my babies slumbered peacefully. To miss this opportunity, flailing along in selfish ambition and vain conceit, would be to thwart God's earthly destiny, possibly even close off eternal salvation for them. I had a brand new yoke, singularly tailored for a new season of life.

"What a difference a day makes—twenty-four little hours—brought the sun and the flowers—where there used to be rain." The white-chocolate voice of Jane Morgan, one of my mother's favorite singers from long ago, welled up inside me. God had met me in a barn, an unassuming place close to my childhood—come to think of it, a place close to His childhood too. He had given me a two-minute dose of wisdom that dramatically redirected my course, drawing me kindly to

repentance and endowing me with the faith to understand that obedience alone would result in the love and peace I sought. I said some imaginary good-byes to Music Row, gave my hoe to God, and hurried home.

It would take a long time for the full meaning of that day to sink in. God had taken my musical dreams and buried them. I didn't know it at the time, but He had not buried them in a graveyard. He had buried them in a garden, where He would faithfully prune and tend them while Bill and I were being readied and our family was maturing. Another day was in the making, a day when He would stand with me at the garden gate, remove His hands from my eyes and say, "Surprise! See what I have made of your dreams." I would open my eyes to behold a musical Eden abundant with ripe and low-hanging fruit, bountiful with noble purpose and godly destiny, a heritage and a legacy grown because one day, I stood in a barnyard and, at the bidding of His grace, let go.

To Kill a Copperhead

Mama Gump: *I didn't know it, but I was destined to*
be your momma. I did the best I could.
Forrest Gump: *You did good.*

FROM *FORREST GUMP*, SCREENPLAY BY ERIC ROTH

I wasn't sure how my new yoke might be configured. The adjustment had been slight, so slight that I had to analyze it to pinpoint its bearing. After all, I had not been a bad mother. My own mother had been a wonderful role model, and her mother before her. Yet, God had brought me to the barn to point out that a piece of my heart was being withheld; a thin slice of irritation, yes, dare I say it, resentment, had kept one foot off the altar and set me scowling at childish interruptions of a personal agenda.

Such a withholding is detected by children when they are little, creating a fissure that grows bigger as they grow. My God-given agenda was to raise children who love the Lord their God with all their soul and all their mind and all their strength, and who love their neighbor as they love themselves. Not a halfhearted dictum. To flounder in the early years, to be even slightly off the mark day after day, translates into a target missed in the trajectory of a lifetime.

I had learned this truth about targets and trajectories long before in a very different setting. When the frightful warnings of practice-room harassment had arisen at OCU—and Mrs. Silberg had recommended I arm myself with a hat pin—Daddy had reckoned she had the right idea but the wrong weapon. He'd figured I should be primed to defend myself not only against attackers but also against intruders and government tyrants, the two sometimes being the same.

He'd asked his friend, Jack Pringle, a retired military man who had been a top marksman on a naval shooting team, to give me lessons. My younger brother, David, would join me.

I responded enthusiastically, having once, at around nine years of age, relished a biography of the sharpshooter, Annie Oakley. Annie's maiden name was Annie Moses, the same as my grandmother's, so in flights of fancy, I figured she would somehow recognize me if I were to meet her. Annie provided income for her family, as a nine-year-old, by shooting fowl precisely through the head. Restaurants paid her top price, as no bullets lay buried in the body of the bird. She later joined Buffalo Bill's Wild West Show and shot such tiny targets as a playing card held on edge, aiming over her shoulder while riding a horse standing up. *How could she do that?* Such marksmanship had to be more than aim. Annie Oakley must have possessed some uncanny, innate sensibility of time, target, and trajectory.

"When I get big," I told David, "I'm gonna find out how Annie Oakley could shoot like that." David, only five years old, slept with his boots on and a toy pistol in his hand. He believed every enemy, even a natural disaster such as a tornado, could be eliminated by pulling the trigger. Though I suspected in myself a latent talent for marksmanship, my tender heart forbade me to shoot anything but paper targets and poisonous snakes, and I preferred commandeering Daddy to kill the copperheads. Like Annie Oakley, Daddy seemed to shoot from *feel* as well as aim, and he could hit some amazing targets.

We had our lesson one weekend when I came home from college. We traveled to a pretty green valley to meet Jack, a Paul Newman of a fellow with blue eyes and a straight spine. He had arrived early to set up the tailgate of his truck with guns, ammo, and earmuffs. The target was attached to a board across a clearing: heavy brown paper with concentric circles and, in the center, a solid-black ring—the bull's-eye.

After a smidgen of history, Jack gave us gun-safety rules, detailed the parts of a pistol; showed us the proper stance, hold, and position; and ended with instructions on sight alignment. "See here," he pointed, "there are two sights positioned on the top of the barrel of this pistol. This rear sight is shaped like a V, and the front sight, here on the end of the barrel, is shaped like an I. He pulled a pen from his shirt pocket. "Now, to properly align these particular sights, you visually center the I of the front sight inside the V of the rear sight." He drew on a scrap of paper as he spoke. "You should see a thin sliver of daylight on either side of the I, front sight, as it appears inside the V, rear sight. That light should be equally divided on the left and the right. If there is more light on the right, your shot will be off to the left. If there is more light on the left, your shot will be too far to the right."

David and I bobbed our heads, eager to understand.

"Once the left/right position is accurately aligned, the marksman must also level both sights so they are flat across the top. If the front sight is higher than the rear sight, the shot will be high. If it is lower, the shot will be low."

I practiced aligning the sights. My arm needed more strength, but I thought I was pretty good.

"Now, don't look directly at the target," Jack said. "If you do, you won't hit it. There's too much distance involved. Instead, look right here." He pointed to the sights on the barrel of the gun. "As you look through the sights down the barrel, locate your target in your peripheral vision and set the middle of the bottom edge of the bull's-eye on the top of your leveled sights. All three must be exactly aligned. If they lack accuracy, even slightly, in your hand, the error is compounded by the distance to your target. To be a tiny bit off here," he pointed at the sights on the pistol in my hand, "is to be way off over there." He gestured toward the target. "So take aim *through* the sights to the bull's-eye. Accuracy happens right under your nose. *It's what you do with what's in your hand that matters.*"

As I absorbed the lessons of the yoke-maker at *Land Between the Lakes*, I thought of those target-shooting lessons of my college days. I realized that I held in my hands a once-in-a-lifetime moment to disciple my children, a moment designed by God who created their young hearts to joyfully and effortlessly receive Him, a moment I had not fully shouldered as my singular responsibility. God had allowed the error of my path to blanket me in discomfort, to become a burr under my saddle, spurring me toward His correction of my heart. Oh, I'd nurtured some big goals and great achievements for my little ones somewhere out in the murky distance. But the daily practices, the sights aligned and adjusted right under my nose that would enable me to hit such a long range target, had lacked step-by-step process and clarity of vision.

Such disconnects seem small at first. The children overlook it. They go back to their play. Little patterns of aberrant behavior are overlooked by fatigued parents who nurture aberrant behaviors of their own. Time passes, the fractures widen. At twelve years old, the blooming complexities of maturation begin. Then thirteen arrives. Overnight, a reality dawns; this person is not a child anymore. Instead, ill-equipped parents encounter a sexually mature young adult who only tepidly cares about the things for which they had intended him to care passionately. The world has wielded more influence than the parent. The trajectory has gone wild, not because of a sudden spiritual blowout, but because we, as parents, were slightly disengaged from the start, allowing small errors committed day after day to compound over the years. Our sights were not accurately aligned, and the distance to the bull's-eye goes on for a lifetime, growing increasingly off target in the scope of time. The years of easy faith and exuberance at the prospect of a godly destiny are behind us.

The early years are so important: Studies conducted by the demographer George Barna indicate that most people die in old age believing what they believed at thirteen.

Only a deep commitment to daily discipleship, with constant adjustment and alignment of heart, can sustain godliness. Perhaps this is why the instruction given in Deuteronomy 6:5–9 (NIV) is so detailed and exhaustive, contrary to a society that shrinks from spiritual passion: "Love the Lord your God with all your heart and with all your soul and with all your strength. These commandments that I give you today are to be upon your hearts. Impress them on your children. Talk about them when you sit at home and when you walk along the road, when you lie down and when you get up. Tie them as symbols on your hands and bind them on your foreheads. Write them on the doorframes of your houses and on your gates."

My shooting lessons were instructive, in more ways than one.

In my lessons with Jack, I caught on quickly, owing in part, I'm sure, to the influence of Annie Moses Oakley. I lined up the sights with strict accuracy, left-right, top-bottom, and squeezed the trigger with a slow and steady pull.

"You should be surprised when the gun fires," Jack said.

I was.

At the end of the round, Jack retrieved my target and analyzed it. My shots had missed the center of the bull's-eye consistently, and were grouped in a cluster, low and left. I was disenchanted, but Jack praised me to the skies. "Excellent," he said.

"You're just being nice," I said. "I missed it every time."

"No, actually, I'm not just being nice," he said. "See how all your shots are in close proximity to one another? With the exception of that one, I can almost lay a silver dollar over them all." He circled his thumb and index finger into the shape of an oversize silver dollar and laid it over the holes. "That's purty good shootin'. He took out a small screwdriver and began to rotate a screw at the base of the rear sight. "If you're shots are all over the place, then there's a problem with your aim," he told me as he worked. "But if you're shooting a tight cluster that isn't centered in the bull's-eye, that means your aim is good but your sights need adjusting. Everyone has a different way of looking down the barrel, so adjust your sights until they guide you to the center of the bull's-eye."

As a young mother, I looked back on Jack's lesson often.

Adjust the sights for *destiny*—every eye is different, so grab the screwdriver and find the personalized plan God prepared just for you.

Align the sights for *accuracy*—a methodology that never changes, like the truths of God.

Aim! "Accuracy happens right under your nose. It's what you do with every moment of today that matters."

Adjust. Align. Aim. Scripture is punctuated with such imagery. "Like arrows in the hand of a warrior are the children of one's youth" (Psalm 127:4).

My quiver was beginning to bulge. I felt an intense urge inside my soul to sharpen my arrows, to align each young life around me with the bull's-eye of God's perfect will, to adjust the trajectory as His guidance directed.

"All have sinned and fall short of the glory of God" (Romans 3:23). *Fall short.* Sights too low. Lift your head.

"Follow the way of love" (1 Corinthians 14:11). That word *follow* means "to hunt, to set love in your sights and pursue it relentlessly."

First item on the docket, I figured, must be to lead my children to salvation. I had known since I could talk that the word "sin" meant to err, to miss the mark or the bull's-eye. Not just slightly, low and to the left, like my first cluster of bullet holes, but so wild that any fool could see I didn't even know the direction of the target—until Jesus swept in to point the Way.

I wanted my children to know Jesus, to experience the beauty of holiness. I wanted them to have the blessings of a godly life. I wanted their gifts and talents to be fully developed. I wanted them to thrive.

Yet all of these noble purposes are an ever-distant target, a target that is only reached by setting our sights on the prescribed daily tasks of discipleship, by "making the most of every opportunity, because the days are evil" (Ephesians 5:16, NIV).

As I contemplated the lessons of the oxen, I vowed that, with God's grace, I would not be distracted, purposeless, or unfaithful with what God had put in my hand. I would adjust, align, and aim. I would shoot straight.

God fueled this passion with a recurring dream. During the "wee small hours of the morning," my mind would find that curious place between cognition and reverie, that strange place of dreaming and, concurrently, watching oneself dream. In this state, it was impressed upon me that one of my children had died without the Lord. My heart wrenched with torment knowing that the child's soul would forever be, as C. S. Lewis wrote in his brilliant essay, "The Weight of Glory," ". . . banished from the presence of Him who is present everywhere and erased from the knowledge of Him who knows all . . . left utterly and absolutely *outside*— repelled, exiled, estranged, finally and unspeakably ignored." I would awake, gripped with a pulsating sense of the eternal responsibility God had entrusted to me in my children.

"On the other hand," Lewis wrote, "we can be called in, welcomed, received, acknowledged. We walk every day on the razor edge between these two incredible possibilities."

"The razor edge." Salvation is the imperative of parenting. Only life is eternal, as the gold record of "Make His Praise Glorious" hanging on the hall wall reminded me daily. The glass inside the frame had cracked on the edge, and dust had crept in. The color had faded, and Sandi's hairdo looked dated. Children—not diamonds, not careers, not fame, not trophies, and certainly not hit songs—are forever.

God loves children. He desires "godly offspring" (Malachi 2:15, NIV). According to Him, they are the content of His Kingdom, the blessings of young men, the happiness of mothers, the crown of old men, the warriors of the land, and the glory of a nation. They are the joy of life—"before the days of trouble come and the years approach when you will say, 'I find no pleasure in them'" (Ecclesiastes 12:1, NIV)—before we begin to shuffle and slump and sag, despite Chuck Norris, Bow Flex, Jenny Craig, liposuction, the red convertible, the saber-tooth necklace, and *viva!* Viagra. We may wield a Botox needle for a season, but the effects eventually fade and…that's that! Death is relentless.

But God has designed a great counterplan. Just when most of our sand has sunk into the bottom half of the hourglass, the sons and daughters born in our youth reach their prime years. Our investment begins to pay off.

First, they step up to pull alongside us. We are shocked by their intelligence and vigor. Then, as we're *rallentando,* they're *accelerando.* Growing ever stronger and more savvy, they surge ahead, leading us onward with exuberance and spiritual fervor. They are more mature than we were at their age, a sign of successful parenting. We are enthralled. Their vision renews our fading vision, their strength imbues our failing strength, and their spirits bolsters our flagging spirit.

Then in-laws appear and grandchildren bounce in and upstage the grim reaper once again. A chuckle returns as they flow into our clotting world, delighted to dance with us, to shake us out of our stupor, and to love us in spite of the gnarly nose, the cactus eyebrows, and the dental despair.

Mingling the very young with the middle-aged and the aged, as God has designed the family to do, dilutes and distracts us from the doom of Death and presents us with a constant reminder that the Kingdom of God is ever young and those who believe in Him will never die.

Robin with newborn Camille and her siblings Annie, Alex, Benjamin.

God has chosen to win the war of the worlds, not with a monstrous manifestation of His scary strength, but through the silky sweetness of a baby. Let your gaze rest upon the innocence of a newborn's face, smell the milky breath, feel the velvety skin, weigh the gravity of an infant's trust. Does that first hint of a smile set your soul worshiping? The innocence, the beauty, the unfettered love a child exhibits: All these painfully gripping attributes are the closest we get to the purity of God from the perspective of Earth. "Whoever welcomes one of these little children in my name welcomes me; and whoever welcomes me does not welcome me but the one who sent me" (Mark 9:37, NIV).

I must sit down to grapple with these words spoken by Jesus. The weight of value He assigns to children is breathtaking. To cold-shoulder the holy assignment to impart faith and cultivate destiny in children's lives is to cold-shoulder God's finest hour in our own lives, to shrug off the mandate of His Kingdom. Children are our delightful, divine responsibility.

Shoot for the Stars

Uncle Louis: *I coulda been a violinist*
but the handkerchief kept fallin' off my neck."
NEIL SIMON "LOST IN YONKERS"

With eternity in my sights, I set about to become the best mother I could be. I knew I had to develop close bonds of love with my children in order to work with them, one on one, day after day, with minimal conflict. I had to get up early every morning and *lead!* That would be hard to do if my children failed to respect me or refused to obey my directions. I knew, from John 14:23–24, that love and obedience go hand in hand, that disobedience comes as a result of a breakdown in the communication of love. I also knew that discipleship is predicated on trust, and that to gain my children's trust, I had to be wise and steadfast.

Moving cross-country to attend the Juilliard School or starting a family band never entered my mind as I took Annie to her first violin lesson. Instead, I was propelled by my newfound momentum as a mother, along with several familial influences: my mother's "sob right here," Bill's skill as a composer and arranger, my love of music, and my desire to see my little girl flourish. The words God had given me as a college student had also drawn me forward. Watching the adorable Asian girl play "Go Tell Aunt Rhody" on her violin, I'd heard the voice: "When you have a little girl, she should do that." For ten years, I had nurtured the prophecy, waiting for the fullness of time.

At last, time was full and overflowing. Currents converged and the energy swept me into the violin studio of Miss Sharon Rogers, head of the Suzuki department at Vanderbilt University's Blair School of Music.

"Come in, come in," Miss Rogers chimed, as cheery as the grandmother clock on her wall. That clock had a stern purpose, though; it would strike on the hour and the half-hour, signaling a necessary "lesson over" to each of her packed line-up of students.

I was a novice when it came to violin, and I was still feeling overwhelmed in our new domicile, as bustling and competitive a musical city as Paris in the Jazz Age. Annie stood at my side, almost five years old, bold and ready, a stance she'd taken from her first day on earth; I gained strength from her aplomb.

"I have a degree in vocal performance, and I play piano, but I don't know anything about the violin," I said.

"Don't worry," Miss Rogers said. "You'll learn with Annie." Her pixie haircut suited her. She was a Tinkerbell of a lady, barely five feet tall, fifty-something, and treble in tone, like the instrument she taught. She had never married and had no biological children but, like Mrs. Johnson, the piano teacher of my youth, she nurtured a packed house of musical children. "A child's success is dependent on the parents, you know," Miss Rogers said. "So, I'll teach you both, right along together."

Right along together? I took a deep breath. Her words raised the curtain on the reality of teaching a four-year-old child to play the violin. Somewhere, in the dim, repressed recesses of my mind, I had always known "together" was the way it would have to be. After all, the "mother-tongue" method of Dr. Suzuki must require both a "mother" and a "tongue." But the imminent demands brought me pause. How good it had felt to sing the final notes of my senior voice recital and end the daily duty of mandatory practice. Now, here I was, signing on for years of daily practice alongside my young daughter. It was a huge commitment. And what about our other children, who would soon be old enough to begin their own studies? "Together" could continue for decades.

I had to take a long, hard look in the mirror to come to grips with the fact that my children's future would be greatly affected by my leadership or lack thereof. I had to deal firmly with *me* in order to lead my children with a wise and loving hand.

I had hated to practice as a young girl and had struggled to enjoy the job in college. The new task at hand presented a great opportunity to analyze why. At the end of my heart-search, I came up with an answer in one word: loneliness.

"Get in there and practice!" my mother would say every weekday as I returned from school, frazzled and dusty from the yellow Bluebird. I hated hearing it, but neither of us knew any other way. Mama would have eagerly joined me in my practice if anyone had proposed the idea. She loved to draw my sisters and me around the piano to sing. But learning to play an instrument alongside one's child was not in the mind-set of this nation's culture until Dr. Suzuki proposed the "mother-tongue" method. If Mama had known to try it—to sit beside me at the piano and learn the pieces with me—the experience might have healed the "sob right here" that she carried in her chest and mentioned so often, the pain of missed musical opportunities. She would have learned loads about music, as I would eventually learn, spending practice sessions working alongside my children. Instead, she relied on a coarse but common parenting tactic: verbal haranguing. "Have you practiced yet? I'd better not hear that your name's on the Black Ribbon!"

Some parents are afraid of the Suzuki mandate to supervise practice every day and to attend and take notes at every lesson, to be able to coach the young student effectively. It sounds overwhelming, and I struggled with the responsibility at first. But soon after I decided to wear the robes, I saw that it is fun, and the rewards become a legacy. I urge every parent to try it. Make the time. Music is meant to be shared.

And so we set out, Annie and I, crafting a temporary cardboard violin, coloring a foot chart to set her feet properly, making bow positions with appropriately positioned fingers and a good bent thumb.

The techniques of playing the violin gave us fits at first. Bow positions that looked simple in Miss Rogers' studio turned confusing and ham-fisted at home. When Annie got her real, quarter-sized violin, she twanged and sawed, trying to pull her bow across the strings correctly while I fixed and fussed, attempting to help her maintain proper form. I pounded out notes on the piano, helping her learn the melody and checking her intonation, and I accompanied her to help her get the flow of the piece.

"Taka-taka-stop-stop, taka-taka-stop-stop," I sang, as Annie plucked on the A and E strings. The rhythm comprised the first variation on the theme of "Twinkle, Twinkle, Little Star."

"Taka-taka-stop-stop. What language is that?" Bill asked.

"It's Suzuki-speak," I said. "You can use any line you want. Some moms say, 'Chick-en-on-a-fence-post,' but I like 'Taka.' It sounds more cultured." Childhood memories of Jane Morgan singing in French and Spanish came to mind—Mama would be proud.

A child's success is dependent on the parents, you know. Miss Rogers' words struck a deep chord with me.

"I've realized lately that I've got to become a better leader," I told Bill.

"I'll lead," he said with a grin: "Tell me what to do."

The leader is the one who leads, who thinks ahead and takes the initiative: the first one out of bed, the first one to cast a vision for the day, the first one to assemble the troops, the first one to make sure the job is done and done right. Practice is a noble task, worthy of structured planning. It requires well-defined intentions interspersed with impromptu fun and promised rewards. It requires leadership. "Just a spoonful of sugar makes the medicine go down," Mary Poppins sang, and she was right. To make peaceful progress, sugar was essential, but so was an equal measure of medicine. I needed Annie's attention, obedience, and cooperation.

I began by instituting the nonnegotiables, which turned out to be unnecessary for her, but would come in handy when her brothers began to study music, and as they grew older: (1) Because music is an imperative of Scripture and helps prepare the brain for every other educational endeavor, you will learn to speak, sing, and play. I will be right here to help you. We'll have fun together. (2) Your intensive study of music will continue until you turn thirteen years old. Please do not ask to quit. (3) At the age of fourteen and throughout high school, the intensity with which you study may be modified, if it is assessed that you will be pursuing a profession other than music. However, you may never, ever, quit while you are down. You may choose to sideline your musical studies only when you are excelling.

These precepts set the boundaries and never failed me. They help a young child to relax, to quit kicking against the goad. They don't need to be spoken harshly. They don't need to be overarticulated. In fact, it is better for them to be seen and not heard, so to speak: understood early as a "given," touched on and reinforced only if challenged. I used a great deal of implied expectation, cheerily overcoming unmerited whining or foot dragging with brisk forward motion.

I'd give an overview of the expectations at the beginning of every practice session so that Annie knew what to expect and what was expected of her. Each week had an overarching goal of achievements assigned by the teacher and implemented by me. Each hour was divided into increments that were marked on the daily schedule. They included reviewing all pieces that Annie had learned in the book being studied, learning the new piece—the most rigorous part—and technical studies, such as bow control and left-hand frame. At times, we measured each increment of the hourly plan with a timer.

Once a goal was accomplished, I marked it with a sticker, and I rewarded accumulated stickers. "Let's start by doing bow positions. How old are you? Four!" My gesture of astonishment would bring a giggle. "Four? How about we begin with four *perfect* bow positions. Then we'll review your pieces and see how *beautiful* we can make them. After that, we'll study your new song! Won't that be fun! Now, let's see how many pennies you can win today. If you can make four perfect bow positions in a row, you'll win *double* pennies!" I put a clear jar on the piano as a penny bank. When the jar contained enough pennies, we went out for a shared treat. It was one of many small motivational goals. The reward system is a wonderful tactic we learn from God, who offers what C. S. Lewis calls the "unblushing promises of reward" to motivate His children.

I did not, however, reward sloppy or careless work. I expected Annie to concentrate, to pay attention, to try her very best to deliver the task I was asking her to perform. Afterward, we both would take time to blow off steam, marching around the room while playing, or setting corny or operatic lyrics to a song's melody. Sometimes we would play really horrible sounds just for fun, then we'd reverse it and play really lovely sounds. It's a great technique, learning how to play by learning how *not* to play.

Whenever possible, we'd jazz it up a bit. While Annie played the "Twinkle Variations"—four different rhythmic patterns built on the melody of "Twinkle, Twinkle, Little Star"—Bill would accompany her on the piano using various musical styles: Country, Asian, Rock 'n' Roll, and, for the grand finale, a sweeping melodramatic version of the "Twinkle Theme." Only Daddy's part changed, but, with Bill's strong rhythmic pulse setting the vibe, Annie thought her playing was spectacular, ready for prime time. This collaboration whet her whistle for more.

She was not the only student to benefit from Bill's shenanigans at the piano. Once, when accompanying for a Suzuki group class at Blair, Bill plowed into his many-styled rendition of "Twinkle Variations." The children looked shocked at first, but they soon got the hang of it and broke into broad grins. After the final flourish, one little boy turned to Bill and yelled, "Let's do it again!"

"That little boy's response said it all," I told Bill later. The desire to "do it again" means you have won the battle of practice.

Sometimes I grew weary and impatient. Then I felt convicted, remembering that patience, according to 1 Corinthians 13, is the first rule of love. Genevieve, my pert little niece with big brown eyes, coined my exact thoughts on the matter. She wanted crayons, and right now! "Be patient," I told her with a disapproving look. "I am," she said. "But I can't do it very long."

"Just continue to correct," Mrs. Rogers advised, and I did: "Curve your pinky. Bend your bow thumb. Flex your wrist...not that much. Play on pitch, please. Fix your feet. Put that chicken wing down. Get your scroll up. Don't squash your egg; left arm under the instrument. Left thumb straight and low, fingers high and curved...and curve your pinky. Bend your thumb. Flex your wrist...not that much. Play on pitch, please..."

How many times must you say this?

Many, many times. When children come to understand that their failure to comply cannot outlast your determination to succeed—that bad form is not an option, and the more difficult they make it, the more difficult it will be—they begin to concentrate and to comply quickly. This creates a virtuous cycle of instruction and implementation—and you're on your way to Carnegie Hall.

Add applause and accolades—"Well done, good and faithful fiddler!"—and the trajectory swings upward into the heavens, where God smiles. A child learns early the freedom inherent in discipline, the power of a strong will harnessed to a godly work ethic, the joy of a passion for doing something right, the intoxicating pleasure of reward.

Rewards are wonderful, and the world doesn't hand out nearly enough of them. Especially honest rewards. I began to look for ways to reward a job well done.

Homeschooling made late morning a perfect time for lessons with Mrs. Rogers. Afterward, I would take Annie out for lunch. Our favorite restaurant happened to be in a mall, a small restaurant that served a great barbecue chicken pizza. The setting allowed for a bit of casual shopping too.

As we strolled, I watched for potential performing opportunities. Before Christmas, I took Annie to the beautiful Laura Ashley store, where she auditioned to play for customers throughout the holiday season. As compensation, she received sixty percent off any purchases, so a brand new Laura Ashley dress became a part of her reward. Feeling beautiful and festive in her new red dress, complete with matching hair-bow, she played with a childlike simplicity and a pure, sweet tone. The guests smiled and applauded, and the work of practice became worth it.

At the end of every book in the Suzuki system, we geared up for a big recital, complete with a new dress and a fancy reception: a linen-covered table set with crystal punch bowl, hors d'oeuvres, and flowers. Her third year, she progressed so rapidly that she was able to give a quite polished recital of two books. "This is the first time this has happened," Miss Rogers told her, proud as a peacock. Out of every performance emerged a more confident, polished performer, for performing greatly enhances and secures the skills being practiced. In performance, the mind enters a heightened mode, and the performer leaves the stage a better player. I had experienced this as a child, long before I ever heard of Suzuki.

My mother held a high regard for performance goals. She was good at finding opportunities for her girls to sing or play in public. As Miss Francis had done for her, she liked to help us choose pieces, and she took our performances seriously. My sisters and I were ready at the drop of a hat to make music for weddings, funerals, revival meetings, camp meetings, and church and social events. Daddy's airplane and evangelistic outreach made the scope of our circuit rather impressive, and Mama groomed us for each occasion.

With Mrs. Johnson as a co-planner, Mama's instinct for public performance found wings; she knew how to make recital days sizzle. Preparations were a defining factor in my musical development, a regime that instilled in me the importance of knowing how to carry myself in public, on a stage, doing my part.

Mama kept us home from school so we would be well rested and freshly dressed for the recital evening. We couldn't be expected to possess the pizzazz to impress a crowd after three hours on the yellow Bluebird bus, and it took all day for us to be properly groomed. Early in the morning on recital day, Mama shampooed our hair, scrubbing hard. After applying the cream rinse, she grasped either side of the towel and buffed our hair vigorously, as if polishing silver. The tresses stood up wildly from the shock until she coaxed them down again, combing and curling them 'round and 'round her long fingers. She secured each wet ringlet with criss-crossed bobby pins or, when we were older, pink foam-rubber rollers. The air dried them as we napped.

But who could sleep, really, with pins and plastic clips painfully positioned between the pillow and the scalp, and with the stressful image of Mrs. Johnson—flapping her ample arms and railing at us to practice—rolling in our minds. Our teacher would not put up with being humiliated by sorry students—and Mama felt her pain. We had to *perform!*

Mama made sure every recital earned us a new, long, formal dress. Mrs. Verena Kinnerson sewed them, stitching her hems while sitting in a rocker beside her lanky husband watching country fare, like the *Johnny Cash Show*. My sisters and I were privileged to pick the patterns and fabrics ourselves. After Saturday music lessons, Mama drove us to the fabric store on Main Street in Mena. Two of my dresses stand out in memory: a dark-green velvet trimmed in Christmas tinsel and a bright white linen blend decorated with swirling butterflies in rainbow colors.

Underneath the fancy dress, I wore all things new: a new slip, new panties, new socks, and new shoes. To enhance expectation, Mama carefully laid out each piece for all-day viewing. She insisted I wear little-girl-styled anklet socks edged with double lace, long after the city girls had exchanged theirs for ladies' hosiery. "You must not grow up too fast," she said. The year she finally allowed me to wear pantyhose, the stockings felt so silky that I knew I would play best of all because of them. The city girls were pretty, with long, blonde Marsha Brady hair and deep dimples. They wore no homemade dresses, but they could not out-play Mama's daughters. Furthermore, I suspected their underwear might not be altogether new.

Mama's dream of magical musical moments, her yearning to perform, the influences of her mother, Mrs. Harris, and Miss Francis surfaced. Now, with her three beautiful daughters standing before her, she had a perfectly fair and noble excuse to revisit childhood dreams. The Christmas recital, held at the grand piano in Mrs. Johnson's Victorian-styled parlor, and the spring recital, held in the Methodist church across the street from her lavender house, plucked us out of the miserable rut of the yellow school bus and made us Cinderella for a day.

Even the stroke of midnight could not break the spell. At the end of a show, Daddy would don his Stetson and proudly crack jokes with the other fathers about having had "a healthy dose of culture." Then he'd load us into the car and drive us to the Triple A Café for a platter of jumbo fried shrimp. Jumbo fried shrimp! Six of them, all to myself. A flamboyant extravagance that our family could not afford except on such a grand occasion. Goldie, the waitress who served us, had hair and skin of the exact same color, a yellow-orange that one might define as "gold." Was there a connection? She looked like something from a wax museum, and I was tempted to scrape her skin gently with my fingernail to see if she was made of wax. My little brain twinkled with such thoughts as I gobbled up the jumbo shrimp. The memories of recital nights remain radiant, painted with primary colors.

The mind of a child soaks up love, as though by osmosis. The images blos-som with time and return to us wrapped in meaning. As the threads are retraced, they lead to the realization of a mother's love, expressed in her devotion to detail, and a daddy's pride in the mother-child dance unfolding before him. Waxed and buffed, a young child may not perceive the point of the polishing as any-thing more than Mama's customary procedure. Yet, the ripening of age softens the heart, and childhood scenes return, bursting with meaning. The liniment of mother-love soothed my young soul. How magically it moved in to assist when the flurry of parenting left me little time to think. My mother's procedures, unappreciated in childhood, returned as a love language. The recital finery, I realized, communicated an underlying message: "I love you. I care about you. I believe you are important." No one had ever conducted a psychological analysis of Mama's parenting. I did not codify it myself, as a young mother. I simply copied her example and combined it with new revelations from Dr. Suzuki and the mother-tongue method.

As Annie's virtuosity grew, I discovered the book, *How to Really Love Your Child,* which underscored, with a child psychologist's learned explanations, the wisdom of Mama's recital conventions and Dr. Suzuki's mother-tongue method. Dr. Ross Campbell wrote the book because he was frustrated by the disconnect he observed between his client-parents' love for their children and their children's comprehension of that love. I soaked in his practical, user-friendly teachings on how to bridge the communication gap.

Love is communicated in three ways, Dr. Campbell argues: appropriate, meaningful touch; focused attention; and eye contact. I recognized in his wisdom the model of Jesus, laying His hands on the children, taking them on His knee, and blessing them.

Dr. Campbell cautions parents against using the three love languages primarily for scolding. As I read the book, a mental picture surfaced of times when I did just that: me, humped like Quasimodo, down on munchkin level, my finger wagging, eyeball to eyeball for glaring effect, at some wrong that one of my children had committed. I would have to correct this in myself.

Only proximity and companionship facilitate cozy conversations, the mingling of minds, the tenderness of touch, the luxury of laughter, the development of discipleship. These moments salve the wounds of the world, the insecurities of purpose and being. Relationship by relationship, they combine to erect the infrastructures of love and thus, of obedience. For love is the bedrock of obedience.

Disobedience displays a breakdown in either the understanding, communication, or existence of love, for love is measured by obedience. Jesus states this truth in John 14:23–24, and Saint John affirms it in 1 John 5:23 (NIV): "In fact, this is love for God: to obey his commands." Because God *is* love, to obey the commands of God is to submit to the actions of love. This God-to-man love relationship is the pattern we follow on earth as disciple and disciple-maker. When a child *feels* loved and sees faithful expressions of love—deeply, thoughtfully, completely—it is easy to lead him.

Practice sessions are filled with great opportunities for touch, focused attention, and eye contact. "Come on, honey, let's practice together." What an enormous difference these words make, especially when coupled with the projection of exciting proposals like, "Daddy can't wait to hear you play your new song tonight. And remember, you're playing the offertory on Sunday. We'll get up early so we can curl your hair." Our schedule included as many performance opportunities as a feisty mama could muster: at retirement centers, family gatherings, and church events.

One day, Miss Rogers phoned to tell me that she would be moving Annie into another class. "Your daughter is doing really well," she said, "and I want to put her with another, more serious student." *Doing really well?* I savored the words as I hung up the phone. Because I had no model with which to compare our progress, the accolade came as a pleasant surprise. I shared it with Annie, giving her a happy hug.

Violin is a rather difficult instrument, and our rookie status kept me constantly looking for clues on how to help Annie succeed in learning. At various intervals each semester, Miss Rogers conducted what she called a "play-in." Students, grouped according to skill level, gathered on a Saturday at her studio and performed together. The Suzuki method accommodates this, because all students learn the same repertoire, collected within a series of books that graduate in skill level.

"Come early, because things can get pretty discombobulated!" Miss Rogers said, enjoying an opportunity to use her favorite word. Annie played with the beginning class, which met in the morning. The older, more advanced students played later in the day.

At one play-in, Annie and I stayed to hear the older children perform. Brooke, a sprightly strawberry-blonde, and Gloria, a slender, Asian girl, played a duet. The complex weaving of the complementary melodies, leading and echoing, held me spellbound. I marveled at how comfortable they seemed, playing together. As I listened, a whole new musical vista opened before me. *So this is where we're going!*

"What is this piece called?" I asked Gloria's mother.

"Eet ees dee Bach Doo-brr," she replied in a heavy, Korean accent.

The Bach what? "We never played this one back in the sticks where I come from," I whispered with a grin.

She smiled politely, looking puzzled.

"Your daughter is very impressive," I said. "You have raised the bar for me today."

She smiled again, a beautiful woman, elegantly dressed, refined and dignified. "Tank you," she said.

During the drive home, Annie and I talked about the "Bach Doo-brr," or "Double," as Miss Rogers later clarified. I told Annie, "Hearing Brooke and Gloria play that duet today has opened my eyes to the real potential inside a little girl like you." She kicked her legs happily as I reached across to pat her hand. "So! Guess what? We have a new horizon! You are capable of great things, and we're going to act like it."

A few weeks later, I discovered that Gloria and her brother, David, both played very well but were not pursuing careers in music. Like their father, they were going into medicine. Mr. and Mrs. Cha set an example for me, taking advantage of both the artistic and the intellectual development afforded by the study of music.

I took mental notes, learning.

Exposure is vital. A musical moment of revelation—seeing the Bach Double played, watching Mr. and Mrs. Cha guide their children to a superior education—spotlighted a new trajectory for Annie and me. *How can one shoot for the stars if one has never seen the sky?* I remembered my feelings of inferiority as a young girl, secluded in the mountains. Things had changed for me. I was enjoying my new musical journey with my daughter. But I realized that the artistic and educational isolation of a mountain hideout like my childhood home of Zafra could also become one's reality in a city replete with artistic offerings. I vowed to become a musical adventurer. Like the *Star Trek* crew, I would "explore strange new worlds."

"You know, we haven't actually heard the violin played very much," I told Annie. "Let's run by and pick up a CD." We chose *Encore!,* a collection of showpieces performed by the Japanese child prodigy who goes by the single name, Midori. I popped it into the player, and Annie and I sat back to listen. The repertoire sizzled, cool pizzicato, triple stops, harmonics, and athletic bow strokes. "Wow! I had no idea the violin could raise such a ruckus," I said, squeezing Annie's hand. "How fun!" Annie chose her two favorite pieces, and I made a mental note to order the music, knowing that doing so would establish an important goal. "It won't be long until you will play these," I said, and she agreed, a natural competitor.

Emily and Katherine, a mother-daughter team much like Annie and me, invited us to ride with them to a concert by Mrs. Roger's performing group. On the way, Emily popped in a cassette, and beautiful, spun sound, with impeccable intonation and lovely lines of phrasing, filled the minivan. After a few minutes of listening, Emily glanced at me in the rearview mirror. "That's a young violinist named Sarah Chang," she said. "She's only eight. She's playing on a quarter-sized violin! Can you believe that tone?"

I checked out Sarah, amazed by her talent. Her album, entitled *Debut,* contained extremely difficult repertoire, including the *Carmen Fantasy,* and she had performed an equally difficult lineup with the New York Philharmonic, with Zubin Mehta conducting. How could that be possible?

You have to be born with it to have what it takes.... I heard that irksome voice again, a déjà vu from my childhood. This time, the future of my little girl hung on my response to it, and I turned to fight the spiritual enemy.

Yes, some are born with it, like my little girl, my mind countered. *And others must take the steady gait of discipline, patience, and hard work. Either way, God is with me, I am up to the task, and you will not win.*

I was learning.

My struggle out of the cocoon of my childhood setting and my striving as a writer living in Nashville had set me on guard against the predators that lurk on the path to musical success—or any success, really. I was savvy to the snatchers who are ready to relegate other people's artistry to somewhere under their feet. Whether they are family members, teachers, peers, parents, a city, demons, or oneself, they must be stepped over, abandoned, fought, rebuked, or ignored.

Over time, I would find out that prodigies are not simply "born with it" but are the culmination of converging influences: a highly educated musical parent, a visionary teacher, and a consistent, rigorous, well-designed methodology of daily practice. Musical success is not a mystery. By God's grace, I would not allow my children to be suppressed by poverty, lack of education, cruel people, or doubt. I could shoot for the stars, because I could see the sky. Out of the millions of lovely lights twinkling there, like crystal dreams, some were twinkling for me and my children.

The Cat and the Fiddle

Alice came to a fork in the road. 'Which road do I take?' she asked.
'Where do you want to go?' responded the Cheshire Cat.

ALICE IN WONDERLAND BY LEWIS CARROLL

Bill and I have been asked repeatedly over the years—and often a suspicious twitch of the eyes accompanies the question—whether our children *had* to play an instrument. The answer is easy: Absolutely! Parenting demands confident leadership. What is a parent *for* if not to discern and implement what is best for the child during the formative years? A four-year-old doesn't assess the future. Such long-range planning was our responsibility.

Even if our children had resisted, we would have overruled and insisted they play an instrument, just as we insisted they eat their vegetables, participate in school lessons, speak politely, and finish their work. Bill and I were loving, kind, considerate, and *strong leaders*. Our children understood that nobody messed with Daddy or Mama.

Children thrive in such safety. They are not qualified to make important decisions, and they know it.

Alex watched his sister's daily musical frolicking: playing along with Daddy on the piano, going to lessons, receiving practice-point rewards such as ice-cream outings, participating in ritzy recitals and post-recital parties, and basking in Mama's focused attention. These musical festivities exerted the pull of a Pied Piper, calling him, and each one of his siblings in time, to join the parade— and sooner than possible. The question of *making* them play music never presented itself. We couldn't *make* them play, because they were *begging* to play.

"You're only two years old, honey. You'll have to wait just a wee bit longer, then you'll get your violin."

One Sunday, Alex exited his preschool Sunday school class bursting to let us in on an astonishing revelation. "Mama, Zach doesn't pay vio-yin at his house," he said. "Nobody in Sunday school pays vio-yin." Then he sat for a moment, pondering. "I thought everybody payed duh vio-yin."

With Alex believing that everybody played the violin, you can imagine how surprised I was when I asked him what instrument he wanted to play and he replied, while doing a little dwarf-sized jump, "Duh fuh-yoot! I want to pay duh fuh-yoot!" I tried to picture him playing the flute but the picture wouldn't develop: the timbre, the lilt, the style of the instrument didn't seem right for his spunky personality.

"I thought you wanted to play the violin, like Annie," I said.

"Duh fuh-yoot, duh fuh-yoot!" One small foot left the ground, as one little fist punched high in the air.

I discussed the prospect with Bill during our Saturday night date. He flaked his baked potato with his fork and thought. "Flutes are sure cheaper than violins," he said, always practical. "But somehow the instrument doesn't fit him."

"Exactly!" I said, happy we were in agreement. "I think he saw James Galway playing on PBS or something. Anyway, it impressed him."

"The instrument or that incredible Celtic music?"

"Maybe both. If we put him on the violin, we can use Annie's old instruments, and I'll know the path."

The question at hand prompted me to take note of other families in our program. One sibling ensemble of five stayed true to the cello, stepping up, one by one, to enter the family's already saturated cello mass. But when the youngest reached his musical startup, he careered out of the cello rut and over to the harp. Harp is beautiful in duet with cello, but the balance seemed a bit off. Five to one? I found myself feeling sorry for the tiny-tot harpist, the odd-child-out. Other two-child families played such complementary instruments as violin and piano—or two violins. Another family, whose mother taught violin, played two violins and a cello. These were logical combinations.

One family chose violin for their daughter and baseball for their son, as if the two were comparable—a common, but short-sighted thought process. Baseball is a game, and has its proper place, but musical expressions when played as praise on the part of every Christian—that's an imperative of Scripture.

After considerable thought on the matter, Bill and I encouraged Alex to take up the violin instead of the flute. He was chomping at the bit to play an instrument of any kind, so he exhibited no grief but quickly took to his fiddle, the moment it arrived. The scratching resumed—only worse. The cat and the fiddle are a natural fit! Annie had taken easily to the violin, once we'd figured out the process of practice and positions. Not Alex. The shocking disparity of natural skill between the two unwound my momentum. I found myself needing new approaches and maneuvers. Alex was exceedingly smart—smarter than the rest of us. But he didn't learn the same way Annie learned. His personality was unconventional, syncopated. The only plan of action that came to mind was to persevere...with a heavy emphasis on the "severe." What I lacked in understanding of Alex's learning style and personality, I supplied in pertinacity. Gradually, I learned that each child needs an individualized approach, and I learned the levels of discernment that such an approach required.

The first helpful advice about Alex came through one of Annie's summer teachers, in the fourth year of her studies. Bill kept Alex and Benjamin at home that summer, while I drove Annie the three hours to Memphis to participate in a two-week string camp. The warm sky of June spread out blue and wide above us, and we sang songs while driving along I-40, so happy to be going to a special event.

Morning assemblies at the camp featured student performances, and the directors selected Annie to perform the first movement of Vivaldi's Concerto in A minor. The day before the performance, Mr. Chang, one of the violin teachers, met us in his studio for a lesson on the piece. He sat in a small, black, padded chair, holding his violin, and his wife sat at the grand piano, ready to accompany him and Annie. They were a brilliant husband-wife team, chipper and smiling, endowed with years of experience.

As I settled into an empty chair, Mr. Chang noticed my pregnancy. "You have many chi-ren?" He asked.

"Yes, this is my fourth!" I held up four fingers to help him understand.

"*Ohhhh!*" He nodded, impressed, and I watched a procession of thoughts parade across his face. "They all pay bio-yin?"

"Well, that's a good question. Annie's little brother, Alex, is paying...I mean, playing...the violin, like Annie."

"*Ohhhh.*" He raised his eyebrows.

"I think...not every chide pay bio-yin!" He furrowed his brow a bit, smiled softly, hoping I would recognize the goodwill behind his words. "The muh-der, she get soooo tired of bio-yin, and the chide not have excitement of new in-straw-ment!" He lifted his eyebrows and nodded, checking to see if I understood.

I understood completely.

Mrs. Chang added, "You not practice so good next time, and this next chide be yid-duh bit not so good ee-der."

Words of knowledge; these two had been around the musical block. Their wisdom confirmed what was already germinating in my heart.

I had noted that Alex had no musical territory he could call his own. Following in Annie's wake, he was perpetually a step behind her, walking in her shadow. I probed about for another year, overseeing his practice on the violin while considering a move to classical guitar or viola. Classical guitar is a beautiful instrument, and the dexterity Alex had acquired in the left hand on the violin would translate.

The viola offered an even easier segue into a new instrumental territory, and it fit perfectly in duet with Annie's violin. I felt a sort of letdown, however, when I considered the instrument's reputation for frumpiness, the backstage jokes insinuating that those who give in and play the viola are really failed violinists; they couldn't cut it in the competitive world of the violin. I observed the violists around me, usually few in number, and I hated to admit it, but I did seem to remember quite a few who seemed slow, or downright lazy. Additionally, because of the size of the instrument, how it's held and the reach involved, viola players seemed to be in chronic need of physical therapy.

I needed counsel, and my friend with the funny double name came to mind. Terry Terry is a skilled violist. I'd once sat spellbound as he performed the offertory at Highland Church; the throaty, woody voice of his instrument floated forth, mellow and easy on the ear.

"Playing viola instead of violin," he said, when I called to ask his thoughts, "is like playing oboe instead of flute, or French horn instead of trumpet. Good viola players are rare and valuable. If he's a good violist, Alex will have some great options for college scholarships and plenty of work. Even if he's getting a degree in something other than music, schools always need more good violas in their orchestra."

I hung up the phone, renewed in my intention to make the change. The dollars spent on childhood music lessons were also an investment in college? This was a win-win scenario worthy of full surrender: spend the bulk of time and money during the prime educational years, from three to thirteen, to cultivate high skill on a rare instrument. Not only would it maximize my child's brain-power, it would aid him in gaining a scholarship to a great college, even if his pursuit was something other than music.

It takes a great deal of discipline and concentration to achieve high skill in playing an instrument. Young people who do so possess a muscular mind, which helps open the heavy doors to such challenging pursuits as law and medicine.

I mulled over Terry's words. "…like playing oboe instead of flute, or French horn instead of trumpet." Strange, isn't it, how each instrument carries its own persona? The field of "lead" instruments—violin, flute, and trumpet—is crowded, filled with egos, while such low, strong, foundational instruments as viola and bassoon attract a steadier, humbler crowd.

Alex took to the viola energetically, and as he grew, I helped tune him in to the advantages of playing an instrument that's not always in the limelight. "Alex, be creative with your viola," I said. "Imagine groundbreaking new ways of using it. Explore new sounds and techniques." This eventually translated, for him, into becoming a gutsy player, unafraid of raw sound and brute power. It is a creativity that has also led to his expertise in additional creative pursuits such as production, arranging, and composing.

Learning to match the personality of a child with the personality of an instrument helped us make good decisions. Annie's undaunted nature fit the competitive, high-strung world of the violin, and she learned to ignore each teacher's idiosyncrasies. Alex loved the down-to-earth community of violists and the rich, midregister voice. The change of clef made perfect sense to him, with middle C being in the middle of the staff. We spent not one second teaching him the new note placements; he somehow grasped the concept immediately and thoroughly.

The body of viola repertoire contains such strong, masculine modern works as the Bartók and Hindemith concertos. It is smaller than the violin repertoire, and thus easier to master. I considered this important for Alex, as I doubted, because of his eclectic personality, that he would enjoy teaching music as a sole profession. If he became a teacher, I felt, it would be as an addendum to another primary profession such as producing or composing.

Annie's violin and Alex's viola merged them into a complementary musical relationship, providing exceptional opportunities for brother-sister collaboration and bonding. We put Benjamin, gentle and thoughtful, on cello, figuring he would love the mellow but rich lower register. I loved the cello and looked forward to studying it with him. I also looked forward to having a string trio in our home, as we combined Ben's new cello with Annie's violin and Alex's viola. Ben's teacher, Mrs. Williams, was unpretentious, sincere, and kind, all of which were necessary ingredients for Benjamin's impressionable and tender-hearted spirit.

A child's dominant learning style, whether visual, aural, or kinesthetic, is an important factor in choosing an instrument. Successfully playing fretless instruments, such as those in the string family, depends primarily on the ear, not the eye. A child with a visual preference will need to strengthen her aural perceptions, and a parent must continuously emphasize pitch and tone, encouraging the student to "tune in" to the sound. This process can be tedious, but success is sweet: A visual learner with a trained ear is a powerful musician who excels at both sight-reading and improvisation. Bill's musical abilities illuminated this precept for me. He is a visual learner who trained his ear to decipher extremely subtle nuance. I love going to the movies with him, listening as he tells me the key signature of the opening musical theme, then proceeds to sing the names of the chord changes, using the bass line for a melody. His job as a music transcriber, editor, and arranger showcases his ability to transfer music, by ear, from a recording and to notate it on the printed page. Such fluency is exceedingly valuable. It should be the goal of every music teacher to groom students who can read and write music with equal ease.

As each of our children came along and we chose instruments, we learned to consider and respect the learning style of each one. Camille, a visual learner like her daddy, naturally gravitated toward the piano, all laid out in black and white. Because many people play the piano, I spoke to Bill about adding a second, more rare, instrument that is akin to the piano. "Remember that sweet blonde at Highland who played the harp in the orchestra every Sunday? Every time I saw her play, I promised myself, 'Someday, I'm gonna have a harp in my house!' Let's start Camille on the harp along with the piano."

"You mean you want to lug one of those around?" Bill said.

"No," I said. "I want *you* to lug one of those around."

Piano and harp are interconnected. Picture the frame of strings housed within the body of a grand piano. Now turn them on their side; the piano has become a harp. As soon as Camille had a good start on the piano, we began harp lessons.

Once a child is functional on her primary instrument, it is fun and easy to add a cousin instrument. Like the harp and piano, violin and mandolin are related, which makes the mandolin low-hanging fruit for a violinist and adds a whole new world of musical possibilities, both in style and color. The instruments are strung exactly alike, so the only new learning is in the right hand: picking versus bowing. Another great combination is the viola and the mandola, which is a rare and utterly cool-sounding instrument that is similar to the mandolin.

Gretchen, our fifth child, expressed a desire, early on, to play the violin like her much admired eldest sister. I had had a ten-year break from teaching the instrument, working instead with viola, cello, and piano, and felt enthusiastic about taking it up again. The lure of rounding out a full-fledged string quartet interested me, as well. As it turned out, Gretchen was extremely easy to teach.

"Wow!" I told Bill. "I must be a master violin teacher! I'm amazed at how naturally she plays it. Her ear…her intonation…they're incredible."

When the basic functions of Gretchen's positions were fluid and natural, I began to teach her to read music. I put the music before her on the stand and was surprised to see her squint her eyes and stick her nose so close to the music that she couldn't open her arm to pull her bow over the strings.

"Gretchen, back up," I said. "Those notes are big. You can read them."

"I tan't see duh notes."

"What do you mean you can't see the notes?"

"I tan if I dit weal tose…." She moved her face so close to the music that her nose almost touched.

Perhaps it was not my expertise that made it so easy to teach her to play the violin. Gretchen took in very little information with her eyes, which, to my surprise, turned out to be quite weak. The way she learned was by analyzing information with her ears. Because of this, teaching her to play the violin was painless. My experience with Gretchen nailed down my increasing awareness that a child's learning style has a huge effect on the process of playing, and especially on a fretless instrument. Parents who take the time to find out how their children receive information will be much better equipped in directing an educational path.

It is important to train a child aurally before the glitz of electronic visual media scuttles the possibility. Parents must speak, recite, read out loud, sing, and play music, because these media forms promote both strong relationships and strong listening skills. They teach a child how the expert rendering of a language sounds, a prerequisite to fluency.

Dawd and Doh-dee-yocks

It is my opinion that art lost its basic creative drive
the moment it was separated from worship.
It severed an umbilical cord and now lives its own sterile life,
generating and degenerating itself.
In former days the artist remained unknown
and his work was to the glory of God.
He lived and died without being more or less important than other artisans...
The ability to create was a gift.
In such a world flourished invulnerable assurance and natural humility.

INGMAR BERGMAN

"I'm so glad God tells us things before we need to know them," Bill said. It's a praise he articulates often. I agreed then, and I agree even more dramatically now, as I see in hindsight how much grace was shown to us during the seasons of our children's development. By this time, the linguistic skills erupting in the brains of our brood were evident all around us in the form of baby talk. "Tum on, Ta-mee-uh Wose!" My thirdborn, Benjamin, would flap a hand to get the attention of his younger sister, Camille Rose. "Yet's pay Wa-bin Hood. You tan be duh Yay-dee. I dit to be Wabin Hood."

"He may wind up needing some speech therapy," Bill observed.

The cherub chatter sounded cheery to us. I often interspersed normal adult speech with clips of baby talk. I liked using phrases of prattle. Words, words, words, whirling through the air. I began to notice the phenomenal way they were captured and assimilated into conversation by my children. Movies, books, songs:

All that was seen and heard found its way into their daily dialogues, splattered with failed fricatives and paltry plosives.

"When Annie and Alex were the age of Benjamin and Camille, they could speak much more clearly," I said one night as Bill and I settled in. "I wonder why."

"Maybe it's because they're learning from each other instead of us."

I considered the kids' speech patterns, counting off each child on my fingers. "Annie has almost outgrown her tendency to stutter. Alex still can't say "yuh" and "thuh," but he talks nonstop. Benjamin sounds like he's speaking a foreign language, and 'Ta-mee-uh Wose' copies him. I had to take Gretchen out of the play-in on Saturday. She would not quit jabbering."

Bill sighed and punched his pillow. "Maybe they'll all grow out of it. Shut off the yight. Yet's doh to seep."

"Dood night."

I lay in the quiet, increasingly curious as to the word-processing power housed inside the brains of our young children. All the time Bill and I were investing in their musical training, we were also nurturing them spiritually. Our daily pursuits were like two streams running side by side that would eventually merge into one. I closed my eyes before dozing off and prayed, "God, please give us a double portion of your Holy Spirit."

As our family had grown, our house had become a blast of energy: The cumulative effect could be potent. After only a few minutes of visiting, Grandmother Jane would fan her face with her hands and exclaim hotly, "This family overwhelms me!" Bill and I learned to instruct our brood to tone it down when Grandmother Jane arrived, telling them, "Grandma needs a chance to acclimate."

Mornings were especially busy. I loved how the family would sit around the breakfast table, clanking their spoons and clamoring, "Torn Sex, Torn Sex. Mommy, pour some mi-yut on my Torn Sex." I would pull the Corn Chex out of the cupboard, fill the bowls, and laugh inwardly as I poured the "mi-yut."

"Lord, help me harness the energy of these voices for Your glory," I prayed.

Our mission was twofold: to groom children who were deeply rooted in a love for God and who possessed the artistic skill to share that love with others. Many godly souls are silenced by fear of public speaking, possessing no skilled modes of artistic expression. Others are thoroughly groomed in the arts—they sing and dance with great pizzazz—but they lack spiritual depth. As their profile rises, they find it increasingly difficult to maintain balance, often with tragic results. Bill and I knew it was important to root our children in spiritual depth, and not just artistic fluency alone.

Homeschooling seemed naturally to facilitate both quests and to make the best use of our time. Besides, the yellow Bluebird weighed heavily on my mind, and my epiphany at *Land Between the Lakes* had powered me up for the task.

I sat with ruler, pen, and paper, ready to construct our daily schedule. Monday, Tuesday, Wednesday, Thursday…*Eeny, Meeny, Miny, Moe*: only a few hours in a day, and the educational options were limitless.

"Lord, show me the essentials," I prayed.

Prayer! God breathed the word into my mind, and I thought back over my own testimony. Just a few months before Bill and I began to date, I had committed myself to daily prayer. Bill's consistent leadership had drawn me further into communication with God. These prayers had given birth to our love for each other, leading to marriage. I had seen how radically transformational, how essential, prayer was to relationships. Why had I not carried the same wellspring of intimacy Bill and I enjoyed into our children's world? Yes, we prayed with them a few minutes before bedtime, before meals, and when specific needs arose. But a morning commitment of extended conversation with our Creator lay in my mind as something I would do one day, when the kids were older and could sit still longer.

Too much chaos, I said to God.

Plant the seeds now, He said. *Do not waste a day.*

I made elongated time slots for family prayer and Bible reading on my calendar.

The day would begin early, at 5:00 AM, following the pattern of King David, who wrote, "In the morning, O Lord, you hear my voice; in the morning I lay my requests before you and wait in expectation" (Psalm 5:3, NIV). One of our family's favorite wall hangings was a rough cedar plaque carved by Bill's woodworking dad:

My heart is steadfast, O God:
I will sing and make music with all my soul.
Awake, harp and lyre!
I will awake the dawn.

Psalm 108:1–2 (NIV)

But let's see, if we intended to arise at 5:00 AM after eight to twelve hours of sleep, depending on age, we would need to be in bed by . . . . I quickly saw the problem. The difficult choice is not what time one arises, but what time one retires. I made a mental note to protect our evenings, and thereby to protect the holy habits of the morning.

Our little house might have looked as if nothing had changed. But dramatic change had come. Oddly, I found that each hour added to our early morning schedule miraculously expanded the functional time within the day. Here's why: Evening hours are often times of weariness, when kids and parents alike become crabby and withdrawn. By using the early morning hours to accomplish the most difficult tasks, we can allow ourselves to relax earlier and to establish calmer dinner and bedtime patterns, which facilitate healthy sleep. It is a virtuous cycle: hearty work during the hearty morning hours, then relaxing into a comfortable afternoon with pleasurable activities such as sewing, reading, writing, and sports. After all, the big tasks are done. The afternoon then segues into a quiet evening, ending in peaceful sleep.

"The wise woman builds her house, but with her own hands the foolish one tears hers down" (Proverbs 14:1, NIV).

Lord, give me wisdom, I prayed.

With my alarm set and our schedule taped to the wall, I set myself to house-building. At 5:00 AM, I rose, dressed myself, and awakened my children. They slept in only two bedrooms, a boys' and a girls'. Friends of ours had refused to have more than two children, citing as their reason a lack of a private bedroom for each. But Bill and I believed it to be short-sighted to inflate the value of a private bedroom over the value of life, and we had come to understand that children who snuggle together in a warm bed grow up to enjoy a deeper and longer-lasting relationship than those who are isolated.

In my house-building, I wanted to cultivate the habit of happiness. So I entered my girls' room with a bright voice, lots of kisses, strokes of the hair, and a gentle tracing of the cheek or eyebrow. As each stirred, I would call her by the name of a fairy-tale princess: Annie, the eldest and hardworking, was Cinderella; Camille, dark-haired, pale-skinned and easy-tempered, was Snow White; and Gretchen, gregarious and difficult to wake, was Sleeping Beauty.

"Sleeping Beauty. Sleeping Beaaauuuuty. Time to greet the dawn."

The boys received a kiss and a grizzly-bear growl. They loved the morning wrestle, the romp and roar of Mama Bear.

In the amber light of God's morning mercies, Bill and I would gather our brood. Those who were cold, I wrapped in a throw. Those who were achy, I rubbed on the back, running my fingers through wild hair, softly massaging shoulders. While the baby tugged breakfast from my breast, the toddlers sat close beside or on Daddy's lap. Bill and I had experienced the intimacy that praying together builds, and we wanted our little ones to learn to associate prayer with the God of all comfort.

I learned to pray with one eye open as our homemade prayer chapel teamed with life, messy and imperfect. God eagerly overlooked it all and met us in full force.

Formal prayers have a proper place, but many families flounder with extended corporate prayer, because they believe they should bring the sanctuary setting home. Remember: Jesus hears above every clamor. He said, "Let the little children come to me" (Mark 10:14, NIV).

We pulled a small wooden rocking chair, crafted by Grandpa Bill and sized for toddlers, alongside Daddy's wingback chair, from which he could place a hand and encourage patience and concentration. The vision of Camille in that tiny rocker especially charms me. So earnestly she prayed, her eyes tightly squinted, her page-boy framing the circle of her plump face: "Dee-uh Dawd...." She solemnly shook her head as she spoke, wrinkling her nose and squinting her eyes too tightly, allowing for fluttery peeping. "Peas help Doh-dee-yocks to not have to tate a nap. And help duh th-wee beh-uhs to not be mean to Doh-dee-yocks...." Annie had been telling her bedtime stories, and Camille felt considerable consternation for the welfare of Goldilocks and the Three Bears. I bit my lip, trying not to laugh or do anything that would make her believe I was belittling her prayer. Bill and I did not correct her personal prayers or try to feed her "proper" prayer lines. Her prayers came from the heart. They would mature with her.

And they have. Camille still has an extraordinary heart for the welfare of others. Once your need is on her list, she prays faithfully, patiently, relentlessly, until the answer comes. Had I stifled her prayers for Goldilocks, I would have plucked the God-blossom flowering in her nature, that special propensity to recognize, analyze, and verbalize the needs of others with unflagging fidelity.

One by one, each voice sounded. We began by reading the Scriptures, then bowed our heads to pray out loud. We prayed for kings, princes, and those in authority, just as the Scriptures bade us. We prayed for each other, our church, our neighbors, friends, relatives, and the sick. We prayed conversationally, each person speaking a theme as it came to his mind and others chiming in to articulate their own particular petition on the subject. We prayed from the top down and from the bottom up, according to age. We learned biblical prayers, like the Lord's Prayer, as well as statements of faith, like the Apostle's Creed and the great confession of Peter, and hymns such as the "Gloria Patri," to speak or sing together. We split up, boys out there, girls in here. We lit candles. We didn't light candles. We knelt. We didn't kneel. Some fell asleep and had to be wakened. Some wiggled and had to be stilled. Some cried and had to be comforted. Diapers were changed during adoration, babies burped over exhortation.

For a season, we prayed first thing in the morning. But I noticed how difficult it was to keep everyone awake. So I began to administer what I called "Pajama Practice," that is, to wake the older children first, offer a short prayer of praise, then fill the first time slot of the day with music. This allowed the younger children to sleep longer, freeing me to focus on practicing. The action of playing music kept the "big kids" from drifting back to sleep, and I could literally feel the Lord's joy as the sounds filled the room. Early-bird neighbors on their morning walks stopped to listen.

We eventually moved our elongated prayer time to after breakfast. This turned out to be our favorite, as we had already completed two hours of practice, straightened the house, showered, dressed, and eaten. It was still early, and we were wide awake and ready as we gathered to praise God, to read His Word, to sing and meet with Him.

Bill's work-from-home business gave him flexibility with his schedule. Most families don't have this luxury, and working out the details of how and when your family will pray varies greatly. Whatever the protocol or time of day, however, the important thing is to make prayer a priority and find the time for *thorough* prayer. I use the word "thorough" because many people pray a little here, a little there, before a meal or briefly before bed, and those prayers are good and should continue. However, they do not realize the intimacy of relationship and the transformation of family life as does a focused time of exhaustive prayer, the conclusion of which might end with Forrest Gump's famous line, "That's all I have to say about that!"

Our prayers escalated. Powerful moments surfaced: Sins were confessed. Problems in relationships were examined and remedies prescribed. We began to grow closer to one another as we grew closer to God.

One memorable day, Bill came to me with these simple words: "I think I am happier now than I have ever been."

"Me too." My heart was blissful.

Prayer as communication with God is the bedrock of knowing *God*. I am not referring to knowing *about* God, but to *knowing* God. In the biblical sense of the word, *knowing* refers to the oneness of sexual intercourse as in, "Adam *knew* Eve, and Eve bore a son." It is this oneness with God that enables the spirit of an individual to *conceive* the truth of God, giving birth to a New Creation. This is a supernatural phenomenon, dependent on the implantation and germination of the Holy Spirit. As this new life matures, it wells up in the soul, filled with spiritual fruits. A child's heart begins to overflow, and she is compelled to find an outlet for the power of her testimony, a toolbox of expression that empowers her to *tell* what she *knows*. Thus a messenger of God is born, equipped to communicate fluently and effectively.

As we prayed, baby talk and childish whims gave way to fluency of speech, a maturity of insight and request. I saw a transformation in my own life as my prayers grew in specificity according to God's Word.

God began to stir His purposes in each one of our children. Unusual curiosities began to manifest as the Holy Spirit led each into the unique quest God had ordained. Ten-year-old Benjamin, for example, began to read voraciously and to be mesmerized by maps. He memorized the geography of ancient Palestine and studied Old Testament stories until he knew who conquered whom, in what order, and for how long.

After church one Sunday, Annie tattled, "Mama, Benjamin corrected the Sunday school teacher today."

"Well, he got it all wrong!" Benjamin frowned. "He said the Israelites defeated the *Hittites*. It was the *Jebusites* that they defeated."

One Sunday afternoon, we stayed at church to prepare for an event we were leading. As I doled out the lunch I had packed, I noticed Benjamin was missing.

Searching the classroom wing, I heard the high pitched timbre of his young voice: "The nation of Israel disobeyed God..." I followed the sound, and when I cracked the door to peep inside, I found Benjamin at the front of the Sunday school room, marker in hand, lecturing to an imaginary class. The board behind him was filled with maps of ancient Palestine he had drawn for illustration.

"Where did this fancy come from?" I asked Bill later. "I didn't assign a study on it in our homeschool."

"You'd think he'd be crazy for video games like every other ten-year-old."

"You'd think so. But today he gave me a list of what he wants for his birthday. It's all these thick books on ancient Rome and Jewish history"—I held up my index finger and thumb to show a four-inch spread—"like you'd put on a coffee table. I'm gonna go ahead and get him a few, but I figure they'll just collect dust."

They didn't. The books were soon creased and grimy with wear. Our family grew accustomed to hearing Benjamin detail the lives of nefarious Roman despots. Instead of assigning book reports, I cooked, cleaned, folded clothes, played chauffeur, and brushed my teeth to an ongoing discourse about Roman history.

Similar developments began to manifest in the lives of all my children, seemingly born out of the blue. I found their vocabulary and word use expanding.

With no prompting from me, Benjamin began to write poetry.

Sonnet for Sequoyah

It rides above the changing of the masses
Strutting forth the hidden lies it sells
With eloquence that sweetens like molasses
And yet the truth it also proudly tells

With its edge it cuts down most convictions
Inflaming passions to the point of action
Like a match that burns with deadly friction
Yet steering to the goal with steady traction

Great nations move at its own beck and call
Past deeds of men will change within its hands
At its signal massive armies stall
Imagining a distant, better land

The written word can rule the hearts of men
Revealing truths that are beyond their ken

"I like your poem." I said, truly impressed. "What inspired it?"

"You know Sequoyah? I read a book about him. There was this one part where he asked his father why the white man had so much power over the Cherokee. His father said it was the talking leaves, the magic of the marks on a page." He shook his head. "Just think. Without writing, we couldn't record our laws or send our thoughts to other people. So I wrote this poem about that."

Bookstores ranked number one on our young family's list of exciting excursions, especially Davis-Kidd, a privately owned store in Nashville. Wide-eyed with sunny windows, the store stood two stories high and thousands of stories rich. We pulled the pretty covers from the shelves, excited to glance through, to see if just maybe we had discovered a rare jewel.

On one particular trip, Bill and I filtered through the fiction as each child found a book and a spot on a bench, engrossed in the pages. My immersion was complete, so it took a couple of seconds to dawn on me that someone was crying. I turned from the shelves as my eyes searched for the sound.

Benjamin!

He was slumped in despair on a low bench, tears pouring. Bill got there first and knelt low. The other children circled. "Benjamin!" "Are you okay?" "What's wrong?"

Benjamin's sorrow muffled his speech, so Bill bent his ear to hear as I made my way to the circle.

Bill's mouth curved slightly in a secret smile as he heard the tale. Then he patted Ben's back and commiserated. "Oh, Benjamin's a little upset, aren't you, Ben?"

Moved by the pity party, Benjamin began to cry again as Bill continued. "He's just discovered that his version of his favorite book is abridged."

I could hardly comprehend the words. "What?"

"Look!" Benjamin came off the bench and pulled a thick book off the shelf. "Right there!"

He was holding a beautiful, thick binding of *The Count of Monte Cristo*.

"It says, *Un-a-bridged*!" He pointed at the word, jabbing his finger in rhythm as he spoke. "Mine was not this thick. It must have been abridged, and...I...I didn't know it." He sank back down on the bench, his little face contorting in sorrow. "It's the best book I've ever read, and I could still be *reading it!*"

Demand breeds supply. I began feeding him—and the others—book after book, like a mama bird feeds worms. I double-stacked our sagging shelves and kept a lookout for bargains. My job as educator changed, as God began to light the fire of His purposes in my children's hearts. Instead of force-feeding a trumped up curriculum, I began to watch what He was doing and to facilitate Him.

All this drive to read, this love of words, of stories, of conversation, of supernatural realities, was born of prayer. It was the Holy Spirit's supernatural flame, sparking the hearts of my children to quest for God.

Slowly the revelation came: Prayer is the greatest language-arts development program available. Think about it. To pray fluently, a child must know what to pray *for*, which requires that she become what the Scriptures call a watcher, a person who is cognizant of what is going on around her (Matthew 26:41; Ephesians 6:18;

Luke 21:36). She must be able to examine what she has observed in the context of Scripture, to see what petitions apply, and to extrapolate the nature of her request. She must formulate the words and speak them out loud to God. It is an exercise involving public awareness, deductive reasoning, analytical thinking, problem solving, good citizenship, concentration, contemplation, focus, logic, forethought, and hindsight. Cultivation of such thinking skills is one of the natural benefits of prayer.

For example, if the one praying commits to the scriptural instruction to "Pray first of all for kings and princes and those in authority," he must know not only what is happening in his backyard but what is happening around the world. He must know the king's name and what request should be made on his behalf. Social and political issues move front and center. This habit of being in the *know* funnels down from the international scene to the national scene, the city scene, the family scene, the street scene, and the personal scene of the individual praying.

Prayer sharpens listening skills, as well: listening to one another pray in order to agree or to augment or clarify the requests; listening to the Spirit of God as He prompts a thought or gives an answer; listening to the Scriptures, to pray them into effect. It is difficult to learn to sit patiently and listen while another person prays in order to agree together about the request being offered. The mind must stay focused on the words being said. Yet it is a powerful mental discipline, because, as we agree together, a unified voice arises to petition the throne of God, to activate saints and angels on our behalf, to change the course of mankind for good.

Listening to the heartfelt prayers of another person requires patience, and patience is the first rule of love, "Love is patient, love is kind" (1 Corinthians 13:4, NIV). Yes, we are speaking and listening to God. Yet at the same time, we are speaking and listening to one another.

"Do you know where your children are?" The question is often asked on late-night television, to encourage parents to impose a curfew. But try asking it in the spiritual sense: *Do you know where your children are?* You do if you will pray with them: You know where they are emotionally, spiritually, physically, and relationally as you listen to them articulate honest, thorough, prayers. You have the sweet assurance that you are participating with them in the most rewarding educational endeavor available. You are lighting the fires of God's destiny in their lives.

This Is My Story

Angels descending bring from above
Echoes of mercy, whispers of love

"BLESSED ASSURANCE" WORDS BY FANNY J. CROSBY

With intimate, bonded, love relationships under construction and prayer as the centerpiece of each day, Bill and I added one more underpinning to the foundational elements of godly artistic success: the Bible. We made the Bible the central textbook of our home and our school. During family prayer times we passed the Book around, and each person read out loud from its texts. Even our very young nonreaders would follow Daddy's finger as he prompted. Then, as their reading skills increased, his input diminished.

Along with reading, each child used the texts of the Bible in learning to write—and to memorize and recite for family and friends. In our family devotionals, we meditated and ruminated and chewed on the mysteries of spiritual things, seen and unseen. Mealtime, bedtime, and road trips surfaced as prime opportunities to deepen our ongoing discussions about the truths and mysteries of God. These spiritual themes lit the atmosphere like a wood fire, their warmth seeping into our souls. We could not get enough of our beloved God.

One Sunday morning, after seeing our family perform as guests at a church in California, a young mother of two middle-school-aged boys approached me. "Your children play their instruments very well," she observed, "but what really struck me is the obvious love they share for God—and each other, to boot!"

"Mom, come on!" One of her sons smacked her on the shoulder and spoke sharply. "I wanna get outta here."

She pushed him away. Another son stood sullenly nearby, but she was determined to have a chat. "What did you do to make them so dedicated?"

I've gotten that kind of question a lot, and I couldn't resist answering with a scriptural prod. "During the formative years, from birth to twelve years old, I followed Deuteronomy 6:7."

"What does that say?" She frowned, as though scouring her mind for long-past lessons.

"We should talk with our children about the Lord, to impress His ways on their hearts"—I made quote marks in the air with my fingers—"when you sit at home and when you walk along the road, when you lie down and when you get up.'" I smiled encouragingly. "That's pretty much all the time."

"Ewww!" she scowled. "I'll bet they just hate you."

I felt a start of surprise. Hate me? My children were constantly tugging at my sleeves, begging me to read to them about God. While riding in the car, we would pull cues for God-centered conversations from everywhere: the full moon, for example, and the God who made it, how it hangs low on the horizon, how it affects the ocean waves, how Earth could not exist without it. We found masterpieces of creation everywhere: in the laws of the universe, in the riddles of physics, in the puzzles of geology, and in the great works of literature, music, sculpture, and painting.

Hate it? El, Elohim, Yahweh, Father, Son, and Holy Ghost were our conversations of choice. (*Oooo!* A ghost? Let's talk about that!)

Young children believe so easily. They embrace unseen, supernatural realities, the mysteries of *being*, without a doubt. If the aforementioned research of the Barna Group is correct—that most people die in old age believing what they believed at thirteen—then we must be intentional about teaching the story of God and His truths during the early years. When a child doesn't know or care about the past—doesn't link himself emotionally with his God, his country, or his family heritage—his understanding of the purpose of existence becomes rootless and he loses equilibrium. If children are to grow into adults who overcome, they must understand and be able to articulate a broad-range personal testimony.

Jesus set up important ceremonies expressly intended to help us remember. He associated icons with these celebrations. The cup, the bread, the wine, the table, the cross, the empty tomb, and the Bible are tangible representations of His story. Samuel, too, raised an ebenezer, a rock of remembrance, as a memorial to the Lord's deliverance. As our family grew, I began to collect keepsakes, personal ebenezers to help me remember the works of the Lord in my life and in the life of my ancestors. I began to impart this knowledge to my children, to help them detail how the Lord had been working throughout their family history to draw them to Himself.

When my friend, Roy, invited our church choir to his home for a dinner party, I got a stark lesson in how easily mankind forgets to honor even the most natural characters in a personal story. Bill and I were choir members and looked forward to the event because Roy has what his family calls "furniture's disease," that is, a discriminating taste for exquisite antiques and a gift for interior decorating. From the moment I stepped through Roy's front door, I reveled in the opulence of his old-south-styled mansion.

A trio of dining tables dressed the oversize dining room, the gleam of their dark mahogany mirroring fresh flowers that cascaded from Victorian vases. The perfume of the flowers pervaded the warm air, wafting up, up, up toward the vaulted ceiling and crown molding, and settling down over us like a sweet potpourri. God is not alone in His love of beautiful fragrances.

As we dined, the clink of fine china, lead crystal, and polished silver mingled merrily with the polite murmurs of the guests: "Thank you." "Yes, please." "More? Certainly!" "Delicious!" Herbed butter and sweet cream comforted tongue and tummy, and I was certain that *Southern Living* couldn't compete.

After dinner, the guests ambled through the mansion to gaze at luxurious draperies, palatial antiques, and—my favorite—bold prints on English-garden wallpapers. The tour of beauty eventually led us into the drawing room, where Bill sat down to play the Steinway Grand, an extraordinary specimen hand-crafted from warm cherrywood with gold-leaf gilding.

"I drove to New York City to pick up this piano," Roy said. "I'm so glad the Lord let me have it." He told us the story of the piano, its design and building, commissioned by a wealthy family.

Bill's fingers burrowed into the keys, pulling out a familiar melody and compelling us to sing. "Amazing Grace how sweet the sound that saved a wretch like me!" As I joined the refrain, my eyes swept the room, and one large painting caught my eye, its massive frame ensconcing a sweep of meadow on a summer's day.

On the left side of the canvas, a stalwart oak sent its shadow across tousled grass. A young mother sat in the grass, her honey-colored hair curled primly over her temples, a slight smile tilting the corners of her mouth. Her eyes looked toward the unseen artist, while, beside her, two young girls, bedecked in ribbons and heirloom frocks, played in the grass. They seemed to lack nothing.

"This painting is one of a kind," I said to Roy later in the evening, as he refreshed Bill's and my coffee. "What an heirloom! Are these people some of your family members?"

"No," Roy answered. "You'll never believe this, but I bought that for three hundred dollars at an estate sale down the road."

"You're kidding!" I gasped. "It must have cost thousands to commission."

"Those two girls in the picture are the ones who sold it. That's their mother." He pointed to the lovely woman sitting on the grass. "She died, and they didn't care anything about it. Can you imagine?"

I could not. "Was something wrong with her, that they wouldn't want an heirloom like this?"

"No, nothing like that." Roy studied the faces in the picture, as if trying to find clues. "Sad, isn't it?"

We stood silently, contemplating.

Then Bill sighed, "I guess you could say… they didn't get the picture!"

We laughed, but the sorrow lingered.

Was there nothing in the relational bonds of these three people that would impart value to such a spectacular icon? Did this original oil painting, in all its beauty and extravagance, not capture and make visible the hidden connections of blood and lineage? Where were the fierce bonds of birth and breast, of lap and laughter, of time and touch? Did no one consider the gravitas, one hundred, two hundred years hence, when a future father would stand with his child and point to the picture and say, "See, there, Isabella, that beautiful woman, there on the grass beside those two young girls? She is your great-great-great-great-grandmother. It is told of her that she was a woman of....That girl there became....Doesn't she look like...."

Such roots pull a child "down to earth," stabilizing her as she faces the world. The further back the story goes, the deeper the roots, the broader the base, the more grounded the child becomes.

We don't reach back to dig up dirt, though the computer age has made everything accessible; we reach back to see how God used the dirt for growing flowers, for transforming the landscape of our lives. This story-time approach to life is not about making things what they are not. It is about seeing things through the lens of God's purposes.

That was good news for me when I began to sort through the generations of my family. Many episodes in my ancestry are downright degenerate: alcoholism, abuse, violence, murder, cheating, poverty, ignorance, adultery, incest, and brutality. In God's hands, however, the darkness serves as a perfect backdrop to display His transformational and redeeming light. I changed my mind about a lot of things as my children grew and I reexamined my life's chapters. I saw that my story churns with cultural charm, rich as cream. I saw that God plucked my father from the fray, saved him, and sent him to Bible college, unlikely though it was that a rough-ridin', pistol-packin', mountain man would stand behind a pulpit. Daddy could have followed many of his elders into a life of debauchery; instead, he used his watchful eyes and powerful parables to pull iron-jawed cowboys and moonshiners into the Kingdom of God. I began, too, to appreciate my mother's determination that her children would study music. Annie Moses and Leona Harris became sources of inspiration to me—two noble women who died before I was born, never knowing the extent to which God would use them in my life and in the lives of others. I wish they could have known.

Instead of seeing the mountains of my youth as a place of isolation and poverty, I came to see them as a chisel in God's hand, shaping in me a heart of compassion for young people in similar settings. My old fear of being unqualified to access the beautiful things most people enjoyed—my feelings of inferiority arising from a lackluster school and a tiresome yellow bus—burned like dross as God began to show me the thread of gold He was weaving through the burlap canvas of my rugged youth. I saw how He brought Mrs. Johnson, clicking her baton and threatening the Black Ribbon, to give wings to my mother's dreams. I saw how He used the revival meetings at midwestern, corn-patch churches to develop my stage savvy, as my sisters and I harmonized old-time gospel hymns.

As shame melted away, God's blessings bubbled up, and everything became part of His goodness—those crazy dreams, warning me to wait for the man God would bring for me to marry; that otherworldly advice that followed the tiny violinist's performance "When you have a little girl, she should do that." I could see that even the malice of Mrs. Daray and Mr. Director had transmuted into a musically gifted daughter named Annie—and that something wonderful was at work in our move to Nashville on the strength of Bill's job and the hit song, "Make His Praise Glorious." I could see how God was honoring my youthful prayer for help: "Father, if there is a place for me in the world of Christian music, I pray you will take me there."

The greatest gift of my reappraisal of the past, perhaps, was my release from the selfish ambitions tied up with those old feelings of inferiority—the tête-à-tête with the Lord at *Land Between the Lakes*. I broke free, then, to focus on my children's spiritual and musical development. It was a pivotal moment that put our family on course to become leaders in the world of the church and the arts.

Every life has a destiny, a purpose, a thrilling plotline if we will only take the time to trace it. As the story of a life is repainted in salvation's colors, the "sins of the fathers" meet their end and a new generation is released to soar to greater heights with the Lord. I have loved imparting to my children their heritage, by way of fireside chats detailing God's faithfulness through the generations.

Their roots run deep, so that when the skeptic clicks his tongue, wags his finger and asks, "Who do you think you are?" they can respond with complete self-assurance, with steady eyes and undaunted moxie:

"Do you have a minute? I'd love to tell you."

This Is My Song

This is my story, this is my song
Praising my Savior all the day long
"Blessed Assurance" words by Fanny J. Crosby

Like Ol' Faithful, a bubbling, vibrant, life story, a testimony, builds in pressure. It becomes the source of a child's artistry, the spiritual and emotional wellspring from which he will draw words, music, and style. As Mrs. Silberg once told me, "Dear, singing is nothing more than speaking rhythmically on pitch." The watcher who knows God sees His work everywhere and cannot help but sing His praise.

The Hebrew people mastered the craft of the story-song, dancing to the jingle of the tambourine and chanting the mighty deeds of Yahweh. King David's music is the consummate representation of a story giving way to a song. David was a warrior, a poet, and a harpist, highly skilled at setting the work of Yahweh to words and music. Because of Daddy, I have had a crush on David since childhood.

Daddy had an unorthodox take on the legendary king. I'd sit on our orange vinyl love seat, my short legs sticking out into the air, while Daddy worked beside me, polishing his beloved boots, footwear that lasted decades—resoled, reheeled, and bedecked with honorable patches. As he worked, Daddy told stories.

"David was ruddy and handsome," he said. "Don't you believe that baloney about him being a runt. He would-a been young, but he would-a been a man's man too." Daddy buffed the black leather vigorously as he challenged the Sunday school felt-board images. "Think about it. King Saul stood head and shoulders taller than everyone else in his kingdom. In ancient times, the big guys were believed to be the natural leaders, and Saul was the biggest of 'em all." Daddy surveyed the shine, dropped the boot with a thud, and stuck his hand into the other boot. His forearm disappeared behind the high top, as he paused to think.

"Now I want-cha to notice something. David tried on Saul's armor, so it makes sense that he was bigger than everybody else too. David had to have been as tall as Saul or he would-a tried on the armor of somebody shorter. Right?" He swiped up some polish and slathered it into the grooves beside the sole of the boot. "I've heard preachers say that David rejected Saul's armor because it was too big. But that's not right. The Bible says he rejected Saul's armor because he wasn't used to it. That's a whole 'nother matter! David didn't want all that metal weighing him down in battle." Daddy applied the polish with a brisk circular motion, then stopped and looked me straight in the eyes.

"Speed and agility were an important part of his style," Daddy said. "David told Saul that he had killed a lion and a bear with his bare hands. Think about that."

I thought, and my admiration swelled. I loved David, just like I loved this Daddy of mine who cared enough to tell me about him.

Daddy set the second boot on the floor and wiped his hands, waiting for the polish to set. "You gotta remember," he said, "Goliath's deal put Saul's entire kingdom on the line. If Israel's man couldn't whip Goliath, everybody became the slave of the Philistines. Let me tell-ya . . . Saul wouldn't have risked his entire kingdom on a little boy!" He picked up the boot and the buffer brush and began to beat a shine out of the leather. *Swoosh-swoosh, swoosh-swoosh.* "David wore that slingshot like the world's first 357 Magnum." Daddy chuckled. "It was his ace in the hole. He knew the best rocks were smooth and round and came out of water. Five of them. Just one bullet short of a six-shooter." Daddy's dark-blue eyes narrowed, as if he were looking down the barrel and through the sights.

"David had to be really good with that slingshot, because the Bible says the rock didn't just crack Goliath's skull. It went all the way through his skull. That's some kinda speed. And his aim had to be perfect because Goliath wore a helmet." Daddy's eyes widened. "David cut off Goliath's head with Goliath's sword!" He held the polishing brush up high, measuring the imaginary sword. "It would-a been huge. No runt could-a wielded it." Daddy closed up the polish and began to sack up the kit.

"David had the perfect life…playin' the harp and singing songs to his sheep, just before he wrestled a bear and practiced his shootin'." Daddy tugged one boot on, then the next, and pulled his jeans down over the tops, slightly breathless from the tussle. "David's songs wound up bein' more powerful than his sling, 'cause Jesus sang 'em when he was hangin' on the cross." Daddy stood, surveying the shine on his boots. "I've always liked the fact that David didn't draw any lines between manhood and music."

Thud—thud—thud—thud, the boots percussed the hard floor, and my lesson was ended.

Years after Daddy's expository lesson on David, Mama told me about Daddy's hidden musical longings, pounding her chest, as always, and saying, "I've carried a sob right here, that I wasn't able to use my talents to the full. But your daddy was talented too."

I understood. Daddy didn't play an instrument, but when necessary, he would lead the singing in the small mountain churches he served. He could start a hymn in the correct key without the benefit of a piano or guitar. The singings of his youth had implanted music in him. Isolated mountain folk used to gather around a pump organ played by his mother, while candles guttered on small shelves to the right and left of the piano, allowing the singers to read four-part harmony from Stamps-Baxter's shaped-note hymnal.

"I don't know if you know this or not," Mama said, "but every now and then, your daddy used to say to me, 'Sometimes, I think I'm just gonna bust if I don't play an instrument.'" Her eyes saddened, and I felt her "sob right here" in my chest too.

I can only imagine what songs my father might have composed from the wonderful stories—both biblical and personal—housed within the wellspring of his heart. I thought of how Daddy dug through newspaper ads to find used, and sometimes abused, upright pianos for any needy young person who expressed a desire to play. That twelve dollars a month he paid for our gutsy, Acrosonic spinet was blood squeezed from the proverbial turnip; it was the sacrifice of a man who could only wish for an instrument of his own to play.

Daddy loved to point out to me the old house where, in his youth, a travelin' fiddler played "Buttermilk Skies" at a country dance. He told me more than once the story of his childhood friend, Jesse Attaberry, who could *really* play the guitar and traveled to Nashville to break into the music scene. He brought a steady stream of guest performers to our little mountain church at Zafra: Ralph Trotto, the blind guitarist; the Rostvitt Sisters, who were mirror twins, one played her ukulele right-handed, the other played her ukulele left-handed; Jim and Jody Pearson, who played the washtub and yodeled, respectively; male quartets like The Gospel Lads; and family acts, like the George Melton Family Singers. Daddy's Zafra concerts were a rollicking good time.

Mr. and Mrs. Elder, my teachers in first grade, added their line-up to Daddy's roster. They had no funding for music, yet they didn't let that stop them. Instead they marched us into the larger of the two rooms of our little rock schoolhouse and led us to sing. All eight grades raised their voices together, and the rafters rang, whether harmoniously or not. Mr. and Mrs. Elder surely didn't know all the theories, but here's what was happening to their pupils:

When we sing, melody, pitch, intervals, harmony, and rhythm combine to demand coordinated, simultaneous action from multiple parts of the brain. We also optimize retention of a text. This is especially true when a song is learned before that magical age of twelve. God has set up our brains so that the information learned by singing is stored in the deepest, most protected reserves of memory. Even the ravages of disease and age cannot fully dismantle this reservoir. A victim of Alzheimer's may not be able to tell you her name, but she can still sing, *Jesus loves me this I know for the Bible tells me so.*

American thinking has relegated the act of singing to the lucky ones who happen to be born with vocal talent or who manage to acquire a record deal and a savvy producer to fix the foibles. But the concept that singing should be practiced only by the talented, skilled, or professional singer is considered strange in many countries. In his book *Your Brain on Music*, Daniel J. Levitin writes of his friend Jim, who, for his doctoral degree, did fieldwork in Lesotho, where the

Sotho villagers asked him to sing with them. When Jim declined, saying he didn't sing, they just stared. "'What do you mean you don't sing?! You talk!'.... It was as odd to them," Jim recalled, "as if I'd told them that I couldn't walk or dance, even though I have both my legs.'"

We are not required to sing skillfully—although we are required to "play skillfully"—but we are required to sing! Singing is free. Singing is easy. Singing is powerful. Singing is therapeutic. And biblically speaking, singing is not optional.

In our early years in Waco, Texas, Bill and I became members at Highland Baptist Church solely because of the power of the Sunday night song service. The church packed 'em in, young and old, rich and poor, happy and sad. Body bubbles burst as members made room for more, complying with the suggestion to "scoot toward the center and leave room at the aisle." The Spirit hovered, as people laughed and chatted expectantly.

A typical service unfolded with a small group of leaders gathered 'round a single microphone, and musicians stationed at their instruments. Bill, sitting at the piano, began to play. The music minister made himself as insignificant as possible, desiring to stay out of the way as he led. Altogether, the leaders acted as servants, assisting but not dominating or calling attention to themselves. Bill followed the signals from the music minister's hand, and he followed the rise and fall of the Spirit's prodding as he wove seamlessly from song to song. He wanted his keyboard offering, like a movie score, to undergird the worshiper's experience without being obtrusive.

Camille, Robin, and Gretchen sing with all their might!

People lifted their faces to sing with their "stomach voices," as Rosemary, my plucky ten-year-old friend, described it. The praise bellowed from pure hearts and unpolluted lungs, rising to adore the Lord. The overtone series soaked the semicircular room with His palpable presence.

Sometimes we finished a song with such momentum that we couldn't stop and would plunge into improvisational singing, an indescribable beauty of sound, nearly a thousand voices that magically fit together, as only a supernatural presence could inspire.

During the latter years of the 1970s, Daddy directed a men's gathering called the "Kiamichi Men's Clinic." As many as twelve thousand participants from across America dodged potholes and cow pies to find the isolated Choctaw village of Honobia (pronounced "Hoe-nubby"). They pounded down tent stakes, propped up lawn chairs, popped open soda cans, and began the fun. In a rash departure from the norm of the times, anyone caught shaving or wearing a tie paid a fine of five dollars. The men loved the back-to-earthiness. Inflating fanny cushions, they padded and perched on the primitive pews that spilled out from under an open-air "steel tent." A long lineup of masterly speakers—governors, country music stars, comedians, and such radio broadcasters as Paul Harvey—mixed with top-of-the-line preachers. The speakers lit political fuses with biblical fire, and Daddy topped them all. The men took to their feet as he mounted the stage, pounding their palms together and roaring. They loved his colorful colloquialisms and outspoken opinions.

But the speakers couldn't hope to compete with the singing. They rode on the coattails of the song service, ten thousand male voices thundering hymn after hymn. All those men, unified to sing themselves hoarse, emitted a joyful roar that couldn't help but "slip the surly bonds of earth."

Nobody wondered about the science. Nobody detailed the chemical recipe that was being stirred up at the Kiamichi Men's Clinic. But the act of singing together spilled a boatload of oxytocin into every man's bloodstream and made the men awash with generosity, good will, and brotherly love. The air grew thick with community, and the laughter surged, as each man slapped his buddy on the back or fumbled to find the next hymn.

The concluding comments commonly cinched it with something like, "The preachin' was powerful. Sure was. But the singing! Oh, Lord . . . !" Tears welled up and rolled down to hit the scruffy beards of the commenters. "The singin' has changed me forever."

Psalm 22:3 (KJV) tells us: "But thou art holy, O thou that inhabitest the praises of Israel." The ancient word on which *inhabitest* is based literally means to "sit." Some translations use the word *enthrone*. The picture is that of our praises moving out into the atmosphere to erect a place, a spiritual throne, from which God, our King, may preside over society. Our "song of praise" flows out into the air to do the job. It's easy and it's powerful to build a musical praise-throne when we drop preconceived notions about singing. A joyful noise will do. Our family song-fests came daily, planned and unplanned. We didn't fuss about accuracy or sound, because children absolutely love to sing and to be sung to and the act of singing is pure power.

So let 'er rip! Sing with all your heart to the Lord. It jump-starts an early morning prayer-gathering and closes out the day with a hearty "Amen!"

Teaching Greatness

I have seen the moment of my greatness flicker,
And I have seen the eternal Footman hold my coat, and snicker,
And in short, I was afraid.

FROM *The Love Song of J. Alfred Prufrock* BY T. S. Eliot

It wasn't until Annie was eleven, and participating in an important master class, that I learned the concept of the Significant Other. I didn't go to the event looking for revelations on such a grand scale, I was scribbling notes on technique, as I always do during such lessons.

"What creates energy in music?" the instructor asked.

The performer lowered his violin, looked upward, and pursed his lips, grappling with the question. Following his lead, I raised my eyes to the large chrome sound-reflectors hanging like massive rearview mirrors above the stage of the Blair Recital Hall at Vanderbilt University. Potential answers fluttered in my mind, but the concept of "creating energy" eluded me too.

A few nervous coughs erupted as the audience anticipated an answer.

From her wheelchair onstage, the guest instructor, Dorothy DeLay, of the Juilliard School, leaned toward the performer and repeated her question. "What are the functions of music that create energy?"

The performer's face contorted, but he found no answer.

Mrs. DeLay waited, smiling patiently. She was a heavy woman with kind, intelligent features that suggested former physical beauty. "We consider the Mendelssohn Violin Concerto to be the most difficult to perform successfully," she said. "The Tchaikovsky, the Brahms, many are more technically challenging. But the Mendelssohn is a favorite concerto. It's requested for professional performance more than any other concerto, and it's extremely beautiful if properly paced. However, if the pacing is not purposefully executed, your audience may go to sleep."

The audience shuffled. The performer adopted a sheepish expression, cocking his curly head to one side. He got it; he had just turned the first movement of the piece into a snoozer.

"A change of tempo can create energy." Mrs. DeLay paused, then smiled encouragingly. "Pick up the pace, the energy will increase. Right?"

The performer nodded.

"What else?" she asked.

"A key change?" the performer offered, thrilled to have thought of something.

"Yes." Mrs. DeLay raised her eyebrows. "Very good. A modulation can certainly refresh the energy, as can any harmonic progression that rises toward a climax." She gestured toward the audience. "Anything else?" No one ventured a guess. "Well…how about a crescendo? Growing louder heightens energy. But if you really want to deliver, then increase both volume and tempo. This doubles the impact."

I scribbled furiously in my notebook. After years of dedication to practice, Annie was an eager and skilled eleven-year-old violinist; she had opened this show with the first movement of Mozart's Concerto no. 3 in G Major. It was her first master class with this well-known Juilliard instructor, but she was used to the rigors of such performances and was excited to play for a famous teacher from a famous school. She had sailed through her piece, then she'd come to sit in the audience with Bill and me. She listened along as Mrs. DeLay critiqued the other performers.

"Or how about a rallentando coupled with a crescendo and a descending bass line? This can create enormous energy." Mrs. DeLay began to sing, drumming on the table beside her wheelchair.

The performer shifted his bow to his left hand and plunged his right hand into his pocket diffidently.

"As the performer, you must study the score to find the patterns that create energy. It's called pacing, and it's vital to a successful performance of any piece, but the Mendelssohn in particular."

I soaked in Mrs. DeLay's words, thrilled to hear this nebulous concept so definitively articulated. "Her teaching is not the same ol' same ol', that's for sure!" I whispered to Bill.

At the end of the class, when a microphone was placed in the aisle and audience members were invited to ask questions, I was one of the first in line. "Mrs. DeLay, you have taught many of today's greatest child prodigies," I said. "What is the primary factor that contributed to their success, especially at an early age?"

"The Significant Other!" Mrs. DeLay leaned forward and spoke without hesitation. "Every child must have the support and guidance of at least one individual who does whatever it takes, really invests herself to see to it that the child has everything he needs for success. For example, Itzhak Perlman's mother brought him all the way from Israel to America to study at Juilliard." Mrs. DeLay smiled, remembering. "Itzak could speak very little English, so when a classmate invited him to a picnic, he didn't know what to say. He came into my studio, told me about the invitation, and asked if I thought he should go. I told him, 'Of course you should go. You will enjoy it very much.' Then he did the funniest thing, he leaned toward me and whispered, 'Mrs. DeLay, what is a picnic?'"

We laughed, enjoying an inside peek at the beloved performer's life. So that's what God did in that ol' barn at Land Between the Lakes, I mused, returning to my seat. He made me a Significant Other!

"I guess it's better than being an Insignificant Other," Bill said.

I laughed, feeling warm and gratified. I was a Significant Other and Bill was my equipper: He made the money and I put in the time. Watching our daughter play, poised and focused, brought us ultimate joy that day at Vanderbilt. I knew the Lord was pleased, and I thanked Him again for redirecting me to capture the budding season of my children's lives.

Dorothy DeLay has since passed away. But on that bright winter day, she was a legend in the world of violin playing. Her profile so dominated the landscape that other violin teachers derided her as overadulated and looked for opportunities to take her, and her students, down a peg. No matter. For decades, Mrs. DeLay, and the "DeLay-Galamian Technique" of violin pedagogy, dominated the market share of concert stages throughout the world. She was the principal instructor of the most celebrated violinists of our time: Itzhak Perlman, Gil Shaham, Midori, Sarah Chang, Nadja Salerno-Sonnenberg. Even today, the performers that command the big bucks and have the mastery to take their listeners on a musical magic carpet ride are her educational offspring. They are adept at reaching beyond the obvious—the notes-on-a-page, the loud, and the soft—to delve into the artistic nuances of a score and showcase not only the intentions of the composer but also their own, singular spirit.

In Mrs. DeLay there was none of the haughty, highbrow conduct of many instructors. Her old-fashioned good manners were refreshing. She relished time spent with her students. Like Inez Silberg, my voice teacher at OCU, the passage of time meant nothing to Mrs. DeLay; she taught until the lesson was learned. The students outside her door simply had to be patient; they referred to it as being "Delayed."

By the time I had children, I had cultivated considerable sagacity with respect to teachers. I had survived Mrs. Johnson's Black Ribbon, Dr. Berg's airy reverie, Mrs. Daray's resentment, and Mrs. Silberg's rescue. I had run the gamut of teacher eccentricities. Or so I supposed. The journey with my children's teachers—some of the world's most exceptional pedagogues—exposed me to all manner of new character quirks, from the Beauty to the Beast.

Annie's first teacher was a gift from God. Thanks to "Make His Praise Glorious"—which necessitated our move to Nashville—we had access to Miss Rogers, who preached the gospel of perfect positions. We obeyed her implicitly. In a world where lackluster teachers abound, God had provided us with one who cared enough to insist that we get it right. She understood the vital role of the Significant Other—me—and we became a team. She kept the technique building, precept upon precept, and I took her plans home and implemented them. Sloppy was not an option. From our beginnings with Miss Rogers, an unimpeded path opened in front of Annie and her siblings. Thanks to our teamwork, Annie could learn increasingly difficult repertoire without hitting the technical blockades caused by incorrect fundamental form or an inability to focus.

Very few children receive the devoted nurturing of a synchronized parent-teacher team. It's not uncommon that students, after years of study, still cannot play well the most remedial repertoire. They never master proper basic technique and positions, so they hit a wall when their repertoire becomes more demanding, and they don't know how to get past it. They want to play well, but the combination of their teacher's ignorance of the fundamentals, and their parents' ignorance of their vital role, holds little potential for success. An age-skill appropriate, organized, incremental methodology, implemented by a synchronized parent-teacher team, is crucial to a child's musical education.

The primary role of a teacher is that of diagnostician. When the skills accumulated begin to break down in the context of increasingly difficult repertoire, the teacher pinpoints the areas of dysfunction and offers remedies. The Significant Other and the child, in their work together as disciple and disciple-maker, focus on these areas of dysfunction and apply the remedies.

This musical exercise holds a powerful underlying benefit that translates into all other areas of life. I once heard Stephen Clapp, instructor of violin and former Dean of Juilliard, put it this way, when talking about the importance of bow control: "The violinist's bow is like life; it wants to go wrong and you must correct it." The disciplines of music are a microcosm of the disciplines of life. Parents who equip their children with the best teachers, instruments, and opportunities are stating, beyond words, that they believe their children capable of refining both their bow and their behavior, and thus life.

Every child carries within himself a voice that cries, "Help me find my greatness!" The high expectations implicit in a teacher's demand for excellence, and the help issued by a hands-on Significant Other, answer that cry. The child learns, "I am valuable. I am capable. Greatness is expected of me, and I am not alone in achieving it."

Once, while waiting in line at FedEx, I overheard a young mother with two children in tow speaking to the older woman in front of her in line. They were intrigued to learn that they lived just one subdivision's distance from each other.

"What do you do?" the younger asked the older.

"Oh, I mostly just stay home," the older replied with a shrug. "I teach a little piano on the side."

"How convenient! I've been looking for a piano teacher for my daughter. Do you have any openings?"

"Of course!" The older woman waved her hand. "I've got lots of time. Just bring 'er over."

Though perhaps unwittingly, the mother was acting on an assumption that all piano teachers are the same, and the subconscious expectation that her daughter's artistic potential was unworthy of research, travel, time, or money. I have spoken with parents who expressed a desire for their "talented" child to do great things, but they didn't have a vision that would inspire them to travel any distance or allocate much money for top-of-the-line teachers or instruments.

Time and money spent are indicators of great expectations.

Not only parents, but teachers too can be guilty of projecting low expectations. Teachers may relegate students to the confines of a "method," feeling secure that they are only required to teach a few pieces from a few books. Methodologies such as the Suzuki System are well planned skill-builders for very young children, but they can become limiting if the teacher is cookie-cutter in her approach and refuses to analyze each child's individual needs and natural abilities. A teacher must be visionary, broad-minded, and flexible, able to customize and fast-track methods when the gifts of an extraordinary child demand it.

Take Miss G., for example. Wave a young Mozart under her nose, and she would not catch a whiff of genius. Her senses were too sluggish in the stale context of her "method" to accommodate a potential prodigy's rush to greatness. I once saw the results when a seven-year-old girl I knew, who exhibited extraordinary natural ability, was assigned to Miss G.'s studio. Like a thoroughbred locked behind a plow, she strained against the snail-paced drudgery. It was hard to watch as she plodded through the teacher's "system." Greatness was not anticipated, so greatness was not accommodated. How different the trajectory of the child's life might have been had her mother awakened to her daughter's potential for artistic greatness and, predicated on that belief, been willing to engage a knowledgeable diagnostician, adjusting her pocketbook and her schedule to the time and money required.

At the age of eleven, Annie joined her second teacher, Connie Heard. Miss Rogers and Mrs. Heard often worked in harmony, like a well-oiled relay team, handing off students when appropriate in the timeline of a child's development. As the Significant Other, it was my job to know when Annie's development warranted a change of teacher; in this case, Miss Rogers and I both recognized it was time.

Warm and congenial, Mrs. Heard agreed to give Annie two lessons a week. In the first, they would study solo Bach, sonatas, showpieces, and technique. In the second, they would work on a major concerto. Skill is cultivated quickly when a student works through études and technical exercises at a brisk clip, while spending more time on longer, challenging pieces. At first, Mrs. Heard was reluctant for Annie to participate in competitions, because she didn't want to impede her movement through repertoire. However, the setup of two lessons a week assuaged her fears and set us on our way. Mrs. Heard was a connected teacher, and connectedness counts. A connected teacher extends her students' scope of awareness, offering—to those who work smart to be ready—a host of adjudications, competitions, and performance opportunities.

During the first summer of Annie's studies with Mrs. Heard, before she would begin the sixth grade level in her academics, I took her to Sound Encounters, a string camp in Ottawa, Kansas. We enjoyed our road trip, driving through rural America while listening to Pinchas Zukerkman play the Mendelssohn Violin Concerto, a piece she had begun to study. The two-week event was directed by violinist and teacher Alice Joy Lewis and her son, Brian. Annie had met Brian the prior summer at a Suzuki camp in Ithaca, New York. An award winning, concertizing violinist and a student at Juilliard, Brian brought a healthy shot of good humor to playing the violin, cultivating a festive atmosphere while homing in on the importance of accuracy and beautiful sound. When I had shared our plans for summer study with Mrs. Heard, she was especially thrilled that Stephen Clapp, her former teacher, was to be a guest clinician at camp and that Annie would be playing for him.

By the end of the camp, I could see that Mr. Clapp was a masterly teacher who articulated with great insight and precision the science behind the forms and positions used in playing the violin. His teaching offered clearheaded explanations of basic technique, form, and function. *This pedagogical approach should be easily available to everyone,* I thought. If the floundering violinists across the world could receive just a few hours of this man's teaching, their playing would be transformed. Imagine antibiotics being discovered, but only Alexander Fleming and his family being privy to the find. That's how I felt about Mr. Clapp's pedagogical light, hidden under a bushel, unavailable to thousands of students. How blessed we were that Annie's teachers shared an illustrious pedigree: Miss Rogers, Mrs. Heard, Brian Lewis, and Mr. Clapp all came from the studio of…Dorothy DeLay. Annie was a partaker of her bountiful legacy even before she'd met her.

That fall, Annie won the Nashville Youth Symphony's Concerto Competition, playing Mozart. She won again the following year, playing the Mendelssohn Violin Concerto, the one we would watch Mrs. DeLay teach on stage at Vanderbilt.

Annie was forced to skip the next year's competition with the Nashville Youth Symphony because the Symphony's board enacted a new rule forbidding any winning student to participate in the competition for two consecutive years. As a result, Bill and I began to seek further opportunities for her. She needed exposure to the greater world of violin playing, to rub shoulders with peers who were equally devoted, to sit under the baton of many conductors in a variety of orchestral settings. Just as dry ground compels a tree's roots to crawl outward as they search for sustenance, I found myself scanning the horizon for a musical watering hole. Bill and I began to take Annie on weekends to the Cincinnati Conservatory to participate in the Starling Program for precollege students. It was a four-hour drive each way but well worth the time and money, as the influence expanded our family's musical perspective, building connections that would eventually chart a path to Juilliard.

The Starling Program was designed specifically for students who aspire to a musical career. Kurt Sassmannshaus, the director, was known for carving out performance opportunities for worthy soloists and crafting around-the-world excursions for his student orchestra. Expectations ran high, and I knew that Annie would benefit from the experiences. However, I didn't want to uproot her from her studies in Nashville. She was still thriving in many ways with Mrs. Heard. Cautiously, I probed the possibility of Mrs. Heard and Mr. Sassmannshaus teaching her in tandem, but high-powered teachers are notoriously territorial and possessive. To my joy, both agreed. My job as Annie's practice coach and note-taker had been lessening for the past two years, allowing me more time to focus on my younger children's progress. Seven-year-old Benjamin was motoring along fine on his cello under the guidance of Blair Suzuki teacher Ann Williams. But I was concerned about Alex. He practiced well but, at ten years old, still struggled in fine motor skills and advanced techniques. Viola teachers were scarce, especially for young learners, and they tended to be abstract in their teaching style: "Play the sunset, dear, just play the sunset," or, "What color is this section? Pink? Yellow?" Stuff-and-nonsense to a pubescent boy.

As Alex's skill plateaued, I soothed myself with the thought that he would probably pursue a profession other than music. I loved this little man with the bowl haircut and the sweet, freckled face. He was plump, talkative, and chipper and, as children do at that age, he was maturing fast. Even though I accepted that he might choose a different path than music, I began to pray directly for a musical breakthrough.

That's when God made a big move on the chessboard.

By the end of Annie's first year in the hub of the Cincinnati Conservatory, I became watchful on behalf of Alex, seeking opportunities for him that could run alongside hers. I spoke to Mr. Sassmannshaus about our dilemma. "We have a wonderful viola department here, led by Catherine Carroll and Masao Kawasaki," he said, in his graceful German accent. "They also teach viola during the summer at the Aspen Summer Music Festival. Will you be going there again this year?"

"We can try," I said.

"Perhaps Alex could begin taking lessons with Dr. Carroll there. He would love her. Try to come for the whole nine weeks. It is the best."

Faculty from both Juilliard and the Cincinnati Conservatory teach at the Aspen Summer Musical Festival, a program that contains multiple orchestras, chamber groups, and big-name performers. Aspen, Colorado, is a remarkable setting, balmy and bucolic in the summertime, with robust rivers, panoramic mountains, and wee, wood-framed houses that sell for a mere two million dollars! Financing nine-weeks of musical studies in Aspen for two children would be no easy task.

Annie had attended the shorter, five-week program the year before, when she was twelve. I had packed her and her two little sisters, Camille, who had just turned five, and Gretchen, who was almost three, into the minivan for the long drive to Colorado. We stopped in Oklahoma to pick up Grandma Jane, who would serve as assistant cook, nanny, and chauffeur. The feminine fellowship of that exceptional summer still shines like a star in the heaven of my memory.

The festival overflowed with amazing performances. One of our favorite venues, and the most affordable, was the giant, open-air tent. It cost a pretty penny to sit inside the tent and watch the shows, but it was free if you were willing to bring a quilt and a picnic basket, perch on the hypergreen lawn, and watch from outside. The lawn must have been a colorful sight from a bird's-eye-view, a patchwork of patchworks, as lovers, families, children, dogs, bikers, and rich bourgeois nibbled and sipped everything from caviar to fried chicken and from champagne to lemonade. Some of classical music's most admired artists came to display their virtuosity: Gil Shaham, Sarah Chang, Lang Lang, the Emerson Quartet, Emmanuel Ax, and Joshua Bell, to name a few.

Bill, Alex, Benjamin, and Grandpa joined us during the last two weeks, giving our extended family the opportunity to go whitewater rafting on the Colorado River and to take a bike trip on the trail that runs along the river. The excitement peaked when Grandma Jane lost her glasses in the whitewater and nearly fell in trying to save them. We squeezed in a couple of viola lessons for Alex, from a master's student who was studying at Aspen. The lack of substance in those lessons only intensified my urge to upgrade Alex's musical studies and interactions. Mr. Sassmannshaus' suggestion resonated. We had to make it work again this summer: two children—nine weeks.

"Why is it that prime educational opportunities are located where only the wealthy can afford to go?" I asked Bill.

"Them that's got are them that gets," he sang, harkening back to Ray Charles.
"Well, it's cruel," I complained.

I took action to see how God would provide for this vision He had laid before
us. Perhaps we could rent a room from a local church or church member. How
about tent camping through the summer? My Eagle Scout husband built expert
campfires and was always prepared! Showers might be rare and cold, but we could
afford deodorant. I called private and public campgrounds, willing to move our
tent-site each time the eight-day limits expired. "Any more time ruins the grass,"
an apologetic camp director explained.

For weeks, I turned over stones, until, one day, my search was answered in
a convergence of three heavenly blessings. First, a new company hired Bill to
put together a huge project. Second, we received healthy scholarships from the
Festival. Third, I discovered Snowmass, a skiing community eight miles outside
Aspen, where prices dropped from hilarious to merely humorous. The apartment,
circa 1968, included a fully functioning kitchen and beds for eight in one big
room plus a loft. With these three blessings in our pocket, Aspen became a great
summer option for us. We could house our family as a group and eat as we would
at home, a much cheaper scenario than paying the individual room and board
prices required by other venues. We would make it our summer home for the
next five years.

Alex's music was going down for the last time, when Dr. Catherine Carroll
of the Cincinnati Conservatory dove into his viola-playing pool to drag him to
safety and resuscitate him. She stood tall and pencil slim with a shapely smile
and even shapelier legs. Alex, still rather short and tubby, gazed upward with
adoration, as she stirred up recipes for success like a master chef, doling out sweet
teaspoons and tablespoons of musicality. At the first lesson, she pulled out a stack
of loose-leaf pages of handwritten and photocopied manuscript, chose a page, put
it on the stand and said, "Okay, Alex, this is your sounding-point exercise. Do
this five minutes in every practice session." Alex nodded, wagging like a puppy
in love. It was as though she had said, "This is chocolate ice-cream, Alex. Eat this
three times a day." He fell more deeply under her spell with each new technique
she demonstrated.

Sounding points—where the bow engages the string—were only the beginning. Page after page of a detailed, micromanaged regimen of viola practice emerged: left hand dexterity, articulation, intonation, scales, arpeggios, vibrato, études, repertoire, bow pressure, and speed. A face can launch a thousand ships, and the kind smile on Dr. Carroll's heart-shaped face, coupled with an impeccable protocol, launched a chubby, eleven-year-old boy into musical greatness. Failure was unimaginable, for to fail would be to disappoint the beloved. What was more, Dr. Carroll believed in him, and he knew it. Teaching Alex a stringed instrument had been difficult for his earlier teachers. His thinking processes were dominated by the left hemisphere of the brain, and he was a visual learner. But as Dr. Carroll's protocol worked its magic, the cerebral coordination that the study of music stimulates began to emerge. Dr. Carroll's deep brown eyes focused, laserlike, analyzing and correcting, until the lesson was learned. Alex began to fly, to soar. I stood in the shadows and watched, astonished at the rapid ascent of his skill. Alex loved his lessons. He loved his viola. He loved his teacher.

Dr. Carroll began playing the viola the year of her seventeenth birthday. Six inches of growth had thrown a kink into her plans to be a gymnast, rendering her too tall for tumbling, beams, and bars. So she'd set out on a quest for a new profession. Viola? How many beautiful, seventeen-year-old women come up with that? Maybe God was planning ahead, setting up answers to my prayers for Alex. In any case, while I was finishing my vocal studies and starting a family, this logical lady was looking for places of opportunity, and good viola players were rare. She approached Masao Kawasaki, a master teacher, and, although she was old for a beginner, he agreed to take her as a student. Upon her graduation, they continued to work together as a teaching team at the Conservatory. The competitive bent she had cultivated in gymnastics made her a voracious practicer and, ultimately, a top-tier player.

I still urge parents to start their children's musical education early. But today, when older children or adults ask if it's too late for them to learn a stringed instrument, I think of Cathy Carroll's story and tell them, flat out, "No. Not at all!"

Soon after Alex began studying with Dr. Carroll, she scheduled his first lesson with "Kawasaki," as she called him. The prospect worried me. Mr. Kawasaki's weekly teaching schedule was staggering: professor of violin in both the collegiate and precollege divisions of Juilliard and professor of viola at the Cincinnati Conservatory, where he worked with Dr. Carroll. Mr. Kawasaki flew back and forth between the two cities weekly, which was good news for prospective students from both areas. But the scuttlebutt had warned me of his stoic manner. Dr. Carroll told Alex, "Some students want to cry in their lessons with him. But don't worry, he just seems scary. You'll learn his mannerisms, and his teaching is world-class."

"We're not paying him to be your best friend," I told Alex after the lesson, underscoring Dr. Carroll's point. "We're paying him to make you the best string player you can be." This posture had served us well. Many of the best teachers are quirky, analytical, critical, ultracreative personalities. Some hail from foreign countries, creating a language and culture gap that will only be bridged slowly. Cultivating a student-teacher relationship based on mutual merit leads eventually to an appropriate friendship. Insisting that a teacher be a buddy from the beginning, on the other hand, can be a recipe for failure.

I followed Alex into Mr. Kawasaki's studio, clutching my notebook. Alex stood woodenly, freckles popped, nerves draining the color from his face, as Mr. Kawasaki explained the process of up-bow staccato.

"In up-bow staccato, you must press with fust feen-gah." Mr. Kawasaki held his violin and bow low to demonstrate at eye level with Alex. Instead of looking at the illustration, Alex studied Mr. Kawasaki's face. "No. Look here." Mr. Kawasaki gestured toward his instrument and played again. Tut-tut-tut-tut-tut! The sound was clipped and measured, like a machine gun.

"Now...you try."

Like a zombie on sleep-aids, Alex lifted his bow but lost his hold and dropped it, clattering, to the floor. Mr. Kawasaki remained stoic, waiting for him to reconstruct. "For up-bow staccato, you must press with fust feen-gah." He demonstrated again: *Tut-tut-tut-tut-tut.* Alex moved like a stroke victim: *Pfft-pfft-pfft.* Mr. Kawasaki turned to face the door. He closed his eyes. "Look here," he said, pointing to the focal point where the bow met the string. "You must press with fust feen-gah." Alex rocked on his heels. *He's about to faint!* I thought. *Pfft-pfft-pfft.* Mr. Kawasaki stepped toward the door as if contemplating escape. Then he stopped, sighed deeply, returned to Alex, put his hand over Alex's hand, and did the up-bow staccato for him, allowing Alex to feel the motion. *Tut…tut…tut.. .tut…tut.* Mr. Kawasaki had digressed from telling to demonstrating, to telling while demonstrating in closer proximity, to taking Alex's hand and doing it with him—the most rudimentary form of imparting technique.

Alex and I left the studio exhausted. Mr. Kawasaki was not sold on Alex's greatness. Not yet, anyway. Dr. Carroll ignored the episode, working like an angel of inspiration. She and Alex moved forward, mastering technique and repertoire. As Alex progressed, Dr. Carroll began to use words to project a vision of him gaining success. "Alex, do you know the Bartók Viola Concerto? You're going to love playing that piece, I just know it. Most students don't play it until they're in college, but I'll bet you'll be playing it before high school." Her easy manner was aided and abetted by the steel in her work ethic. What she really meant was, You can do anything you want to with this instrument. And you'll be great, too, because I'm here to help you.

Dr. Carroll's faith transformed my son's life. I still nurture the mental image of them together, Alex's round, freckled face staring up in adoration.

While Dr. Carroll worked with him weekly, the stoic Mr. Kawasaki saw him monthly.

There is a great difference between teachers like the Kawasaki-Carroll team and a teacher like I had in Mrs. Daray. The first are professional and intent on creating truly great players. For every problem, they find an answer. The second are personal, pointing the finger, offering no remedy, and implying that the student is simply inferior. Most teachers fall somewhere in between, not genius, but not cruel either. Finding a genius is always worth the effort.

As Alex progressed, Mr. Kawasaki came around to Dr. Carroll's way of thinking, saying, "Cathy, you were right about Al-eex. He will make exceptional play-uh."

But Mr. Kawasaki never falsely praised Alex. Dry and persistent, he always told the truth. "Al-eex, you play off-pitch about seventy-five pa-cent of time!" he said, in one of their earliest lessons. "You must play on-pitch ninety-five pa-cent of time."

The truth is beautiful. The truth will set a student free to clear out impediments.

It didn't take long to understand why Mr. Kawasaki is one of the highest-paid violin and viola teachers in the world: His diagnostic skill works marvels. Many times, Alex would enter his studio, unable to play a difficult passage. By the time the lesson concluded, the problem had been identified and the remedy received, and Alex was well on his way to executing the passage. No abstract concepts like "play the sunset" for Mr. Kawasaki. His teaching stocked a player's artistic toolbox with an array of high-quality, concrete skills for extraordinary music-making.

A truthful teacher analyzes a student's playing, diagnoses the ills, and prescribes the right medicine. I backed Mr. Kawasaki, making sure Alex understood that a good teacher won't dish out empty praise or intentionally overlook problems to coddle a child's ego. Such falsehoods only create a future stumbling block.

Mr. Kawasaki and Dr. Carroll were inspirational teachers, the kind who stand arm in arm beside their students; who keenly articulate the refined science and technique of the instrument; who refuse to settle for the inept and inferior; who cast a big vision and provide exciting performance opportunities; who understand the inner workings of rhythm, beauty, and grace; who reject jealousy and hype. Such teachers should be the stars of any culture.

Find them. Pay them. Stand beside them. You will not be sorry.

The Extra (Ordinary) Mile

I have promises to keep
And miles to go before I sleep
And miles to go before I sleep

FROM "STOPPING BY WOODS ON A SNOWY EVENING" BY ROBERT FROST

As co-winner of the Blount Concerto Competition in Montgomery, Alabama, Annie received a scholarship to a two-week chamber-music camp at Tanglewood, home of Boston University's summer-music enterprises. Our sixth and final baby, Jeremiah, precluded me from going along, so Grandmother Jane accompanied Annie. At the conclusion of the camp, I packed up Jeremiah and flew to Tanglewood to join them for a drive down to Manhattan and a tour of the Juilliard School. For more than twenty years, the world-renowned conservatory had hovered in my thinking, impenetrable by sheer reputation. It was housed in the high and mighty Lincoln Center, home to the Metropolitan Opera, the New York City Ballet, and the New York Philharmonic Orchestra. As far as gaining admittance, it was listed as the second most difficult college in the United States. I have learned, however, that walking through a place, feeling it out and praying it in, deflates the hype and places it within my vision and, thus, my grasp. For many people, physical contact—not Internet research or gossip—makes fears dissolve and dreams come true. My children needed these doors to open.

As we entered Manhattan, God affirmed His presence and His provision so dramatically that I think of the episode as one of my life's miracles. Driving into the city was nearly the death of us. We didn't know where we were going, and other drivers were not sympathetic toward Grandmother Jane's rural-mountain-road driving style. Cars blazed by, blasting their horns, whipping around us in an attempt to avoid a collision, as she braked hard on the freeway to inquire of us, "Is this the right exit?"

"Drive on, Mama!" I yelled, "or we'll all be killed."

We flailed around north of the city, until I spotted a sign for Broadway. "This is the street Juilliard is on," I said. "Let's see…we're at about the 180th block, so let's just stay on it until we get to 66th. That's around 120 blocks; it shouldn't take long."

We could have walked the distance faster. The traffic burped and wheezed, crabbing at us as Mama eased her Buick through the messy masses. Pedestrians darted like minnows.

"This is actually a foreign country, you know," Mama said, her knuckles white on the wheel. "They may not admit it, but it's true!"

"I believe this is Harlem," I said, looking at the map. "I wonder where folks around here buy diapers. This baby is wearing his last one, and it's sagging with wealth."

"Where do they buy food, for that matter? I don't even see a grocery store," Mama said.

I watched the storefronts flap by, seeing nothing I recognized, and certainly no place that would sell diapers. Dusk rolled in, and we were skittish. I bowed my head and prayed a simple prayer, "Lord, keep us safe. And please provide some diapers."

I recalled the words Bill had left me with: "'Don't spend money! Things are really tight, right now.'"

A money crunch in Manhattan? Bad timing.

"Lord, show us Your provision," I added.

We eventually found our hotel, a few blocks from the school. I was used to Holiday Inn-styled edifices surrounded by generous parking lots and beautiful landscaping. This hotel, fed by a single door, seemed to suck in its stomach and squeeze into the slender space between adjoining, equally skinny, storefronts. Mama pulled curbside, and I got out of the car, gingerly holding Jeremiah in his dirty diaper. My mind searched but came up empty. Manhattan and diapers: unlikely partners. What to do?

As I shut the car door, something moved in my peripheral vision: a young woman approached. "Excuse me," she said, "would you happen to have need of these?" I stared in astonishment as she held out a package of diapers, the right size and a top brand.

"Thank you!" was all I could mumble.

She looked a bit embarrassed, "My cat grew ill, and needed them at the end. I only used a couple."

What were the odds? I was supremely grateful for the diapers and the kind stranger but more grateful for the miraculous message the diapers represented: God was with us. He would provide for us in our mission to "Play Skillfully" and "Make His Praise Glorious."

The next summer, after the extraordinary teaching of Dr. Carroll and Mr. Kawasaki had begun to pay off, Alex won the position of principal violist with the Disney Young Musicians Symphony Orchestra, a select group of very young players who rehearsed for two weeks, then filmed a television special of Disney music. Annie went without him to Aspen, then he joined her there, after the conclusion of the Disney event. That fall she began flying to New York to continue her studies with Mr. Kawasaki. Bill, meanwhile, drove Alex to Cincinnati to study viola with both Mr. Kawasaki and Dr. Carroll.

"This is like musical cities!" Bill said. "Annie is only fifteen, and New York isn't Grandma Jane's house, you know." It scared him that Annie's planes kept getting grounded overnight, forcing her to stay in a hotel by herself. Annie and Alex both studied with Mr. Kawasaki. Wouldn't it be a lot easier if she could take a violin lesson right after Alex's viola lesson in Cincinnati? Then we could all drive home together.

The Conservatory didn't work that way, though: Mr. Kawasaki's Cincinnati studio was limited to viola. She had to travel to Manhattan to take a violin lesson with him.

It was Annie's participation in the Kingsville Concerto Competition, in Kingsville, Texas, that brought our crazy travels to a head. Young players from across America gathered to participate in the annual string competition. Annie played Mendelssohn's Violin Concerto exceptionally well, capturing so much momentum at the apex of the piece that the surge of energy derailed her.

"There are concertizing performers out there who play weekly with symphony orchestras without slipups," I said to Bill. "How can we help Annie develop that kind of security in performance?"

Stephen Clapp, the professor of violin at Juilliard, served as one of the adjudicators that year at Kingsville. His interest and kindness testified to his life as a Christian. "Annie has to develop a rock-solid technique," he said, when Bill called to consult him, "so that even if she stumbles—as every player does at some time or other—she can correct so quickly that it is almost unappreciable to her audience."

Dean Clapp's words generated in us a swelling resolve to see our children develop that "rock-solid technique." We needed more. As we sat in our poorly lit, burgundy-and-brown hotel room in Kingsville, I gave in to the urgency I felt and spouted, "We need to move to New York!"

Bill blinked. "What?"

"College is too late. I've had Juilliard's precollege program in my sights for a long time. Annie and Alex are both studying with Mr. Kawasaki. If they are accepted into Juilliard, moving to that area will end the split-city travel. And I believe Benjamin can get in on it too. He's only ten, but his cello playing is coming along. We need to go where the action is. The kids need to see the scope of opportunities. They need more exposure."

"New York City! *That* is a huge undertaking."

"Your Living Stone work can be done from anywhere, with FedEx and e-mail. We have everything to gain and nothing to lose."

"New York is expensive!" Bill shook his head. "It's as bad as Aspen."

"I know," I said. "But remember the diapers."

He sat silently for a moment. Then the boyish enthusiasm that I'd always loved spread over his face. "It actually sounds sorta fun!" Laughter melted the strain and left us in whimsical anticipation.

Bill called a high-school buddy who had settled in Manhattan. "So…how much for an apartment that sleeps eight, with enough square footage for a home business and home school?"

"Three words of advice," his buddy said. "Bring yer money!"

Fueled by faith alone, Bill and I researched homeschooling laws to help us choose between the states of New Jersey, New York, and Connecticut. Connecticut won. We researched real estate prices just outside Manhattan and learned a new phrase, "The Gold Coast." Like Aspen, Connecticut's housing prices ranked high on the hilarious meter. When we went for a look, it seemed like the gum-drop-sized dwellings only waved and snickered at our low-budget frustration.

We drew a bigger circle and came up with the city of New Milford, just outside Danbury. "It's like Aspen and Snowmass," I told him, "cheaper, but functionally close. We'll still need a miracle, though." I packed up the faithful four: Annie, baby Jeremiah, Grandmother Jane, and myself, and we flew to Connecticut to choose a house.

Look out, Elijah! Another miracle was about to burn water.

Our real estate agent was a sniffy fellow who held an excessively fluffy, cute but ill-tempered lap dog. We used a foolproof method in choosing him: He was the first person we saw when we walked into a random real estate office. "I need a house, today!" I said. "Let me see what you have for not much money. It needs to be big enough for two parents, six children, a home business, a home school, and a golden retriever. Shacks qualify. We are relocating to access opportunities for our children's musical pursuits. 'Whatever it takes,' you see."

The dog scowled at us as his owner printed a few pages from his computer. Then we were off, for a wearisome morning of dead ends. Back at the office, the agent scratched his furry friend on the top of the head, sniffed, and sighed, "There's just nothing. I'm sorry."

"I don't believe you." I walked around the bannister that fenced off his desk and shuffled through the papers for myself. He set the dog down and followed my lead, picking up some sheets, rifling through them, and pulling one out of the pile. "This one just came on the market," he said. "None of us has seen it, and there's no picture." He scowled. "And it's all electric."

"Don't even look at it," growled a crabby coworker at a desk nearby. "You'll pay through the nose for heat."

"Look," I said, pointing at the description. "It has a fireplace. I'm a mountain girl, and a fireplace works for me. I don't care what it looks like. Let's go."

We were the first shoppers because the house had come on the market the day after local realtors had taken their tour of new listings. It looked well kept—except for a few carpenter ants and a scary creep of ivy—and big enough for all eight of us…if we cleared out the basement.

The Realtor shook with excitement as he held out the spec-sheet and pointed to the price. "Unbelievable! Well below market value." He leaned over and whispered, "The only reason this house is not in a bidding war is because the market doesn't know about it yet. We realtors literally race back to our offices to phone clients about deals like this."

We made an offer and bought the house before anyone else had seen it. When we sold it a few years later, we made enough profit to reimburse ourselves for the entire NYC excursion.

Once, while engaging in my favorite pastime—wandering through bookstores—I happened upon a biography of Mia Hamm, doyenne of soccer. I picked up the book and thumbed through, jealous of Mia's muscular legs and rippling abs. A caption, artistically framed on a page, pulled me from sorrowful thoughts of my melting, multipregnancy middle. It read, "It's okay to obsess."

I love this book! I chuckled, propping it open to the quote about obsession as I sat it back on the display. Muscled Mia, admired by the masses for kicking a soccer ball better than any other woman in the world, was giving me permission to obsess. Thank you, Mia! I thought for a moment of those who might consider our family obsessive in pursuit of musical excellence. Perhaps they didn't believe musical excellence to be a worthy obsession. Well, I didn't consider champion ball-kicking to be a worthy obsession. Yet, even with my abysmal abs and slack athleticism, I had cheered like a soccer-mom in 1996, when Mia led the American team to a historic victory at the Olympics. I realized that I admired Mia, champion ball-kicker. Why? Because she sacrificed greatly to be the very best female ball-kicker ever. Why did she do that? I don't know. Perhaps some ancient gene of Spartan asceticism sparked her athletic passions.

As for my family, I knew why we were willing to sacrifice greatly to be the very best musicians we could be: because God had placed a gift of music in Annie Moses' life, and then, a longing for musical skill and opportunity in my mother's heart. That longing had been answered as God opened a professional path in music for Bill and me. With all our hard work and sacrifice, we were following and discovering God's purpose for our family. More than following a biblical imperative about music, we were engaging in a spiritual discipline of excellence in life, pushing back the enemy, and building a throne from which God may occupy society. It is a call worthy of our all. King David said it best, "I will not offer Yahweh that which costs me nothing."

"It's okay to obsess!" Wearing my new motto like a girdle, I tightened my abs and drove home from the bookstore feeling a surge of moral support. As I opened the door, I saw, hanging above the piano where I practiced with my children, the original   it's-okay-to-obsess pronouncement from God, Colossians 3:23–24, a Scripture so important to me that I had been moved to cross-stitch it years before, using brown boxy lettering against a strong green-and-rust border. Matted and framed, it hung before me, in a new light: "Whatever you do, work at it with all your heart, as working for the Lord, not for men, knowing that you will receive an inheritance from the Lord as a *remard*." In my eagerness, I had accidentally stitched an "m" instead of a "w" in the word, "reward." But the error only endeared the wall-hanging to me, heightening the power of the command, reminding me of the last line sewn, the gavel that pounded the King's proclamation: "It is the Lord Christ you are serving."

"Work at it with all your heart," I whispered. "It's okay to obsess."

The Annie Moses Band

The only way to fail is to quit!
UNCLE GEORGE MOSES

In a flurry of packing and practicing, we prepared for our move to Connecticut. Annie and Alex, playing Paganini and Weber, respectively, had been selected as winners of the Nashville Youth Symphony's Concerto Competition. It was Annie's third win, and Alex's first. Performing in the Symphony's spring concert would cap off their final year of study in Nashville.

Bill and I were pleased that all three of our oldest children had been admitted with scholarships to Juilliard's precollege division: Annie, fifteen; Alex, thirteen; and Benjamin, ten. The younger children, Camille, seven, and Gretchen, five, would study a few blocks away at the School for Strings, and twelve-month-old Jeremiah toddled from instrument to instrument as the children practiced, claiming each one as his own.

The first movement of the Bartók Viola Concerto that Dr. Carroll had encouraged Alex to play had gained him his scholarship and his position as principal viola player of the Juilliard Symphony. While he was in the practice rooms, warming up the piece for his audition, the door had burst open, and a violist from the college division had marched in, demanding, "How old are you?"

"Thirteen," Alex said.

"Man! I'm way older than you, and I didn't play the Bartók until college." He shook his head and backed out the door. "Embarrassing."

Alex beamed when he told us, and gratitude for Dr. Carroll filled my heart. She had set the vision and developed the technique. Alex had polished the piece by recording it relentlessly, listening to and critiquing his own performance, eventually raising it to maturity.

Many of the auditions for our musical goals—camps and competitions—had required recordings. I used the opportunity to build my children's endurance in performing a piece without stumbling—with professional execution throughout.

"Just edit something together," one studio engineer said. "No one will ever know."

"*I* will know," I said. "And so will they. A live performer must be able to play through an entire piece without major problems. We may as well face the music."

I took my children, first Annie, then Alex, to record in churches, in schools, at the Blair Recital Hall at Vanderbilt, and at the Scarritt-Bennett Center in midtown Nashville. We'd set up the microphones, adjust the levels on the console, and go at it in the cavernous space, one performer, one audience member, and the recorder whirring. When fatigue set in we'd go home and sleep, then find a new venue on another day and go at it again. We'd listen to the product to analyze the performance. Recordings don't lie, and the sooner a student learns to judge his own playing, the sooner he will move up the ranks to professional. It is the mark of maturity to correct oneself. I had heard Mr. Sassmannshaus, Chairman of the String Department at the Cincinnati Conservatory of Music, comment on this during one of Annie's lessons. "Annie, you are advanced enough to analyze your playing for yourself," he said. "Listen as you play, and make judgments about your playing. What is good? What is not good? How can I make it better?"

Recording develops a confident, self-critical ear. Put an important person in the control booth, someone the performer desires to impress, and the brain engagement skyrockets. Recording is extremely beneficial in developing a budding artist. Practice alone will not achieve high performance skill. Each link in the chain—practice, performing, recording—develops a different aspect of a well-rounded musician.

By the time Alex auditioned for Juilliard, he had recorded the Bartók dozens of times, playing it all the way through without stops. The training put the piece in his pocket with full ownership; it is fire in his fingers to this day. After his time at Juilliard, he used the piece for a competition and won. The scholarship to

Juilliard and the award money later amply compensated him for the time spent learning it. But the joy in proficiency is his lasting reward.

The summer of our move, as Bill and I heaved boxes and arranged furniture, Annie and Alex traveled to Aspen with Grandma Jane as chaperone. Each did what they do best: Annie and Alex practiced, Grandma Jane cooked. Brown bags stuffed with sandwiches, fried chicken, deviled eggs, chips, fruit, rice pudding, homemade pies, cobblers, and cookies traveled with Alex and Annie to the practice cabins. Six to seven hours a day, they practiced, breaking occasionally to go to lessons and rehearsals—and, at Grandma Jane's insistence, to eat. "So you'll gain some strength!"

I noticed that the word "pudgy" applied when they returned to our new home in Connecticut. I also noticed an incredible new level of virtuosity in their playing. Six to seven hours of practice a day? Completely self-driven, at fifteen and seventeen years old? The level of discipline pleased me, and I realized that they had grown into it from the age of four. The daily exercise of practice had, over the years, developed thick muscles of self-discipline and had made the weight of practice easy to lift. When translated into the heavy lifting of life, such discipline becomes broad-shouldered strength—relationally, emotionally, professionally, and most important, spiritually. The writer of Hebrews summed it up this way: "No discipline seems pleasant at the time, but painful. Later on, however, it produces a harvest of righteousness and peace for those who have been trained by it" (Hebrews 12:11, NIV).

I understood this passage of Scripture differently after reading Dr. Campbell's book, in which he explained that discipline and punishment are not synonymous. Discipline has to do with training the will; picture the Shepherd reaching out His rod to correct the path of the wayward lamb, illustrating the words of Psalm 23, "Your rod and Your staff, they comfort me." Discipline is freedom and safety. Punishment, on the other hand, is the infliction of a penalty, administered with specificity and only in response to the most egregious crimes against love.

I was pleased to know that my children were ready for the rigors of the Juilliard School.

On the first day of lessons, we set out early from New Milford, our new hometown. During the night, the area had been hit by a major fall storm, which deposited debris all over the highways. Relax! I told myself as I navigated fallen trees and swollen streams. Some roads were closed, forcing me to find alternate routes. *Why is driving into Manhattan always so perilous?* I was thankful for the ample vehicle our family size demanded, and my skillful steering, learned from splattering cow pies in Oklahoma, helped out too. We arrived intact.

The school was mostly empty. Being significantly more relaxed than I was, the other parents had anticipated delayed classes in the wake of the storm. I went outside to feel the bright, crisp air that had breezed in, as if the temper tantrum of the night had never happened. I sat in the sunny courtyard at Lincoln Center, closed my eyes for a moment to shed the tension, then looked around. The Metropolitan Opera stood to my left, her high, arched windows, like a beautiful woman's face, welcoming me with eyebrows lifted, eyes wide in pleased astonishment. I thought of Mama, what it would have been like for the ping of her crystal-clear singing voice to resonate through that hall, over the balcony, around a room so naturally reverberant. How the people would have loved her! I pictured her at curtain call, in a red velvet gown more grand than the outfit Annie Moses made for her as a child. A red velvet gown that went plunging from off-shoulder to accentuate her graceful neckline, the bodice cut deeply to cradle her breasts, the skirt billowing all 'round as she bowed to the applause. Bravo! Bravo! I could see the radiance of her skin and smile as red roses, elegantly tossed, landed around her.

"Of all sad words of tongue or pen, The saddest are these: 'It might have been!'" The line from John Greenleaf Whittier's famous poem, "Maude Muller," spoke my mind.

Behind me, beautiful young girls—their hair in tight buns, their toes turned strangely outward, their necks lifting straight off their shoulders with extraordinary poise—hurried through the doors of the New York City Ballet. Body type, in part, had gained them admission to the Ballet's preparatory division. Daddy's mean friend had been right when she had patted my hips and said, "You'll never be a ballet dancer. You're too heavy here." These ballerinas' bottoms *were* tiny. I smiled inwardly, remembering my childhood dream of dying like a swan.

Oh well, I will die like a saint instead.

A few blocks away, the theater district lights gave the streets a circuslike vibe. A handful of graduates from Oklahoma City University had done well there. I didn't envy them. I loved to watch the shows, but as far as working the same show, day after day, Ethel Merman could still have it.

The Juilliard School rose before me, here and now, her arms wide open, welcoming my children. Four generations of love and sacrifice had laid the stepping stones to her door. The musical horizons were expanding more than I ever could have thought possible, and I knew that God's unusual call for our family was continuing to unfold, as long as we obeyed. I said a prayer of thanks and drew my heart into the potential of the present. Time passes so quickly; it seemed only yesterday that I was watching that tiny violinist in Music Survey class at OCU and heard the voice of God speak, "When you have a little girl...."

I looked back over the musical paths my children and I had walked together, years of laughter and camaraderie, of striving for excellence, of refining beauty, of learning patience and kindness, the essence of love. As their artistic skills blossomed, so did their spiritual voices, their ability to express their thoughts and dreams, their capacity to bless others from the deep, rich wellspring of love housed in their hearts. These relationships, developed during the summertime of my life, were now the gold in the beginning of my autumn years, and they will be the celebration of my life's winter. I had found more joy, honor, and wisdom in the squeak of a tiny violin and the prayers we'd said together than I could have in any accolade Earth could offer.

We had embarked on a holy and heavenly musical adventure, Bill and I, working side by side. He had never faltered, funding our needs with a father's hearty generosity: packing, composing, driving, writing checks, serving his family with a love and patience that mirrored the Lord's. When finances grew thin, or I became weary, he made it his particular aim to make me laugh. Wrapping his arms around me, he'd whisper in my ear, "Don't worry, I'm your Balm of Billy-ad!" or "Never fear, Emmanu-Bill is here."

For five years, he had been arranging music for our children, tailoring the parts to fit the skill level of each one. Annie and Alex, mature and virtuosic, received demanding parts, while Benjamin and the younger ones received simpler parts. As each child's proficiency grew, Bill rewrote the parts to challenge them again. Thus our little family ensemble took shape.

About a month before Christmas, the music minister at our church in Connecticut asked if we would play a thirty-minute preshow to the Broadway-styled Christmas production the choir was performing. We were more than ready to play. We were not more than ready for the overwhelming response. The folks loved it, and wanted to know if we taught; if we traveled to perform; if we had recordings; how we chose instruments; where we purchased instruments; what methods we used; how we got our children to practice—and did we make them start; did we let them quit; who were our teachers; and could we help them ascertain if their children were "talented?" Parents were thirsty for clues...directions...answers...anything that would help their children accomplish success in their artistic pursuits.

At the prompting of these parents, Annie, Alex and I began to teach. Ours was a spirited group of students, some homeschooled, some private or public schooled. The homeschoolers were quite a study: I admired their moms, carrying little black books detailing a predetermined daily regimen, the type of moms who—as humorist Erma Bombeck once wrote—"wax their garden hose" and approach bedtime with their husbands as an opportunity to pencil in procreation. Children who learn within the safety and structure of such a home make remarkable progress: They peel out, speeding through the beginning books, mastering the details of form and function.

"Our church could have a phenomenal chamber orchestra in just four years," I told Bill. "Imagine the evangelistic possibilities of such outreach."

The Lord constructs His Kingdom by establishing single family units, joined house to house. These individual cells, when grouped together, create a community of faith that supersedes all earthly governments and thrones, a community in which His precepts, His ways of living, are revered and enacted. It is a beautiful way of life, saturated with love, strong familial bonds, and the comfort of the Holy Spirit. It never ends, but carries the faithful onward from Earth into eternity. I have experienced it, and I cannot be dissuaded from its reality and goodness.

Where love reigns, the family flourishes. Where the family flourishes, society flourishes. Where society flourishes, the arts flourish.

The inverse is true as well. Where love wanes, the family fractures. Where the family fractures, society fractures. Where society fractures, the arts rot. The arts measure the vital signs of a society's spiritual health.

No fulfillment tops that of empowering the single-unit family to take up the God-ordained responsibility of making disciples of each new generation. How can we hope to evangelize the world if we cannot succeed at evangelizing our own children, if we neglect the opportunity to empower them with the fluency and eloquence to articulate, in word and song, the love that they have experienced and the truth that they have learned?

From my new vantage point in Connecticut as both parent and teacher, I began to envision the power of a coalition united in the common purpose of equipping a new generation with the skills necessary to "Make His Praise Glorious." I saw the church community joining with pastors and music ministers to support the families who were investing in their children's artistic training: applauding, volunteering, and subsidizing. I saw the joy becoming contagious.

I thought of Leona Harris and the impact her interest and attention had made on my mother's life. She had pulled my mother out of the rut of poverty to introduce her to a world of beauty and art. Her gift had become a legacy. My children and I were partakers.

Historically, patrons were invaluable visionaries. They generated and funded the work of many of the classical composers and performers we esteem today. If the church hopes to reclaim artistic leadership in the world, congregations must revive the role of the patron—the godly patron.

I began to envision a whole new job description emerging: a music minister who would serve the future, not the past. Instead of focusing assets and energy on adults who had already passed their prime, he would appreciate and engage the musical skills of the young children committed to his pastoral care. Under his leadership, the adult choir and orchestra would turn their interest and the bulk of their resources to nurturing and disciplining the young children of the church. They would capture young minds during the season when they are sharp, spinning, and eager to learn.

In doing so, the music program would generate a feeder stream of powerful musical skill, as preschoolers grew into the adult programs. The artistic options would multiply. All sorts of musical styles and configurations would begin to form. As the young artists matured, they would form a highly skilled adult program that would understand and take on the responsibility of nurturing and mentoring the next generation of musicians. The program would become proactive, a circle of love, offering multigenerational performances so compelling, so excellent, so exciting, that people of all persuasions would be drawn to see the beauty.

I envisioned the six "P's" in action:" Pupil, Parent, Professor, Pastor, Patron, and the Public, joined in holy purpose, pulling together toward a day when the earth would ring with the glory of God, when excellent, continuous praise would flow from the fingers and mouths of a new generation. The guidance of a wise pastor and music minister, championed and subsidized by visionary patrons, would work together with parents to build a strong community of loving families. The whole body of Christ would funnel its attention and resources to the children, to say in word and action: "We have assessed and appreciate your potential. We believe in you and are here to ensure that your gifts and talents are fully realized. We are thrilled to spend time with you, to teach you the ways of the Lord and how to communicate His praise, to help your parents understand the gravitas of their role."

By the time we landed in Connecticut, I had been studying the violin for a decade. I had sat in on hundreds of lessons from the best teachers in the field. I had taken notes, practiced with my children, read books, driven thousands of miles to access the best programs and schools, then moved halfway across a continent, bent on the noble mission of teaching my children to "play skillfully" and to "make His praise glorious" (Psalms 33:3, 66:2).

As our family pursued this divine call together, we were also getting to know the Lord. We were praying, centering our lives around the Word, reading, and learning who God is and why He is worthy of glorious praise. Spiritual life had bubbled up and begun to overflow like the "cup" of Psalm 23.

Toward the beginning of our third year at Juilliard, the children began to express a desire to perform more. "We practice all the time, but what are we practicing for?" Annie said. "I want to play more than chamber recitals and orchestral performances. I want to sing and make albums and write."

I turned to Bill. "The Lord has been urging me in this very thing. The opportunities to use our music are so few! How about we start a band? We could put together a show, maybe do a few open mic nights, be ready for parties, receptions, that sorta thing."

Being a band-man from high school, Bill caught the wave. "On the way home from the City the other day, I heard Annie singing in the van," he said, as we retired to bed that night. "She's a great violinist, but she's a talented vocalist too. God impressed on me that we have a responsibility there. I think the band idea might be a good one."

"Well, I know we can do it," I said. "After all, we have you, Mr. Piano-man." The idea was sparkling, for both of us. "What should we call our band?"

"Something about strings," he said. "How about Pop-a-String? Or String-a-long, or Heart-Strings?" He paused to think. "I've got it! We'll be a grunge band and call ourselves Stringy Hair! No, no, wait! This is even better: String Bikini! Just think of all we'll save on wardrobe. With a specimen like me to front the group…!"

"*Biiillll!* I'm serious!" I laughed, despite myself. "We have such a wonderful musical legacy on both sides of the family. Why don't we go back to our roots? Annie is named for my grandmother, Annie Moses. She did so much with so little, to be true to her daughter's potential. Since she started the legacy, why don't we call our group, The Annie Moses Band?"

The name opened depth and meaning, and the coining of the title seemed to stabilize our vision. Perhaps I could write a song telling her story. It would paint a backdrop for our family's music, explaining the legacy, God's powerful work through the generations.

Annie Moses. I love how her eyes still hold the same intensity of spirit.

The next morning, I awoke early. A vision of Annie Moses—straw hat, bent back, rough hands—hung like a Rembrandt in my mind. What words would adequately paint that picture to an audience? How could I express the gratitude I felt for her faithfulness and humility? I picked up a notebook and pen from the nightstand. At the top of the page, I wrote, "Love's Legacy." I would begin by using large strokes to paint the big picture; to tell the generational impact of her devotion. Annie Moses was a planter of seeds, small seeds, pushed deep into the fertile soil of my mother's heart. Had she turned to the right or to the left, had she abandoned the way of faithfulness, how different my destiny would have been. An image came to mind of my daughter Annie, standing center stage with her violin, confident, poised, rooted and grounded in the love of many generations. I began to write the words as she would sing them, chorus first...

> *Planting the seeds of Love's Legacy*
> *Passing her faithfulness right down to me*
> *Writing the song of my destiny*
> *I stand here because of her love's legacy*

Then I began to contemplate the verses. Sad, that my children had never met their great-grandmother. They had only my commendation and their grandma Jane's memories on which to base their understanding. I wanted them to know and respect Annie Moses as I did. But I had never met her either. She died so young. How could I best describe who she was? I began the wordplay: daughter of the black dirt; child of poverty; planter of the furrowed fields; mother of my mother; faithful in the small things. The lines began to emerge…

> *Oh, my great-grandma Annie, we never did meet*
> *But the song of her legacy plays on in me*
> *Her life was a hard one, she worked in the fields*
> *To see how much cotton an acre could yield*

> *A husband, some children, and an old clapboard shack*
> *Sun beating down on her young, aching back*
> *As her hands lost their beauty in the black Texas dirt*
> *Right there beside her the Lord was at work*

As I wrote, Bill intercepted the children and herded them to the kitchen for a cold breakfast. He was eager to put music to the lyrics and wanted to protect my time so I could finish. The morning grew late as I continued writing the second verse. I wanted to focus the lines on the music of Annie Moses, stifled by poverty and negligence, then given a second chance.…

> *On a hot August evening, a fine baby girl*
> *Was born to young Annie, and a song filled her world*
> *The angels crept closer as she made a vow*
> *This little girl's life would be better somehow*

> *As her daughter grew older, Annie rejoiced*
> *To hear the rare beauty of her little girl's voice*
> *She found a piano, she pinched every dime*
> *And started a symphony dancing through time*

The song brought a central pillar of purpose to our mission as a musical family. We began to put together a concert, learning repertoire, taking pictures, building a Web site, and—here's the kicker—recording an album.

We had recorded a lot, but not to make a real, true-blue album for sale. We purchased a computer and a recording system, and Alex, barely fifteen, stuck his head into the manuals and didn't come out for weeks. Our friend, Doug, a true music lover and our first guitar player, helped us hang some old woolen army blankets in the basement. They made a cozy, star-spangled sound booth as light glowed through the moth holes. After a few hours of recording vocals behind the woolly blankets, however, we decided that some natural reverb might sound better. Clapping and shouting, we toured the house to find the best resonance.

The sun room stepped up for the job, the glass bouncing a Bee Gee's sort of sound, such as one might hear in a stairwell or concrete bathroom. From the control board in the basement, we routed cabling up to the room on the first floor, and set up a rented mic. The birds found out what we were up to and fowled the airspace, out-twittering us in their raucous registers. Remembering the proverb about the early bird and the worm, we attempted to beat their alarm clock. Five in the morning, four, three: how early would one have to rise to beat the birds out of bed? Annie would pull herself to the mic, hair wild, headphones askew, singing blearily. When an error demanded a retake, she'd run down the stairs to awaken Alex, who slumbered like an old man in a church pew, dampening the control board with drool. Finally, we surrendered to the early birds and reversed our strategy; we began to record late at night after they went to bed, plopping down on an air mattress to snooze between takes.

When it came time to record the strings, we pounded the countryside until we found a great space, one rich with sonic sweetness but that didn't require much cash. It was a historic rural church, right across the street from designer Bill Blass's home. Gardeners mowed, mulched, buzzed, and blew his tournament-size lawn, and we attempted to record between the start-and-stop rhythm of their engines. The church seemed to have time-traveled from yesteryear, with candlelight colors and an echo chamber: The area behind the pulpit looked like God had taken a big ice-cream scoop and carved the wall and ceiling into a big, sound-propelling curve. A rusty old bell squeaked in the tower, while, déjà vu, baby birds nested in the window, screaming for food.

"The birds are following us," Alex said. "It's straight from Alfred Hitchcock."

"Maybe they want to sing on the album too," Annie said.

The church had no restrooms, so we played while doing the potty dance, which was particularly difficult for Benjamin, who had substantial cello solos. "One more take. Hurry! Just one more take," he'd yell, determined to finish before scurrying to anyplace Mr. Blass's gardeners couldn't see.

There is no education like the school of hard knocks, and with a little punning, that can be construed biblically: "Knock and the door will be opened." Our knuckles were red, we knocked so hard, and at the end, we had a boatload of memories that still bring laughter. We also had our first album in hand, and the recording process, so hyped and forbidding, had lost its power to intimidate. Nothing builds a player's chops like recording, performing the lines over and over and over again until they're exactly, perfectly right. We had sweated the small stuff, we had paid our dues for years, and we were ready to play.

By this time, our Juilliard experience was quite rich. Annie had graduated from the precollege division and was enjoying her freshman year in the collegiate department. She had served as Concertmistress of the Juilliard Orchestra—leader of the first violins and assistant to the conductor—and Alex had continued to serve as principal, (sectionleader) of the violas of the Juilliard Symphony. Both she and Alex were still studying with Mr. Kawasaki, violin and viola respectively; his teaching had massively honed their skill.

They had attained high honors and opportunities in chamber music. When the two walked on stage together, the musical telepathy was uncanny, electric. Their group had distinguished itself by being selected to perform in Alice Tully Hall, at Lincoln Center, and at Juilliard's commencement ceremonies. Alex had been chosen to play in a string quartet coached by Itzhak Perlman, a highlight of his Juilliard experience. Benjamin, too, had found a niche, under the instruction of Ann and Ardeth Alden, and he was maturing rapidly. The younger children, Camille, Gretchen, and Jeremiah, were progressing beautifully as well. The children's grades were great, and their reputation as hard workers and solid performers was growing.

The Annie Moses Band is formed, at first including the three older children along with Bill and Robin. Left to right: Bill; Alex, 15; Annie, 17; Benjamin, 13.

Annie and Alex's experience and success playing in chamber-music groups influenced the Annie Moses Band's style. Instead of sitting like a traditional group, we stood. We got rid of the chairs, but we kept the intensity of connection, of eye contact, the handing off of lines, and the sense of ensemble. Then we added vocals and a rhythm section. The effect was a sort of musical punch: some classical, some jazz, and some mountain music thrown in for fun.

Our first gig was a freebie, an ice-cream social to raise funds for homeless senior citizens. The director pointed us to a six-foot-by-eight-foot deck, where we set up our skeletal sound system. We could hardly move, the space was so small, and the bows poked dangerously toward faces as the sweat ran, creating a roadmap through the girls' makeup. The homeless seniors didn't seem to notice the music much, but they enjoyed the ice cream.

We tried open mic nights at cafés, coffee shops, and opera houses, but I kept having to hurry the kids outside when lyrics became lewd or blasphemous. Not for us. We quit the scene and waited.

Our first big opportunity came through Tom Fettke, a good friend and fellow composer, who had heard of our venture and said, "I'm gonna tell Jerry Evans about you guys. He hosts the J&J Music Conference in Manhattan every year, and it's expensive getting groups there to perform. Since you're already there..."

Jerry called a few days later and invited us to play. "There'll be around three hundred music ministers there. You'll be the first thing they hear, let's say about forty-five or fifty minutes of music."

We loaded our trailer and ventured through Manhattan traffic to the convention center. Once again, God had stayed a step ahead of us. We held out hope that out of the three hundred music ministers attending the conference, some would call us for a concert at their church. That hope was well-founded: We booked an eleven-week tour, spending that entire summer on the road. Positive feedback flowed, alerting us to the compelling nature of our work. One dad wrote, "After seeing your family play tonight, I suggested to my family on the way home that we all take up an instrument and start a band. To my surprise and dismay, they all heartily agreed." Parents waited in line to meet us, voicing a determination to get their children started on music right away. God had begun to issue His promised "reward," or as my incorrectly cross-stitched wall hanging read, my "remard."

"This is fruit that will last," I told Bill. "Both parents and children have been inspired. We are affecting the future of the Kingdom of God here."

Bill took my hand. "You have done a good work, my dear."

"We're a pretty good team, you and me." I smiled. "Do you ever think that we are doing to our audiences what that little china doll of a girl in Music Survey class did to us?"

The Juilliard School offers a one-year sabbatical to college-level students who need time to try out other opportunities. With the satisfaction of the summer tour fresh in our hearts, we took it—and we didn't go back.

The Wolaver family. Left to right: Jeremiah, Bill, Gretchen, Robin, Annie, Camille, Alex, Benjamin

It was time to craft a professional path, to use our music for the purpose for which we'd received it. Our adventures with God would take us around the country, across the ocean, to such odd and mysterious places as North Korea. But that is another story. For now, Bill's jazz, my mountain music, and our children's classical chops would meld into a fusion of sound, appealing to a wide range of ages and tastes. We would return to Manhattan to play at Carnegie Hall— Mama's yearning—and just a short time later, we would receive a standing ovation and an encore at the Grand Ole Opry— Daddy's dream.

Four generations of godly legacy had taken us from the cotton patch to the concert hall. It is a big climb up the ladder by the world's standards, but God is no respecter of persons, and He is not impressed by spotlights. He is searching the inner chambers of our hearts, looking for humility and faithfulness, everlasting values that He can mine like gold and credit to the account of children yet unborn. Such is the economy of His Kingdom.

I have heard it said that God will measure our lives by what we have done with what we have been given. If so, Annie Moses is rich. In her short life, she laid a foundation of inexhaustible love, a rock so steady that every subsequent generation has built upon its strength. It is my passion to sing the song of her legacy: a song of faith and family, of love and loyalty, of investing in the future by nurturing the promise inherent in a child.

APPENDIX A

First Things First

A dialogue outlining the process of artistic discipleship

PARENT: How do I nurture artistic success in my child?

COUNSELOR: First, commit yourself wholeheartedly to the raising of a godly child. Make it your aim to equip your child with the stability of the two-legged stance: (1) to know her God; and (2) to develop a toolbox of highly skilled artistic voices to tell what she knows. Thus, a messenger of God is born.

PARENT: How do I begin?

COUNSELOR: Upon your baby's birth, do everything possible to build the strongest possible bonds of love and good health and to maximize the natural timeline of speech and language development. The first three years are crucial, especially breast-feeding, closeness, eye contact, and verbal interaction with the parents, both in speaking and singing.

PARENT: What else?

COUNSELOR: You must include your child in the practice of prayer as soon as he can speak. Prayer is the greatest word-processing curriculum available to mankind. It activates the Father's destiny in children's lives while teaching them to recognize and fight evil.

PARENT: What else?

COUNSELOR: Practice Deuteronomy 6:4–9, where we are exhorted to love the Lord our God, with all our heart, soul, and strength, to take His commandments to heart, and to impress them on the hearts of our children.

Talk about the Father constantly, teaching the Scriptures and the story of salvation. Impart to your child a keen understanding of her own personal legacy as designed by her heavenly Father. Let her know that He has written the book of her life and has prepared good works in advance for her to do. Tell your child that God will never leave her or forsake her, and that her life will be abundant and joyful if she will obey God's will. Repeatedly point out to your child that her perfect destiny originates with God, that God's ways are light and life. Become a conduit for the Lord, equipping your child for that destiny through prayer, study, and discussion. When your child receives the salvation of Jesus, her experience will become a first-person, eyewitness account of Who God is and what He has done in her life. Then her testimony cannot be shaken because she has experienced it personally. It will be her strength when doubters attack or persecution arises. Remember: "They triumphed over him by the blood of the Lamb and by the word of their testimony" (Revelation 12:11, NIV).

PARENT: That's a big assignment.

COUNSELOR: Yes. But it grows wings as you proceed. As you and your child draw closer to the heavenly Father, you will also draw closer to each other. Your relationship will flourish: a lifelong bond.

PARENT: Okay, so we're bonding, praying, studying, talking about the things of God. Then what?

COUNSELOR: Then you must sing with your child!

PARENT: Sing?

COUNSELOR: That's right. You and your child must sing new songs, composed from the Father's transformation unfolding in your lives. This is My Story. This is My Song. That's what one of our finest saints wrote, and it's true: Story and song become one, overflowing from the wellspring of the heart.

PARENT: Then what?

COUNSELOR: Somewhere between the ages of three and five, you and your child should begin music lessons.

PARENT: Me? Do you mean me, take music lessons?

COUNSELOR: You will become your child's equipper and practice coach. All children should take music lessons, regardless of their talent or anticipated line of work, and because they are children, you'll need to be involved to guide them. Remember, the cultivating of musical skill is not about becoming a "star," or a professional musician; it's about being a fluent messenger of God. Furthermore, music maximizes the brain, preparing it for every other educational endeavor.

PARENT: But I can't play an instrument or sing.

COUNSELOR: You can learn enough to guide your child. Your child is the player; you are the coach.

PARENT: When should we start?

COUNSELOR: If you are praying and singing, you have already begun. Add to those scriptural mandates formal lessons on a chosen instrument during the "window of opportunity." This will build and network your child's brain, increasing his capacity to learn in every area. It will maximize communication skills, verbally, vocally, and instrumentally. Now your child's artistic toolbox is beginning to fill up. He will have four powerful voices with which to glorify God: speaking, singing, playing, and composing.

PARENT: What do I do first to get the lessons going?

COUNSELOR: Choose an instrument.

PARENT: Okay. Then what?

COUNSELOR: Find a good teacher, one who understands the high calling of her task and how the parent fits into the picture.

PARENT: That sounds good. Then what?

COUNSELOR: You and your child become a team, practicing together. Your child is the player and you are the note-taker and coach. Practice sessions are a wonderful opportunity to communicate love and caring. It's also a wonderful time to build the relationship of disciple and disciple-maker.

PARENT: All right. What else?

COUNSELOR: Create a coalition. One of the reasons students don't want to practice is because they are lonely. Music bonds people, and it is meant to be shared. You must bring together a coalition of supporters and fellow musicians to undergird and encourage the process. It's a noble job.

PARENT: Okay. And after that?

COUNSELOR: As your child's skill grows, find opportunities for her to share her music. With performing experience, she will become a confident communicator. Because she "plays skillfully," her performances will be beautiful and winsome. Other children who hear her play will ask to begin lessons. They'll say, "I want to play like that!" Parents will ask how to do what you have done. Furthermore, their hearts will be drawn to the beauty of the relationship you and your child share. They will thirst for what you have. It is the essence of evangelism. As you point them to God, the heavenly Kingdom is advanced and His praise is made glorious.

PARENT: And that's the whole point.

COUNSELOR: That's the whole point. Remember to hold in reverence the God-given blessing of leading your children to maturity as skilled and articulate adults. Let them hear you speak thanksgiving to God every day for allowing you to be a part of their lives. Let them know that you consider it a privilege to spend time together with them, making music in the adventure of life. But there's one more thing…

PARENT: Yes.

COUNSELOR: As your child becomes skilled and polished, she must remember to abide in the Father as the source of life or her art will become self-centered, making her unhappy and unbalanced. Remember the two-legged stance? A popular artist might play before millions of screaming fans. She may begin to suppose herself worthy of such exaltation. But she is not. Only the Father is worthy because He has created (Revelation 4:11). No one on Earth is an original creator. Mankind is only subcreator. We paint a sunset. The Father creates a sunset. We sew a doll. The Father creates a baby. We compose a song. The Father created music. Our goal is to let our light shine so that mankind will see our good works and glorify the Father. In that process, we become a partaker of His glory, and therein find contentment and the fullness of joy.

Choosing an Instrument

Choosing an instrument that fits the child, and the family framework in which the child will learn, is vital to success. The point is to establish a craft to which both child and family will enjoy committing for the long term. Flitting from instrument to instrument or "taking breaks" is counterproductive and delays the accrual of skill.

Six Overarching Essentials

- All unborn children hear their mothers read and sing to them, from the womb.
- All children speak, first informally, then formally, in family, church, and community settings such as prayer groups, Scripture memory groups, poetry recitals, and theater.
- All children sing, informally with their family and formally in choirs or ensembles, then as soloists.
- All children attain a level of proficiency on the piano.
- If the child's primary instrument is suitable only for study by older beginners—such as trumpet—begin piano first, then add the primary instrument. The child may discontinue piano once a suitable level of proficiency has been reached, and then focus on the primary instrument.
- If the chosen instrument is suitable for study by a very young beginner, add piano after the fundamental positions on the primary instrument are well established.

Considerations in Choosing an Instrument

1. AGE OF CHILD—KEY MOMENTS IN DEVELOPMENT

Prebirth: Musical training starts in the womb, as simply as with the mother's own singing. Babies love music and are born showing favor toward the songs and voices they heard while in the womb. The unborn child responds to sound by twenty weeks gestation, and increasingly thereafter.

Birth to Eighteen Months: Mother's singing is the most natural and ready music. Simple, easy songs will intrigue and bring joy to both mother and child. Encourage children to sing from birth. You'll be astonished how early they will attempt, and even succeed, in joining you.

To this natural listening scenario, add Bach, Handel, Mozart, Beethoven, Debussy, and other great composers, along with folk songs and nursery songs that lighten the sound and add fun and variety.

Avoid overly loud, aggressive styles such as pop, rock, rap, and heavy metal, even recordings that are labeled "Christian" or "Praise and Worship." Remember, a child's ears are very delicate. A peaceful, comforting atmosphere filled with beautiful, tonal sounds is the goal.

Toddler (Eighteen Months to Three Years): As the baby's coordination grows, he begins to play with musical toys, beating and banging, singing along with Mama, and making his joyful noise.

At around eighteen months the left hemisphere of the brain begins to surge. This development unlocks the code of speech and brings a startling upswing in vocabulary. The two-year-old child knows around three hundred words but the three-year-old child knows some three thousand words. It's a miraculous burst of brain capacity. Capture nature's momentum during this period by teaching music in the same manner as speech, by informal trial and error. Use poetry, singing, rhythm, movement, and listening.

The "mother-tongue" method of Suzuki, which starts children as young as age three or four on instruments, flows from the understanding that the three-year-old child's brain is optimized for the assimilation of language—and likewise music. In this way, he cultivates not only words, but also nuances of accent, timbre, inflection, and tone. It makes good sense to seize this opportune season to teach the language of music, primarily through speaking, singing, clapping, listening, and free motion.

Very Young Child (Three to Five Years): Children differ in maturation and personality, so observe and experiment to ascertain if your child is ready to begin learning an instrument. It is best to get a good start on only one instrument that is conducive to study by very young children. Make sure that the methodology used is appropriate for the size of the child and the child's hands. The hands, at this age, are equipped to execute the single notes of a melody rather than chords.

The Suzuki Method is structured for very young children. However, it does not replace speaking and singing. As a Suzuki mom, I added lyrics to many of the songs in the series, which made them fun to sing. It's great to engage the ear before the eye, but be wary about waiting too long to teach the child to read music.

Older Beginner (Eight to Twelve Years): All instruments are ripe for the picking during these years. Some become available for study later than others. Brass instruments, for example, must wait until a child gains adult front teeth.

For an older beginner, instruments like piano and guitar are great choices. The guitar is a popular instrument, and lessons pay off quickly. The child can be playing a popular song in no time, and many favorite songs contain only three or four chords. See the section on guitar, under "Instrument Requirements," for more information.

2. INSTRUMENT REQUIREMENTS

Voice: With few exceptions, usually for medical reasons, everyone has a voice, and everyone is designated to "sing to the Lord." Not necessarily in public or on stage, but the Bible does describe some pretty specific places, like "on your bed." I love Zephaniah 3:17 (ESV), which describes God as he exults over us with "loud singing"!

Just as few aspire to dance professionally, but everyone can dance, few may end up singing professionally, but everyone can sing. Some children have great natural ability, while others must hire a teacher and practice to cultivate a similar ability. Some will become exceptional, while others will attain only limited skill, because in both singing and dancing, one's body is one's instrument and some carry within themselves greater natural potential than others.

While everyone loves to hear a skilled singer, some of the most successful popular singers are not skilled by most voice teachers' measures of range, placement, breathing, volume, and control. Nevertheless, they clue us in to the amazing truth that singing is not just about beautiful sound, but other worthwhile and meaningful aspects like timbre, message, passion, and personality. Audiences want to relate to the songs they hear. Maybe that's why the Bible does not require that we sing skillfully. It just directs us to "Sing!" So if you are a worshiping, obedient occupant of the Kingdom of God, you are a singer.

Singing together bonds people chemically, as it releases oxytocin into the blood. Singing utilizes words; it is more powerful than an instrument in that it conveys a message. Singing is free; it can be done anywhere at any time, in sickness and in health, in joy and in sorrow.

Piano: For a young beginner, learning piano requires a specialized methodology that includes pieces that are age-appropriate, for example, forgoing widely spaced intervals that small hands cannot execute.

Plain to see in black and white, piano is a fundamental instrument, and constructs a visual representation of the math of music. At the keyboard, the pianist may do much more than play solo pieces. He may accompany, improvise, or program electronic music. Fluent pianists—those who can arrange, write, orchestrate, and produce—have many wonderful musical paths open to them. Their fluency undergirds the musical efforts of others: ensembles, bands, soloists, and choirs, in rehearsals and shows. I am amazed how a weak and unstable ensemble performance, either vocal or instrumental, instantly takes forceful, coherent shape when a skilled pianist adds a strong, rhythmic groove and increases the range of sound in the melody and harmony. Such a breadth of mastery at the piano is becoming rare—and thus an increasingly valued musical commodity.

Guitars: Small children will often begin with the ukulele. However, guitars come in small sizes and work well for very young students. As at the piano, a very young beginner's methodology must focus on single-note melodies, allowing small hands to mature before graduating to chords and intervals. Guitar, as noted, is great for older beginners. It pays off quickly, as a vast popular repertoire is composed of a handful of simple chords that are easily learned.

The downside is that it is difficult to distinguish oneself, because there are so many guitar players. A skilled guitarist must determine to explore the vast breadth of the instrument, becoming familiar with many styles and all types of guitars. Finding a teacher who can instruct a young student on this path takes research. Look for someone who uses a codified methodology appropriate for a young child and teaches classical guitar. It's a bonus if a teacher can grow with a child into jazz, blues, rock, country, and bluegrass—and cover electric as well as acoustic instruments.

Strings: Dr. Suzuki's method has encouraged production of instruments in the string family that are playable by very young children. Instruments are available in fractions—one-eighth, one-quarter, one-half, and three-quarters—to fit a growing child's needs. While some parents begin their children at the age of three, a four-year-old may learn in only a few lessons what a three-year-old may take an entire semester to learn. I began my children the fall of the school year when they turned four, so some had just turned four and others were almost five. I had filled the earliest years, before formal lessons began, with casual introductions to the instrument, coupled with listening and singing.

It is vital to size the instrument accurately to fit the child. Proper left-hand frame is impossible to accomplish if the left arm is overextended or the bow is too long for the arm's reach. A distorted bow position is counterproductive. Many parents and teachers, impatient for improved tone, give in to the temptation to give a child an instrument that is too large. Mature sound will come with time and skill. Shop for a high quality small instrument whose strings are easily pressed by the left hand and whose bridge is properly curved so that the bow can navigate clean string crossings. Good violins sell easily, appreciate in value, and, if the policy of the dealer permits, may be traded in for bigger ones as the child grows.

Brass: Brass instruments, as mentioned, necessitate an older beginner, between eight and eleven years of age, with adult front teeth. Trumpet students may begin on the cornet, which is easier to hold and gentler in tone. French horn is great for older beginners, and, if played well, may win the player a hefty college scholarship, as it is more rarely played than trumpet or trombone.

Winds: Flutes have been modified to accommodate young beginners. However, other wind instruments pose challenges and are best taken up when older. Young children may begin the study of clarinet on the recorder.

Percussion and Drums: For the older child, the drum "kit" is the most visible component of the percussion family. It is a favorite for boys. However, percussion includes a broad array of instruments, such as bells, triangles, cymbals, tambourines, shakers, and ethnic drums, to name a few. An older child may desire to play the drums as a primary instrument, but a child interested in drums should have focused instruction on "tuned"—or "classical"—percussion instruments, as well—like the xylophone, marimba, vibraphone, and tympani. The study of tympani helps to develop a keen sense of pitch, timing, and musical phrasing, while the study of marimba (similar to the study of piano) develops the ability to read music, understand harmony, and perform melodically. I highly recommend that percussion students also study piano.

Instruments Featured in Competitions: Some instruments are more competitive than others: voice, piano, and violin rank at the top, as instruments that are featured in high-profile competitions, some of which offer a big cash award to the winner. Violin and piano are also the most commonly featured in concerto performances. Most instruments, however, offer the possibility of at least some organized adjudications.

Combinations: Encourage children to find the instrument they love to play and to stay with it until the fundamentals are set; then add any instrument that dovetails. For example, the violin and the mandolin are strung alike, so they finger the same in the left hand. The fingerboard on the mandolin is fretted, which makes the left hand easier. The mandolin is picked, however, so the right hand has to learn a new skill. A violist might want to consider taking up mandola. Studying more than one instrument expands a player's musical options, allowing him to use a wider palette of musical styles and timbres.

Another great combo is piano and harp. The harp and the grand piano are strung the same; the harp is a piano turned on its side, so the strings can be plucked instead of hammered. The harpist will have to learn to use pedals for key changes, and to pluck using eight fingers, because pinkies aren't used in playing the harp.

Guitars are versatile, affordable, and used in a wide variety of styles, genres, and methods of playing: classical, electric, twelve string, and hollow body. The electric guitar is a world in itself, with a multiplicity of sounds, and gear to create them. The scope for virtuosity is broad.

Many players of wind or brass instruments play multiple versions of their genre.

It is important for a student who enjoys conducting, composing, orchestrating, or producing to learn the mechanics, ranges, and clefs of each family of instruments, as well as the method of notating each.

3. PERSONALITY AND LEARNING STYLE OF THE CHILD

Each instrument possesses a unique personality, as Prokofiev's *Peter and the Wolf* cleverly showcased. Tuba players usually aren't given to superiority complexes, and violinists have been known to be elite and high-strung. Sound strange? Not at all. It's a commonly accepted proposition. Qualities including timbre, repertoire, style, demands of performance, and cultural or musical settings help determine which person will gravitate toward which instrument. Some instruments have a broad array of styles and ensemble settings, while others are used quite narrowly. For example, repertoire for the violin can be feisty and fiery, romantic and passionate, flighty and birdlike, fun and frolicking, or soft and comforting. Violin is a staple in a wide range of musical settings: country, jazz, classical, bluegrass, and folk. The violin is small and easy to carry but expensive to buy if you want your child to have a chance at being a contender in the non-amplified world of classical music. Violinists at the top levels need a big sound that can project over an orchestra and articulate a wide range of emotion and color.

Brass instruments, piccolo and flute, and percussion instruments are the pillars of high-school marching bands, which complement football games.

This performance outlet creates robust and readily available brass and percussion programs across the country. Jazz band lends itself to a wonderful ensemble experience, and teaches improvisation as well. A social butterfly will enjoy the community found in both opportunities. Private lessons on the instrument of choice are highly recommended, in addition to ensemble classes.

If you are hoping your child's instrument will gain her a college scholarship, choose one that is important in an ensemble setting but rarely played: viola over violin, French horn over trumpet, and oboe over flute. Cello is more rarely played than violin, but is still popular as a solo, concertizing instrument. Viola and double bass are much rarer in solo performance with orchestras. Players of many less popular instruments, such as viola, will find that there isn't as much varied material for their instrument, leaving wide-open opportunities to innovate: to compose and explore new styles for their repertoire-thirsty fellow-players.

Learning Style: In choosing both an instrument and the approach to be used in teaching that instrument, it's helpful to be aware of a child's dominant sensory receivers. Many methodologies exist to help a parent categorize and understand their children's learning styles. One of the most simple and common, and the one that most easily applies to our purposes here, breaks learning into three components or modalities: Visual, Auditory, and Kinesthetic (VAK).

One or two of these modalities may dominate the way a child receives information. This will affect how a teacher or a practice coach best presents material. For example, when learning a non-fretted instrument, correct intonation is primarily recognized by the ear, not the eye. An aural child, when playing off-pitch, may wrinkle her nose and move her finger to correct the intonation herself, while a child who is visual or kinesthetic may not be listening at all, much less to categorize the intonation as correct or incorrect. Put the visual child on a visual instrument like the piano, however, and he will appreciate the black and white of it right away.

This is not to say that an aural child should not play the piano and a visual child should not play the violin. It does indicate innate areas of strength and weakness that may manifest as the child begins. Ultimately, all three sensory receivers must be engaged and educated.

The Suzuki method relies heavily on aural and kinesthetic stimuli, introducing note reading after form is well established and the ear is firmly engaged. Aural learners, as mentioned, are especially adept at studying stringed instruments. But don't allow the ear to get so far ahead of the eye that the child is delayed in her ability to read.

While kinesthetic learners may resist learning the finely detailed etiquette of a stringed instrument, they love such athletic instruments as drums and percussion, or trombone. In the string family, a parent may want to direct these active little people toward cello or string bass over violin or viola, because these instruments are more forgiving, and positions are more user-friendly. Kinesthetic learners may enjoy a big, happy, lumbering tuba more than a delicate flute. They may enjoy the rock-star persona of the electric guitar more than the refined intricacies of the classical guitar. It's often easy to spot a kinesthetic learner: He flowers when the school day is over and he is set free of the classroom chair to explore and *do*.

4. FAMILY DYNAMIC: INTEREST AND TASTES OF THE CHILD AND PARENTS. INSTRUMENTS PLAYED BY SIBLINGS.

Expose the child to many instruments by attending performances at church and elsewhere, and listening to recordings and watching videos. While listening, observe his or her response. Very often, a child will clearly prefer one over the others. The best decision, however, will be filtered through the good judgment of wise parents, who will weigh all the parameters that are unknown to the child.

Siblings may want to choose complementary instruments in order to form a band or chamber group.

The family may have deep roots in a particular style of music, such as classical, country, bluegrass, or jazz that would indicate a particular instrument of study. Ethnicity—Irish, Scottish, African, and so forth—is also a factor in some families.

Parents are wise to select an instrument they will enjoy teaching the child to play, since they will put in many, many hours before their job is done. Choosing a different instrument for each child is refreshing. It offers each child an individual sphere of musical expertise and expression, and lessens competitive behaviors and comparisons.

5. FINANCES AND RESOURCES

The nice thing about starting on an instrument while a child is young is that small instruments are usually a fraction of the price of full-sized, professional instruments. Some instrument dealers, as mentioned, allow trade-in value. The parent buys the initial instrument; then, when the child needs to move up a size—or needs a better, more expensive, instrument—the price of the old one goes toward the purchase of the new. In that way, as a child moves up, the parent builds equity in the instrument.

Good news on the violin: The good ones appreciate in value with age, and are an outstanding investment.

A low-quality instrument is one of the biggest deterrents to success. It's like dressing your child's talent in musical rags. It doesn't matter how skillfully the student plays, he cannot rise above the quality of the instrument.

The price of an instrument varies greatly, within a given musical genre and across genres. Guitars, for the most part, are cheaper than pianos. Sometimes the price varies according to the professional demands made on the instrument. If a violin is to project over an orchestra without amplification, to execute an array of emotional timbres, and to respond quickly to a variety of bow strokes, it will not be a cheap instrument. Stringed instruments, in general, are not expensive to start, but can become quite expensive if the child grows up to become a concertizing, professional player. A student may begin on a spinet piano, but she will need a nine-foot grand for a Rachmaninoff Concerto.

Professional level brass and winds are more affordable than top-notch violins. However, sometimes these instruments carry a more limited range of musical settings. Be sure it's what you want. I recently heard the director of the music program at a large conservatory say, "I have twenty-three freshmen oboe players. When they arrived, I wanted to hang a banner saying, 'There are no jobs!'" It's true. Many musicians work at an unintended occupation—a "day job"—because they didn't project beyond college. Even if the degree is from the Juilliard School or the Cincinnati Conservatory, or another esteemed program, graduation day may leave a student unemployable in the world of music. Double that dilemma if the student plays an instrument that is not widely used in popular music.

As a practical matter, encourage your child to take up the instrument that offers the richest source of opportunity *in your location*: a great teacher, a prep program in the local college, a sound methodology, an outlet for performance. Before involving your child in a search, peruse your town's opportunities. If you have a great piano teacher and not much in the way of guitar teachers, steer your child to piano. Gain your musical bearings and plug into the richest source.

Appendix C

Finding a Good Teacher

Go to musical events that showcase your child's chosen instrument of study and analyze the fruits of the teachers represented. You will soon see a pattern. The teachers who inspire their students to practice, who establish exciting performance opportunities, will be evident in the quality of their students' performance.

A Good Teacher...

Is *there:* When a young child is just beginning to study, proximity is important. A beginner who is still securing the fundamentals will gain huge advantages by participating in at least two lessons per week. Let's say a child really wants to play cello, but the closest cello teacher is two hours away. That's not too bad for an older child who is motivated to make the long drive and whose skill has progressed, but it's a lot to expect for a young beginner. Likewise, carpooling works well once children are self-sufficient—practicing on their own—but it doesn't work very well in the beginning, when the parent, whose role is vital at this stage, needs to sit in on the lesson.

Teaches: Understand that many teachers lack strong purpose and focus, wish they were doing something else, and will sometimes find ways to fill the time with something other than teaching: telling stories, looking for music, writing out charts, performing for the student. Teachers who love to teach, who love their instrument and the music it plays, will spend the lesson teaching. Such teachers inspire their students, and inspiration is a vital ingredient in success.

Is appropriate for the student's stage of development: Secure a teacher who understands how to work with the age and skill level of your child. Some teachers are great for beginners, other are great with students of intermediate skill. Rarely will one teacher take a student from a young beginner to an older, advanced student. With rare exceptions, it takes a team of teachers to go the distance from preschool to college. Don't be afraid to make the move from one teacher to the next as your child matures.

Understands the role of the parent: A functional teacher-parent-student combination is vital to a good start, especially when the student is very young and the parent is not a musician. The teacher must be organized and able to set a clear agenda from week to week. She must work with the student, while training the parent to be the student's practice coach. Discern how a teacher views the role of the parent in a child's musical journey. This can be done through interviewing both the potential teacher and other parents who are familiar with her studio. Parental involvement is crucial when a child is young. It begins to decrease around the age of nine and ends at the age of twelve, by which time a child can be taking full responsibility for his music, having established the discipline and protocols of perfect practice.

Isn't necessarily a "best friend": Many parents look primarily for a teacher who is "nice," and certainly a professional attitude of mutual respect is commendable. Some students are more sensitive in personality and have a greater need for nurturing from a teacher than others. Parents who supply plenty of nurturing themselves, however, will do well to put "nice" on the back burner and look instead for a great teacher who has high expectations and a well-codified methodology. Many effective teachers have personality quirks, to put it plainly. If they are great teachers, put up with the quirks.

Is flexible: A great teacher assesses a student's learning style and adjusts her methodology accordingly. She considers and adjusts her teaching to accommodate special needs and challenges, personality traits, and family settings.

Is a diagnostician: A physician may have a less-than-perfect bedside manner, but if she is a genius at diagnosing and prescribing, the rest may be forgiven. The same is true with a teacher, who, like a physician, diagnoses problems and prescribes remedies. When a child has difficulty playing a section of music, a good teacher

will analyze why that particular section doesn't work, and prescribe good remedies. If a teacher neglects this function, focusing instead merely on the learning of
notes, a student's progress will be technically impaired, especially as the repertoire
increases in difficulty.

Knows the science of her instrument: To analyze, diagnose, and prescribe, a
teacher must know the fundamental form and technique for playing an instrument. This is why public schools—which often expect one or two teachers to
teach all instruments—can only take your child's skill to a certain level. A great
teacher knows his instrument and is capable of conveying to the student basic
form and technique. A great teacher insists on establishing the fundamentals,
never allowing a student to sink into bad habits, however difficult the work may
be. The parent-child team falls into line with the teacher's demands. With the
basics in place, the horizon keeps lifting, as the student progresses into increasingly difficult repertoire.

Knows the repertoire of an instrument: Has a thorough grasp of the lineup
of educational repertoire, plus a creative and eclectic stash of repertoire that she
shapes to suit a child's taste, adding personality, fun, and flavor to the child's
routine.

Builds morale while demanding accuracy: Articulates to the student her faith
in his ability to accomplish what she has assigned.

Is truthful: Makes an honest assessment of a child's performance, and then offers
appropriate compliments and critique. It is very dangerous, musically speaking,
to hear only superficial accolades. The profession of music is brutally honest, and
to be employable, you'll need real, indisputable skill. Remember: "The truth will
set you free." Teach your child to love correction. "Iron sharpens iron. So one man
sharpens another."

Is structured: A good teacher builds precept upon precept, following a well-
structured methodology. Look out for the teacher who moves at a snail's pace,
as well as the one who gallops ahead, pushing the learning of notes without
allowing basic form and technique to solidify. A good teacher keeps the child

tiptoeing, neither bored nor frustrated but challenged—and equipped to meet the challenge.

Recognizes and accommodates both special needs and giftedness: Beware of a teacher who is so bound by her "method" that she doesn't recognize when she should speed ahead on the wings of a gifted child's natural ability and when she should slow down to focus on a challenged child's special needs. You can detect such a teacher when she either underwhelms or overwhelms your student.

Exposes: A good teacher issues listening assignments, and makes her students aware of performances in the area that would be beneficial to attend. Before long, her students have seen the top players in their field, both amateur and professional. Such exposure gives students musical goals. Thus, you avoid the big-fish-in-a-little-pond mentality. A good teacher also mixes advanced students with beginners at play-ins and recitals, setting a vision for the younger, less skilled players.

Thinks big and projects vision: "I expect that, within two years, you'll be ready to audition for the youth symphony. In three years, I'd like you to audition for the concerto competition. Let's begin by learning this piece. I'd like you to master it within three months, so we can move on to this next piece. Then you'll be ready to start a concerto...."

Sets goals: A good teacher knows where to send her students for adjudications, competitions, performance opportunities, special events, and such summer extras as camps and workshops. Goals infuse lessons and practice with purpose. A good teacher sets small goals such as performing for family members, as well as large goals, such as an end-of-year solo recital or participation in a competition. A good teacher ensures that the goals serve the progress of the student and are natural outlets for the music being learned. Progress is impeded when the requirements of a performance goal fixate a student's attention on a few pieces of repertoire for too long.

Provides performance opportunities: A good teacher hosts exciting recitals, concerts, and musical excursions. She innovates, grouping students into duets, trios, and quartets. She is familiar with the competitions and adjudications in her region and state, and makes sure her students know of these opportunities.

Inspires greatness: Uses words to infuse a child with a sense of the high call of his artistry and the love and appreciation of a well-performed piece.

Is connected: Interacts with other studios and teachers, and is a member of local, regional, and national music associations and societies.

Promotes healthy attitudes: A good teacher never, ever holds back a hard-working, talented child so that the child's peers won't feel threatened. She avoids comparisons, and encourages the parents in her group to do so as well. She has no tolerance for jealousy, selfish ambition, or vain conceit. She works hard to offer all children, both the challenged and the gifted, opportunities that are tailored to fit their needs and abilities.

Is not possessive: Recognizes when a student has grown beyond the teacher's own level of expertise, and aids him in moving to the next tier of opportunity.

Educates in all areas of fluency: Music is a language. As in any language, fluency is exhibited in three forms: speaking (singing and/or playing); reading; and writing. Many music teachers deal only in the first two, playing and reading. A good teacher educates for fluency in writing as well, through the study of theory, composition, notation, and improvisation.

Knows skill builders: A good teacher recognizes that practice is only one method for building skill. She will encourage her students to perform with other students, to perform for audiences, and to record themselves playing their pieces. These are superior methods of building skill.

Is pleasant to be around: A good teacher avoids distracting habits and arbitrary rules. Examples: pets in the lesson, chewing gum, poor hygiene, a television on in another room.

Appendix D

Practicing Well

Tips on maximizing the time spent

Space: First, establish a bright, cheery, space in which to practice, a space that is clean, orderly, quiet, and set away from distractions such as the television and the game room. When possible, schedule practice with older children early in the morning while younger children are still sleeping, or during nap time.

Keeping Company: Loneliness is the greatest impediment to success in practicing. Learning to play should at least be a duet, and on occasion, it's important to call the whole family in for applause and encouragement. Children love to please those whom they love, and their audience might start with just mom and dad, then grow to include the entire family, the Sunday school class, and the whole church or community. Whatever the size of the audience, children will benefit from being reminded of the point of their practice: to bless others and the Lord with their music.

Love Languages: Practice time is a wonderful opportunity for filling your child's emotional needs, communicating your love through focused attention, eye contact, and appropriate, meaningful touch. So add a bountiful serving of these elements to practice time, along with lots of prayer for God's blessing and aid. Be sure to point out to the child how God answers prayers. Nothing builds intimacy like prayer and music.

Pajama Practice: "I will awake the dawn!" (Psalm 108:2, NIV). "We are children of the day" (1 Thessalonians 5:5, NIV). These are just a few of the Scripture quotes that encourage us to "Arise and shine" (Isaiah 60:1, NIV) to greet the Lord's mercies, which are "... new every morning" (Lamentations 3:23, NIV).

Whether your children crawl or bounce out of bed, give them big hugs, brush their hair out of their eyes, pray a prayer of thanksgiving, and hand them their instruments.

Here's the secret. A child's brain is fresh as sunshine in the early morning, ready to store new information, and the best part is, when children practice in the morning, their brains don't stop when they put down the instrument, but keep processing the information.

In the early afternoon, hold another practice session, spending about half the time of the morning practice. Then again, right before you tuck your child into bed, practice once more, about half the time of the afternoon practice.

For example, if you and your child practice thirty minutes in the morning, practice fifteen minutes in the afternoon, and seven or eight minutes before bedtime. Thus, the child's brain is categorizing the music, even as she sleeps.

Listening and Exposure: Listening is a critical component to success in any musical endeavor. How can a child play beautifully if she doesn't know the sounds of beautiful playing? A great time to turn on the music device is while your little musician is dressing for bed and dozing off to sleep. Through listening, the child will develop an aural goal, understanding how pieces will sound when they are polished and ready to perform. Begin with the music the child is learning, then add the pieces that make up the bedrock of repertoire for her instrument: show pieces, concertos, sonatas, and suites. Play videos of great performances, and take trips to the symphony. Exposure to live performances, especially those by individuals who are around the same age as the child, is inspirational. For best results, stick with classical music in the early years, then branch out as the child matures.

Singing: Before you play it, sing it! It's fun. It's educational. It's free of charge. And most of all, it's biblical. The Scriptures instruct us numerous times to "sing to the Lord!" Science reinforces this good idea by informing us that singing is stored in the central, most protected portion of the brain. That's why so many stroke victims and Alzheimer's patients, who have impaired speaking ability, can still remember what they learned to sing when young. Singing utilizes both sides of the brain simultaneously, networking the left and right hemispheres.

Unfortunately, some children are labeled "tone-deaf." Don't let that stop you. Work on teaching your children to move the voice up and down the scale and to connect the voice with the ear as correct or incorrect intonation is determined by the ear. With time and practice, children can learn to match pitch.

The Significant Other: The Significant Other is the all-important person—usually a parent—who takes on the responsibility of nurturing and overseeing the training of the child, of structuring time for practice, and insuring that all key factors for success are provided. If you are the Significant Other and you have limited musical knowledge or skill, don't worry, you will enjoy learning along with the child. It is not necessary that you become a virtuoso, but you will, by the end of the journey, know a lot about your child's instrument.

The Bunny Rule: Growing up on a farm, I learned the "Bunny Rule" from our long-eared donkey, Bunny. If I pulled hard on Bunny's rope, she stuck her chin in the air, pulled backward, and sat down. If I pushed from behind, she refused to budge.

The only way to gain Bunny's cooperation was to stand close beside her head, hold her halter, speak gently to her, and coax her along. On difficult days, remember the "Bunny Rule." Resist the urge to push or pull your child. Instead, try drawing close and talking in a friendly and understanding manner. After all, you are partners in your pursuit of musical excellence.

Brain Time: Skill is the sum of practice plus time. Six hours are required for new information to make its way from the temporal frontal lobes to the back of the brain, where the deep stores of memory reside. If, soon after a lesson with a teacher, you and your child carefully go through the assignments, your child's brain will reap the benefit of plenty of processing time. Procrastinating, then attempting to cram a lot of information into the few hours before a lesson, doesn't allow the brain time to assimilate the information. It only adds a heightened level of fear and stress, and lessons become frustrating. So take time soon after a lesson to make corrections and to begin to learn new assignments.

Practice Doing It Right: When playing any instrument, correct positions are fundamental to success. It is imperative that children practice methodically and correctly to establish habits of good form and posture. Practice doesn't make perfect. Perfect practice makes perfect. Incorrect practice reinforces incorrect habits, impeding progress and frustrating both child and parent. Avoid getting really good at playing wrong. Give attention to detail, right from the start. Stop the motion when it loses its form. Start over. Drill the same procedures until they are established. Only then, move on.

Avoid Comparisons: Don't allow comparisons to tempt you to forgo good fundamental form in the interest of keeping up with the crowd. Questions about what song or piece a student has progressed to, should be avoided. Accuracy is vastly more important than speed.

Setting the Boundaries: It is important to implement consistent, accurate, and disciplined practice protocol from the beginning, so that a child knows what to expect. Lead your children toward positive attitudes and away from complaining, distractions, and resistance. Children find security in boundaries, and upon discovering that the lines will not be shaken or moved, they will cease to push against them. As children begin to enjoy the fruits of their labor, they will no longer want to challenge the lines. Learning to play an instrument well takes patience and persistence, but the rewards are great.

Skill Builders: Practice is beneficial in building skill. Other types of musical activities, however, enhance the foundations of daily practice. For example, in performance, the brain takes on heightened awareness. Performing consistently builds skill on a different scale than practice, acclimating the child to an audience. Playing in a group, especially beside other, more skilled and experienced musicians, or alongside peers, can be exhilarating, lighting a fire in a child's heart—a desire to get better and gain more such opportunities.

Drill Bit: Isolate difficult sections and practice the spots repeatedly, as long as progress is being made. Most pieces of music consist of easily attainable passages glued together by difficult passages. It is these difficult passages that determine who will command the big stage and who will be a parlor performer.

Slow to Fast: Begin practicing slowly, with a metronome. It is critical that your child learn to perform to an external source of timing, and a metronome is the simplest, most direct way of doing so. The recording industry—and collaboration in bands with a rhythm section—demand a keen sense of rhythmic accuracy.

Back to Front and "Spot Practice": Rotate the portion of music that begins your practice session. If you always begin at the beginning of a piece and work your way to the end, you will have a strong beginning and a weak ending. "Spot practice" difficult places so that the song does not have a lag at any point in the performance. A performance needs to gain energy as it proceeds, and to end in a blaze of glory. The audience will hardly remember how it began.

Review: The most important part of a practice routine is the review of the repertoire being studied. Once the notes are learned, the child is able to concentrate on other components of polished performance—phrasing, dynamics, pacing, intonation, and beautiful sound. This practice supersedes all others in creating a fluent, expressive player.

Recording: Recording is the most powerful and nuanced skill builder available, especially when performed in the presence of someone the performer wants to impress. The playback doesn't lie; it gives students a real assessment of the sound they are creating. Music, after all, is sound, and recording teaches students to tune their ears and really listen. A beautiful, error-free recording of a piece of music is an inspirational achievement, and the effort leaves the student on a whole new plane of playing.

Dessert Music: Pieces learned just for the fun of it. Add them often.

Visual and Verbal Affirmations: It is good to take pictures and video to reinforce your children's vision of themselves as instrumentalists, singers, and speakers. Articulate, for the child, a clear vision of where their musical studies are leading. Keep the picture realistic and rewarding, a musical quest that builds in joy and excitement.

Playing to Win: Imagine a football team that practices relentlessly—learning plays, building muscle, and donning uniforms—but never plays a game. We would never entertain such a waste of time in the world of sports. Unfortunately, it's commonplace in the world of musical arts. No wonder young people grow discouraged and lose interest. Who wants to sit all alone in a room, practicing unpopular music for no one to hear? Group activities, competitions, and performance goals keep musical purpose concrete and attainable, leading students onward from "glory to glory," just as the Lord leads us.

Setting Performance Goals: Both parent and child will find excitement, motivation and anticipation in practicing toward short- and long-term goals.

Short-term Performance Goals: These should come often and be easily attained. One method is a penny bank: A child receives a penny for each correct bow position created in a row. Use the child's age as a guide: five bow positions for a five-year-old child, and so forth. Give extra pennies if the child does all five bow positions in a row correctly. You will be amazed at how hard children will concentrate to win the bonus. The pennies go into a penny bank. When enough pennies have been collected, the child and Mama go to the ice cream shop and split a cookie shake, or Daddy takes the child on a trip to the park as a reward for extra-good behavior and concentration during a lesson. Small rewards say to the child, "I am watching, and I see your good work." Remember, even God is saving up to reward His children. So be creative.

Long-term Performance Goals: These are loftier and take longer to attain, requiring vision, checkpoints, and persistence. A good teacher will be thoroughly involved in such adventures, directing students to appropriate opportunities regarding solo and group recitals, adjudications, competitions, and group outings to such friendly venues as nursing homes and clubs, church events, summer camps, and, eventually, competitions.

APPENDIX E

Creating a Coalition

The church has long been a powerful patron, recognizing that the arts are a vital purveyor of His Word. But when modern congregations abandon a serious commitment to the arts—and music in particular—their mission falters. Today, the arts are more powerful than ever before, and the church has an opportunity to reclaim territory. The way forward is to raise a new generation of artists dedicated to the truth of God and educated in artistic languages.

A successful church arts program comprises an admiring audience delivering enthusiastic applause for young children who have displayed skill in worship of God. To cultivate a robust, energized, mutually supportive artistic hub, multiple tiers of people must be engaged to interact. It takes a network of what I call the "Five Ps": *parents, professors, pastors,* and *patrons* to hone *pupils'* skills, organize publicity, make donations, lend instruments, and educate as to the importance of the program.

PUPIL: The child is the inspiration for creating a coalition—a network of support that undergirds the study and showcasing of the performing arts.

PARENTS: Parents must be educated as to the spiritual, developmental, social, and educational benefits inherent in the artistic development of their children. Only then can they see to it that their children have everything they need for success. They are the vision casters, with a twofold objective: (1) to root their children spiritually in the love of God; and (2) to equip their children with an artistic toolbox so that their children can effectively communicate that love to the world.

PROFESSOR: The teacher must understand the vital role of the parent and work with the parent, as well as the child, in a methodical way, to establish good fundamental form and function. The trinity of pupil-parent-professor is powerful when each one does his/her part well.

PASTOR: It is up to the music pastor to follow the biblical mandate that his flock should "play skillfully" and "make His praise glorious." The music pastor of a church body must understand that the performing arts—playing, singing, and dancing—are a spiritual discipline. Instead of working with only a few volunteers and skilled church members, the music pastor must accept responsibility for the artistic dreams and abilities of the entire flock given into his care. Once he accepts that role, he will educate parents. He will provide graded programs of musical development—choirs, lessons on instruments, performance opportunities, service participation, and seasonal and nonseasonal productions—creating a feeder stream from preschool to elementary school, middle school, high school, and onward to adult programs. The bulk of funds available will go to the earliest years of education, when the spirit and mind are optimized by the study of the arts.

All sheep entrusted to this music minister's care will *sing!* And by singing they will be bonded; they will find their connectedness; they will feel goodwill and generosity toward one another. The primary pastor will understand the importance of musical events, and services will be planned accordingly. The church stage will be utilized as a grooming ground for young voices: speakers, singers, and musicians. The leadership will realize the powerful effect of raising a new generation of fluent, artistic, creative voices that love to tell the good news of God's love. Therefore, adult musical programs, choir, and orchestra can play a role in organizing and shepherding the young.

PATRON: Historically, patrons have been central to the artistic splendor of churches, cities, or nations. Bach's music-making, for example, was rooted in the church and funded by patrons. For the church to thrive and revive, patrons must be educated, alongside parents, as to the essential part the arts play in community and society.

Few arts programs today enjoy the reach and vitality generated by the converging influences of parents, pupils, professors, pastors, and patrons. But it is worth making it happen. If any one of the tiers in your church can manage to activate the others, a powerful voice will emerge. Healthy programs strengthen and grow our churches, creating hope for the glory of God, who is worthy of praise.

Acknowledgments

A hearty thank you goes to my husband, Bill, who tells me daily how I should write! And thanks to my six children—Annie, Alex, Benjamin, Camille, Gretchen, and Jeremiah—who have taught me so much about love. Thank you, Mother and Daddy, who never grew tired of listening to chapters read over the phone. And to Meg Knox, a brilliant mind and ready editor, thank you for your professionalism, skill, and friendship. And thanks to my agent, David Shepherd, for being steady-on, capable, and persistent. Thanks to Lawrence Kimbrough for his encouragement and elucidation as to the protocols of book publishing. To David Morris and the team at Guideposts Books and Inspirational Media, thank you for taking on this rather unusual project and for your excellent, professional work.

About the Author

Robin Donica Wolaver is a singer, speaker, and writer living in Nashville, Tennessee, with her husband and fellow composer, Bill Wolaver. They are the parents of six children: Annie, Alex, Benjamin, Camille, Gretchen, and Jeremiah. Robin holds a bachelor's of music degree in vocal performance from Oklahoma City University and travels with her family in a group called the Annie Moses Band, performing over eighty concerts annually. The group's PBS special, "Christmas with the Annie Moses Band," received over 1,200 hours of airings. Their Christmas album, *This Glorious Christmas*, reached the top ten on *Billboard Magazine*'s classical crossover chart.

Robin's passion for arts restoration has led her to speak publicly across the United States, encouraging families to pursue spiritual and artistic excellence and to disciple their children through the common bond of music. Together with her daughter Annie, Robin has codified a curriculum for beginning violinists called the Annie Moses Method. As the artistic director of the Fine Arts Summer Academy with the Annie Moses Band, held annually in Nashville, Robin enjoys mentoring and grooming young and aspiring artists.

An award-winning lyricist, Robin earned the honor of Gospel Song of the Year by the American Society of Composers, Authors, and Publishers (ASCAP), as well as the Nashville Songwriters Association. She has been twice nominated for a Dove Award in both the Song of the Year and Best Children's Musical categories.

Explore the music of the Annie Moses Band, the Fine Arts Summer Academy, Robin's children's musicals and curriculum, and many other publications at AnnieMosesBand.com. Get to know Robin and her family or check out new information and materials at RobinWolaver.com.